Developing Critical Languaculture Pedagogies in Higher Education

LANGUAGES FOR INTERCULTURAL COMMUNICATION AND EDUCATION
Series Editors: Michael Byram, *University of Durham, UK* and Alison Phipps, *University of Glasgow, UK*

The overall aim of this series is to publish books which will ultimately inform learning and teaching, but whose primary focus is on the analysis of intercultural relationships, whether in textual form or in people's experience. There will also be books which deal directly with pedagogy, with the relationships between language learning and cultural learning, between processes inside the classroom and beyond. They will all have in common a concern with the relationship between language and culture, and the development of intercultural communicative competence.

Full details of all the books in this series and of all our other publications can be found on http://www.multilingual-matters.com, or by writing to Multilingual Matters, St Nicholas House, 31–34 High Street, Bristol BS1 2AW, UK.

Developing Critical Languaculture Pedagogies in Higher Education

Theory and Practice

Adriana Raquel Díaz

MULTILINGUAL MATTERS
Bristol • Buffalo • Toronto

Library of Congress Cataloging in Publication Data
Developing Critical Languaculture Pedagogies in Higher Education: Theory and Practice/
Adriana Raquel Diaz.
Languages for Intercultural Communication and Education: 25
Includes bibliographical references and index.
1. Language and languages—Study and teaching (Higher)—Case studies. 2. Language
teachers—Training of. 3. Language and culture—Study and teaching--Case studies.
I. Title.
P53.755.D53 2013
418.0071'1–dc23 2013022860

British Library Cataloguing in Publication Data
A catalogue entry for this book is available from the British Library.

ISBN-13: 978-1-78309-035-8 (hbk)
ISBN-13: 978-1-78309-034-1 (pbk)

Multilingual Matters
UK: St Nicholas House, 31–34 High Street, Bristol BS1 2AW, UK.
USA: UTP, 2250 Military Road, Tonawanda, NY 14150, USA.
Canada: UTP, 5201 Dufferin Street, North York, Ontario M3H 5T8, Canada.

The policy of Multilingual Matters/Channel View Publications is to use papers that are
natural, renewable and recyclable products, made from wood grown in sustainable for-
ests. In the manufacturing process of our books, and to further support our policy, preference is given to printers that have FSC and PEFC Chain of Custody certification. The FSC
and/or PEFC logos will appear on those books where full certification has been granted
to the printer concerned.

Typeset by Techset Composition India (P) Ltd., Bangalore and Chennai, India.
Printed and bound in Great Britain by Short Run Press Ltd.

Contents

Figures and Tables

Figures

Tables

Foreword

This book emerges at a time when language education is confronting a period of change and it seeks both to document and contribute to that change. New forms of communication, greater mobility and the emergence of language as a critical form of capital in the knowledge economy have all placed pressure of language educators and language programmes to develop learners with intercultural capabilities. This represents a challenge for language educators as they respond to new needs and new contexts in their practice.

The idea that language learning prepares students to understand and communicate with members of other cultures is hardly new. Language educators have long included the development of intercultural capabilities as a rationale for language teaching. However, although intercultural capabilities may have been an aim for language education, teaching approaches have not typically focused on these, seeing them rather as implicit in any form of successful language learning. The recognition that language education is to be successful in developing intercultural capabilities is much more recent and has led to a radical rethinking of the nature and processes of language teaching and learning. Central to this rethinking is the idea that intercultural capabilities need to be foregrounded in language teaching and learning at all points in language education programmes.

The reason for this rethinking has been a realisation that language learning without a specific intercultural focus has not developed the sorts of capabilities that language educators have claimed. Negative attitudes, problematic stereotypes and limited abilities to adapt to the languages, cultures and perspectives of others may persist throughout the learning of a language and, in some cases, may intensify through the processes of learning. This is because the development of intercultural capabilities is not inherent in the acquisition of communicative competence as represented by the grammar and vocabulary of a language. Rather it is something additional to these.

The realisation that language teaching needs to be adjusted to achieve what language educators have claimed as a goal of teaching and learning has led to rapid changes in the ways in which culture is integrated into language education. Although culture has long been present in language programmes, the cultural component of teaching has usually been separated from the language itself and has been seen as an additional dimension of learning, either communicated outside the target language or reserved for advanced level students whose language abilities were considered adequate for dealing with complex content. This separation of language and culture has effectively limited what can be achieved in language programmes in terms of intercultural learning. Recent thinking has called for a more integrated approach to language and culture in language education.

Revising language education programmes to integrate language and culture has not proved to be easy. This is because such integration does not simply involve a revision of language curricula but a complete reconceptualisation of the nature of language teaching and learning. This reconceptualisation involves new understandings of some of the fundamentals of language education, notably how we understand the core concepts of language, culture and learning.

The reconceptualisation of language has involved a shift from seeing language only in terms of code (grammar and vocabulary) to a view that integrates the code with social practices of meaning making and interpretation. Language is therefore not simply understood as the building blocks of communication, but as the processes and products of that communication. Understanding a language is therefore not simply a feature of proficiency, but a complex interpretative act that recognises language as constituting and constituted by the social actions of communicators. Learning a new language therefore involves more than the acquisition of new grammar and vocabulary as it requires the language learning to engage with the culturally positioned nature of language in use. In such a view of language the learners' first language and the target language do not operate independently – the practices and processes of meaning making and interpretation in each language are always potentially present in communication. A new language therefore needs to be understood in relation to the practices of meaning making and interpretation that are already available for the learner.

The impact of this reconceptualisation has been significant for understanding the nature of language, however, it can be argued that it more significant for how language educators have come to understand the nature of culture. The typical way of dealing with culture in language programmes has been to focus on culture as artefacts and information developed by another culture, typically understood and a monolithic national culture. Culture has been presented as uniform and immutable. Understanding a culture has meant knowing about cultural products of others. The shift to interculturally oriented language education has entailed a shift in views of culture from artefacts and information, to a view of culture as symbols and practices that are constituent elements of the social world. Learning in relation to such an understanding involves engagement with practices in processes of meaning making and interpretation. Concomitant with this shifting focus in the nature of culture has been a realisation that language learning needs to engage with culture as situated, variable, plural and contested – a dynamic creative processes of human social interaction rather than a static representation of undifferentiated national representation.

As languages do not exist in isolation from each other, so too are cultures brought into the relationship through language teaching and learning. The learners' own cultures are a powerful component of the ways that they make sense of their world and communications about it. These cultures cannot be excluded from the communicative practices of second language users, but need to be brought into relationship with them. The learning of culture cannot therefore be isolated from the symbolic and interactional practices that constitute the learners' existing cultural repertoires. For this reason, language education has come to emphasise processes of decentring – stepping outside existing cultural assumptions to view the world from different perspectives – and mediation – interpreting cultural realities across cultural boundaries.

Finally, the view of learning involved in language education has been enlarged. Since the 1980s, language education has favoured the idea of acquisition – the unconscious development of language through comprehensible input – over conscious learning. However, such a view of learning does not allow for the development of the more complex needed to develop intercultural capabilities. Interculturally oriented language education has, therefore, developed an expanded theory of learning that integrates acquisition and learning in mutually supporting ways. The focus on learning allows for a sophisticated involvement of language learners in refection on processes of meaning making and interpretation.

The reconceptualisation of language learning found in interculturally oriented forms of language education has resulted from an ongoing consideration of theoretical concepts in language teaching and learning, but the development of practice has tended to lag behind theoretical development. The introduction of any new way of working in education requires dissemination among those whose experience, both as teachers and as learners, has been developed in different contexts. Developing practice, therefore involves working with practitioners to engage in change both in conceptualisation and practice.

In interculturally oriented language education, developing practice is complex because intercultural language teaching and learning does not provide a methodology for teaching that can be adopted into practice to transform education. The fact that intercultural language teaching and learning is not a methodology results from a view of practice that maintains that there is no ready-made, one-size-fits-all way of developing intercultural capabilities through language education. Rather teaching and learning processes need to be understood in context. Therefore it is more appropriate to consider intercultural language teaching and learning in terms of a perspective on, or stance towards, learning in which the conceptualisation of the nature and purpose of language education leads to practical responses. The emphasis on stance or perspective entails the development, by individual teachers, of a comprehensive approach driven by reflective practice informed by theory, which can be used to scaffold the systematic integration of a coherent language and culture pedagogy.

This book represents an early investigation of the complexities of developing practice in intercultural language teaching and learning. It presents a coherent framework for approach curriculum and pedagogy, and documents the experiences of a group of teachers in developing their practice in response to emerging ideas of interculturally oriented language teaching and learning. In so doing, it addresses the pervasive theory/practice gap in language education by providing a comprehensive conceptual discussion of emerging critical themes in intercultural language teaching and learning supported by empirical accounts and case studies from the classroom. By evaluating theoretical and practical issues, this book identifies viable, sustainable innovation strategies for systematically integrating critical pedagogies in university language programmes.

Anthony J. Liddicoat
University of South Australia

Preface

This book was born of a desire to articulate the perceived gap between theory and practice in language and culture pedagogy. This gap, which seems unbridgeable at times, surely needs to be narrowed if we are effectively to address what is widely acknowledged to be one of the key competences for the 21st century: the development of intercultural competence. This has been the subject of countless scholarly publications, from monographs to journal articles, textbooks and conference proceedings. Many of these have become seminal works that serve as the foundations for this book. And yet, this subject continues to mystify theorists (i.e. linguists and applied linguists) and practitioners (i.e. teachers, teacher trainers and curriculum designers) alike. The volume of work available is all but testament to this.

In my own case, this gap continues to manifest itself as a chasm in personal and professional interactions. Earlier it was through my experiences as a learner of the English language in Argentina and subsequently, for over a decade now, as a foreign language teacher living in Australia. At the core of my concerns and frustrations has always been a fascination with language and culture, how they co-relate and how this relationship manifests in interaction.

This book has been, therefore, a way for me to pursue my own quest to help bridge the theory/practice gap in language and culture pedagogy. In so doing, I seek to help other language teachers and curriculum developers, like myself, to rethink their language and culture teaching practices and develop ways to articulate these into principles that may be adapted to the diverse and imperfect nature of the everyday language classroom. Principles that may also be relevant beyond the classroom, to best serve us in the increasingly globalised world in which we live. Indeed, because of the global shift in higher education and the consequences of this for pedagogy, these principles also need to be embedded in the international context that is currently shaping the higher education policy agenda, and, in turn, ineluctably shaping our practices.

I could not have completed this book without the support of a number of people and I extend my most sincere gratitude to all of them. This book draws from the empirical research I conducted as part of my doctoral dissertation, so I begin by acknowledging the guidance provided by my supervisors Dr Susana Eisenchlas and Dr Sue Trevaskes. I sincerely thank them both for being devoted mentors to me in my career as a beginning academic. I am also indebted to Ms Maureen Todhunter, who edited and proofread this manuscript diligently, and provided invaluable support in conceptualising this book as a coherent whole. I would also like to thank the editorial staff at Multilingual Matters, as well as the reviewers of the book proposal and final manuscript, their input and suggestions were invaluable to completing this work.

I thank all the participants in my empirical study for the time, ideas and support they provided in our meetings and interviews. I am particularly indebted to the teacher–participants, who by sharing insights into their experiences and teaching practices were instrumental in enabling me to bring this investigation to fruition.

Last but not least I acknowledge the valuable contributions of my loved ones. My parents, Sofia Luna de Díaz and Carlos Daniel Díaz, enabled me to make my dream of studying in Australia a reality and continue to encourage me in my academic endeavours. Above all, I thank my husband, Fabio Caruso, for always being there for me, for motivating me and inspiring me to never give up on my dreams.

Introduction

In many ways it is a truism that the world is more globally interconnected than even before. The last few decades in particular have witnessed profound changes in population mobility, technology enabling instant international communication and the ever-increasing frequency of intercultural encounters. These changes impact significantly on the employment market, where many prospective employees are expected to have skills and knowledge to enable them to deal competently in a wide range of situations and with people who have diverse language and cultural experiences and communication styles. In this context, higher education has become central to developing these skills and to providing graduates with competitive advantage in the international labour marketplace (Paige & Goode, 2009). Yet despite this imperative and the opportunities it presents, as Lee *et al.* point out, institutions 'are not doing an adequate job' (Lee *et al.*, 2012: 1).

According to the latest Global Survey conducted by the International Association of Universities in 2010, the top rationale driving internationalisation processes in higher education institutions is 'improving student preparedness for a globalised world'. The second is 'internationalising the curriculum' (Egron-Polak & Hudson, 2010). Many educators acknowledge that preparing students for this globalised world hinges largely on integrating students' intercultural competence across disciplines, course curricula and degree structures (*cf.* Lee *et al.*, 2012). This approach extends to the study of languages (Dlaska, 2000, 2003), which is widely acknowledged as integral to raising awareness and understanding about underlying cultural values and beliefs reflected in communication (*cf.* Byram, 2009b; Della Chiesa *et al.*, 2012; Risager, 2006b; Sercu & Bandura, 2005; UNESCO, 2009).

However, strategies responding to internationalisation have largely overlooked the role of foreign language education[1] in preparing graduates for engaging in an intercultural dialogue with and in this globalised world (*cf.* Bergan & van't Land, 2010; Byram, 2012b; Dlaska, 2012; Klee, 2009; Warner,

2011). This is clearly reflected at the macro-level of policy statements at transnational, intergovernmental levels (Bergan & van't Land, 2010; Chambers, 2003; Egron-Polak & Hudson, 2010; Tudor, 2005) and in numerous reports and scholarly publications at national level – particularly in the United States (AACU & National Leadership Council, 2007; CIGE, 2012; Modern Language Association, 2007), the United Kingdom (Coleman, 2011; Worton, 2009) and Australia (Nettelbeck et al., 2007; Pauwels, 2007; White & Baldauf, 2006) to name but a few. These reports and publications paint a paradoxical picture: a firmer focus on internationalisation of higher education against reduced offering of foreign language education.

At the core of this paradox we find a field in transition. Over the last few decades the field of languages education has changed significantly, especially through redefinition of the underlying goal of language learning. Leading scholars in the field (cf. Byram, 1997, 2001; Feng et al., 2009; Kramsch, 1993, 1998a; Liddicoat et al., 2003; Risager, 2006b; Sercu, 2004) claim the underlying goal of language learning is no longer primarily defined in terms of the acquisition of *communicative competence* (CC) (Hymes, 1972) in a foreign language, but rather, the development of *intercultural communicative competence* (ICC)[2] (Byram, 1997). The latter encompasses the skills, knowledge and attitudes that may help learners to communicate effectively across languages and cultures and thus become 'interculturally competent speakers' (Sercu, 2005: 2). This transformation has in turn called for reconceptualising teaching approaches and syllabi to address the development of students' intercultural competences, and above all has called for teachers to revisit their role in promoting the development of these competences in the context of higher education.

Overall, despite widespread agreement at macro policy and discipline level that languages education should seek to develop interculturally competent speakers, how to achieve this goal at the micro-level of curriculum development is still under debate (Houghton, 2012; Parmenter, 2010). This discrepancy between expected goals, and teaching approaches and practices in place to achieve them, is reflected in the failure of both theorists (i.e. linguists and applied linguists) and practitioners (i.e. teachers, teacher trainers and curriculum designers) to traverse the theory/practice divide. Theorists continue to advance models of language, culture and their interrelationship, along with ways of conceptualising intercultural communicative competence and all-encompassing teaching approaches to address it in practice. Yet practitioners continue to struggle to translate these models and teaching approaches into actual classroom practice. While theoretical models for language and culture teaching have been made ever more sophisticated over the last few decades, implementation of these models still fails to address the imperfect nature and limitations of the everyday language classroom.

Published research into reconceptualising language and culture pedagogies in theory and practice serves as the springboard for this book. This research can be broadly grouped into three interrelated areas of inquiry: (1) the vexed relationship between language and culture (*cf.* Byram & Morgan, 1994; Kramsch, 1998a; Risager, 2006b); (2) potential pedagogical manifestations of this relationship (*cf.* Byram, 1997, 2001; Liddicoat & Crozet, 2000; Liddicoat *et al.*, 2003; Risager, 2007; Sercu *et al.*, 2005); and (3) implications for language and culture learning goals in the internationalised context of adult education (Byram, 2009b, 2012b; Trevaskes *et al.*, 2003). However, these areas of inquiry are sometimes not articulated in a complementary manner or with a view to offering explicit practical guidance in the current context of higher education. Since current developments in the internationalisation of higher education globally underscore the importance of developing intercultural communicative competence, these aspects need to be addressed as part of a complex whole with their inter-relationships clearly understood and articulated.

The stage is set for a clarion call. Higher education institutions (HEIs) around the world face imperatives to rethink their approaches to internationalisation *vis-à-vis* their stated vision of developing interculturally competent graduates. As part of this rethink, institutions need to reconsider their commitment to revising the internationalised curriculum that currently neglects the integral role of language studies in the development of intercultural competence. Similarly, the field of language education needs to revisit what is now widely acknowledged to be its ultimate goal – the development of interculturally competent speakers – *vis-à-vis* emerging research on how to realise this goal in practice.

This book sets out to engage in this critical examination and, in so doing, to identify avenues conducive to narrowing the gap between how this goal is conceptualised and the practices pursued to achieve it. I argue that to reconcile everyday practices with top-down forces at both policy (international, national and institutional) and discipline (theoretical and conceptual as well as practical) levels, we need to formalise and scaffold strategies to reform the current language and culture curriculum in higher education. This entails generating a comprehensive curriculum development framework driven by *praxis* – reflective practice informed by theory. Engaging in development of this framework may help both theorists and practitioners to traverse the perceived theory/practice divide for the benefit of all involved.

Main Features and Aims of This Book

The title of this book, *Developing Critical Languaculture Pedagogies in Higher Education: Theory and Practice*, encapsulates its main features and aims. The three main features of the book are interrelated. One is its *critical* approach. Criticality, that is, critical thinking, critical self-reflection and critical action is emerging as an integral force traversing every aspect of language and culture pedagogy in adult education (*cf.* Byram, 2012a; Guilherme, 2002; Houghton, 2012; Johnston *et al.*, 2011; Levine & Phipps, 2012; Yamada, 2010). In this book, it manifests as an underlying thread woven into conceptualisation of (1) the proposed curriculum development framework; (2) the language and culture learning goals; and (3) the very nature of research conducted in the classroom. The second feature is use of the portmanteau term *languaculture*[3] to conceptualise and refer to the relationship between language and culture. In the field of language pedagogy, this term has been extensively examined and used by Risager (2005, 2006b); I use it as an overarching term to include Risager's and other relevant language and culture conceptual frameworks that reflect linguistically mediated cultural meaning and behaviours in interaction.

The third feature is concerned with the principles of a curriculum development framework I have conceptualised as possible *pedagogies*. Acknowledging 'pedagogy' as a contested term, in this study it is understood as the purposeful articulation and enactment of the *why*, the *what* and the *how* of our teaching practices, that is: goals, content and methods as they relate to our specific educational context with all its structural, logistical and organisational limitations and possibilities. Above all, this understanding of pedagogy is underpinned by epistemologies of practice as *praxis* – reflective practice informed by theory – to promote innovation (Murphy, 2008). Indeed, according to Guilherme, 'the articulation between reflection and action provides for the nullification of the dichotomy between theory and practice, thus changing the educational practice ... into a *praxis* ...' (Guilherme, 2002: 37).

As a guide to practice, this book takes the perspective of teachers and foregrounds their paramount role as curriculum developers and potential agents of educational innovation. It is thus primarily intended to help university language teachers in developing and implementing sustainable curriculum innovation, and above all, to inspire change in the academic community at large. Indeed, coherent articulation of the various elements involved in developing intercultural competences through language education requires action from policymakers as well as curriculum developers and theorists.

Here guidance is provided through a threefold process. The first critically re-examines discrepancies between the expected goals of languages education and higher education policies in relation to intercultural learning, and the teaching approaches and practices in place to achieve these goals. The second articulates a curriculum development framework that aims to address these discrepancies. The third critically analyses the proposed framework's implementation, through four case studies of curriculum innovation in the Australian higher education context. These case studies are underpinned by a critical, constructive and transformative stance toward language and culture pedagogy, as well as professional development in higher education. As such, the case studies represent both 'units of study' as they embody the various educational contexts in which the framework was implemented, and 'end-products' as they comprehensively describe and analyse the findings from each unit.

The case studies included a Participatory Action Research (PAR) component, which enabled me as the researcher to engage collaboratively with the teacher–participants in innovation through a scaffolded cycle of inquiry within the context of their own subjects. The argument supporting this PAR component is that good practice is only as good as its potential to be transposed to other contexts, and this can be made possible only through collaboration. Qualitative data from interviews, field notes from classroom observations, as well as classroom-work samples offer a holistic view of the teachers' curricular innovations.

Rather than serving as yet another prescriptive model, this *praxis*-driven curriculum development framework presents a pedagogic blueprint. It is made up of interrelated building blocks that both theorists and practitioners should consider when engaging with processes of curriculum innovation to better develop interculturally competent graduates. While underpinned by current theoretical trends in language and culture pedagogy, these building blocks also address the intrinsic structural features of university degrees and, in particular, of their language programmes. Thus, in its overall conception, this framework considers both top-down and bottom-up perspectives on the limitations of sustainable curriculum innovation. Most importantly, it critically considers the conceptual, logistical and organisational features common to the everyday classroom reality. It recognises teachers in their key role of curriculum innovators while considering sustainable avenues for continuing professional development. Therefore, this framework should not be conceptualised as immutable, procedural or 'one-size fits all', but as a pedagogical blueprint and guiding compass for theorists and practitioners to consider the variables involved in the complex process of traversing the theory/practice divide in language and culture teaching.

Overall, the results of this study aim to contribute to the development of deeper reaching and more effective processes of internationalising the higher education curriculum through critical *languaculture* awareness in knowledge and practice. By encouraging readers to reflect critically on their assumptions about language, culture and their inter-relationship, and on their own teaching and learning practices, this study may help to generate the kind of personal and professional reflection that is at the heart of both intercultural learning and the development of intercultural competence.

Overview of the Book

This study is organised in three main parts, the first predominantly critical-theoretical, the second empirical, and the third a synthesis of the two. Part 1 opens with Chapter 1 where I examine the theory/practice gap from a top-down perspective. This perspective explores two paths – the current theoretical and conceptual concerns in the field of language and culture pedagogy, and the internationalised higher education context. They enable identification of the main 'stumbling blocks' or obstacles to narrowing the theory/practice gap, to enhance the development of intercultural speakers. In Chapter 2, I consider how to turn these obstacles or 'stumbling blocks' into the principles or 'building blocks' of a pedagogical framework. I group these building blocks into three categories: theoretical, pedagogical and institutional.

In Part 2, with its empirical focus, I present applications of this framework in practice. I explore the interface between theory, practice, reality and possibility, through four case studies of curriculum innovation in two language programmes at an Australian university. These case studies explore the challenges faced by language educators as they sought to enact the development 'critical *languaculture* awareness' in the curriculum and in the classroom. Even though these case studies are set in an Australian context, as I explain throughout the book, they reveal processes that mirror trends common in the literature and in the international context. Chapter 4 takes up the empirical findings to extrapolate exemplars of good practice, while acknowledging recurrent limitations in the framework's building blocks. Finally, this chapter articulates good practice *vis-à-vis* current demands in higher education.

Part 3 of the book is devoted to Chapter 5, which, on the basis on the empirical findings, explores the mechanisms at play in promoting and ensuring that the kind of *praxis*-driven pedagogical innovation proposed in this book can be sustained over time. It thus revisits the role of the teacher as curriculum innovator, the need to scaffold their professional development and the urgency of designing active dissemination and embedding strategies for the future of the field. This chapter also considers the role of HEIs in supporting these mechanisms and pays particular attention to the overall vision for intercultural graduate outcomes *vis-à-vis* current demands in the internationalised higher education scene. Finally, the Conclusion draws together the most important findings of this book for reflection and action. It uses this base to explore the research prospects for a field in transition, as well as the implications for language and culture pedagogy and the international higher education sector.

Notes

(1) Pauwels (2011) acknowledges the considerable debate over terminology used to refer to 'languages additional to one's 'first' language' (p. 256). While the term 'Languages Other Than English' (LOTE) was used in Australia for a considerable period of time to refer to these languages, policy documents from the *National Statement for Languages Education in Australian Schools: National Plan for Languages Education in Australian Schools 2005–2008* (MCEETYA, 2005) have opted for the more inclusive term 'languages' (RCLCE – University of South Australia, 2008: 3). In this study, I shall alternate between 'languages' and 'foreign languages'.
(2) Intercultural Communicative Competence (ICC) should not be confused with Intercultural Competence (IC). The former refers to an overarching model in language pedagogy, while the latter is one component of this model. I discuss their meaning and relationship in detail in Chapter 2.
(3) In this manuscript, in line with Risager's earlier publications (Risager, 2005, 2006b, 2007), I have opted for the use of *'languaculture'*, and its adjectival form *'languacultural'*. However, it is important to note that in more recent publications Risager favours the use of *'linguaculture'* (and *'linguacultural'*) (Risager, 2011, 2013), 'as perhaps a more straightforward term for linguists' (Risager, 2013: 3419).

Part 1

The Theory/Practice Gap in Language and Culture Pedagogies in Higher Education

1 Stumbling Blocks to Bridging the Theory/Practice Gap

Introduction

Foreign language teachers in universities around the world find themselves at a crossroads. They are required to reconceptualise their role and teaching practices, as well as specific curricular content and objectives, within a paradoxical educational landscape: an increased focus on internationalisation of higher education parallel with a decrease in university offering of foreign language education. Disconnection between the internationalisation strategies of higher education institutions (HEIs) and the provision of language education has emerged as a major gap in the internationalisation rhetoric (Byram, 2012b; Crichton & Scarino, 2007; Pauwels, 2011; Trevaskes *et al.*, 2003). This rhetoric reflects serious discrepancies between an interculturally aware vision for graduates and the practices in place to realise it.

My aim in this chapter is to begin to articulate the pervasive nature of these discrepancies, which I conceptualise as 'stumbling blocks' to narrowing the theory/practice gap in language and culture pedagogy. Here 'theory' refers not only to theoretical concepts and frameworks in the field of language education, but also to the rhetoric endorsed in policy documents, institutional mission statements and descriptions of course curricula. Both aspects represent a top-down perspective on examining the problem. The bottom-up perspective is provided through the actual realisations of 'theory' in the everyday classroom, which is explored in Part 2 of this book.

I begin this chapter with a critical examination of what is now widely acknowledged to be the ultimate goal in language education: the development of intercultural competence. I consider this goal in the context of a field in transition and in light of the imperative currently driving higher education to develop interculturally competent graduates. I then shift the spotlight to examine the international backdrop against which this goal is avowed in various policy documents and institutional mission statements. The underlying argument here is that identification and critical assessment of these 'stumbling blocks' can constitute a suitable starting point to uncover grounds more conducive to innovation and, ultimately, to sustainable achievement of this goal in practice.

Language and Culture Pedagogy: Facing Some Inconvenient Truths

It is undeniable. The last few decades have witnessed the emergence of globalisation processes that have fundamentally changed the nature of human communication and, in so doing, have reshaped, redefined and reconfigured communication across languages and cultures: from population mobility to instant international communication and the ever-increasing frequency of intercultural encounters. Languages education, as an inherently intercultural activity, has been called upon to equip learners to deal with this new reality, heralding significant changes to the field. The most fundamental change is reflected in the underlying goal of language learning, no longer defined primarily in terms of the acquisition of *communicative competence* (CC) (Hymes, 1972) in a foreign language, but rather as the development of *intercultural communicative competence* (ICC) (Byram, 1997; Byram & Zarate, 1994). The concept of ICC, now widely spread in the context of foreign language education, signalled a landmark shift in the way language education approaches the integration of a cultural dimension. This competence model attempted to operationalise the place of sociocultural knowledge in the development of learners' linguistic proficiency. As such, ICC is conceived as comprising of four subcompetences, three of which were included in previous models of CC: linguistic, sociolinguistic and discourse competences (Canale, 1983; Canale & Swain, 1980; Hymes, 1972; Savignon, 1983), and, as a new element: intercultural competence (IC). The last of these is conceived as encompassing a set of practices that can be grouped under three dimensions: *cognitive* (knowledge), *behavioural* (skills) and *affective* (attitudes), all crucial to helping learners communicate effectively across languages and cultures and thus to become 'interculturally competent'.

Byram and Zarate (1994) explained these dimensions using the French term *savoir*, which can be translated as 'knowing'. They identified four *savoirs*. The first, *savoirs* or 'knowings', represents the knowledge of self and other in interaction, both individual and societal. The second, *savoir comprendre*, or 'knowing how to understand', concerns the skills for interpreting and relating information. The third, *savoir apprendre/faire* or 'knowing how to learn/to do', concerns the skills for discovering new knowledge and for interacting to gain new knowledge. The fourth, *savoir être* or 'knowing how to be', concerns the attitudes involved in relativising the self and valuing the other. Byram (1997) later added a fifth component, *savoir s'engager* or 'knowing how to commit oneself', which concerns the development of 'critical cultural awareness'. Byram compared this last component with the purposes of *politische Bildung* in the (West) German education tradition, in which the goal is to encourage 'learners to reflect critically on the values, beliefs and behaviours of their own society' (Byram, 2009b).

Since its emergence in the field of language education more than 15 years ago, 'intercultural competence' has largely eclipsed its overarching ICC model to the point of achieving a ubiquitous yet somewhat elusive presence. IC's ubiquity may be attributed to various factors. One is its significant impact on the field *vis-à-vis* emerging processes of globalisation, such as the ever-increasing frequency of cross-cultural and cross-linguistic encounters. Second, as a direct corollary, is the influential adoption of it at macro policy level in various educational contexts. IC has been widely adopted as a desired goal for language education in the United Kingdom and across the European education policy context. The Council of Europe's Common European Framework of Reference for Languages (CEFR) has endorsed this model within the compulsory education system as a framework to prepare learners:

> ... for interaction with people of other cultures; to enable them to *understand* and *accept* people from other cultures as individuals with other distinctive perspectives, values and behaviours; and to help them to see that such interaction is an enriching experience. (Byram *et al.*, 2002: 6, emphasis added)

At university level, Deardorff's Delphi study[1] on university administrators and leading intercultural experts led to the identification of Byram's IC definition as the most applicable for formulating university goals in United States tertiary institutions:

> Knowledge of others, knowledge of self; skills to interpret and relate; skills to discover and/or to interact; valuing others' values, beliefs and behaviours; and relativising one's self. Linguistic competence plays a key role. (Byram, 1997: 34, cited in Deardorff, 2006: 247)

Yet IC is till elusive, which may be associated with the complexities involved in articulating its manifestation in practice. Overall, despite widespread agreement about its central role in language education, IC remains a largely uncontested concept. Byram himself noted that his model has been 'widely cited, and less widely, critically evaluated' (Byram, 2009b: 322). In so doing, he motivated much reflection on the matter, by both himself and other scholars. As a result, in recent years various aspects of this concept have come under increasing scrutiny (cf. Byram, 2009a; Byram, 2009b, 2012a; Coperías Aguilar, 2007; Harden, 2011; Houghton, 2010, 2012; Witte & Harden, 2011, inter alia), gradually giving shape to criticism that I aim to articulate in this section as theoretical and pedagogical 'stumbling blocks'. I have grouped these criticisms under three interrelated categories: (1) conceptual; (2) relational; and (3) developmental.

At the core of this critique lies a pressing question recently posed by Harden (2011: 75). The question asks whether or not it is feasible to continue pursuing IC as an educational goal, as it is currently conceived, when it is diminished by considerable limitations across these categories. These limitations ultimately call into question the reliability and validity (cf. Vijver & Leung, 2009) of the very research that aims to develop IC in practice. In light of this discussion, I argue for a shift away from IC and towards the notion of criticality. This shift foregrounds a key notion already integral to IC (Byram, 2012a) that also seems to underlie common understandings of what it takes to become interculturally competent across disciplines. I argue that a focus on criticality can give shape to a renewed teaching and research agenda driven by critical trends in language and culture pedagogy, which have already been gradually generating theoretical and paradigmatic changes in this field (cf. Byram, 2012a; Dasli, 2011a, 2011b; Houghton, 2010, 2012; Johnston et al., 2011; Levine & Phipps, 2012; Yamada, 2010).

The purpose of this discussion is not to replicate reviews of the literature on conceptualising 'intercultural competence', which are already available in a wide variety of disciplines within and beyond the field of language education (cf. Spitzberg & Changnon, 2009). Rather, here I aim to articulate a formal critique of the limitations of 'intercultural competence' as it is currently conceptualised and applied to research in language education. In so doing, I seek to address the tensions between the field's vision for the development of intercultural speakers and the difficulties of realising this vision in everyday practice.

Theoretical and pedagogical 'stumbling blocks'

Conceptual

This first category concerns the conceptual nature of 'intercultural competence' as articulated in Byram's work (Byram, 1997, 2009b, 2012a;

Byram & Zarate, 1994) and as it relates to the ontological assumptions about application of this concept. In unpacking this term, the individual notions of 'intercultural' and 'competence' may be considered separately or as a whole. Ontological assumptions in the use of the term 'intercultural' alone have been widely addressed in the field of intercultural communication (cf. seminal works by Bennett, 1998; Gudykunst et al., 1988; Gumperz & Hymes, 1986; Scollon & Scollon, 1995, among others).

In the context of language education, assumptions about the 'intercultural' are largely underpinned by how 'language', 'culture' and their interrelationship are conceptualised, together with their role in communication and in pedagogical applications for developing 'intercultural speakers' (cf. House, 2007; Kramsch, 1999; Lo Bianco, 2003). The relationship between language and culture and its place in language teaching have long been a focus of discussion (Brooks, 1968; Damen, 1987; Liddicoat & Crozet, 2000; Risager, 2006b; Seelye, 1984). While these discussions continue, the general consensus is that language education can no longer be conceived devoid of an (inter)cultural dimension (cf. Arabski & Wojtaszek, 2011; Byrnes, 2010; Kramsch, 1998a, 1998b). While Byram's model stresses the inseparable relationship between language and culture, it ultimately lacks a systematic view of this relationship (Risager, 2007) in a way that can be mapped onto the mechanics of everyday practice. This is highly problematic.

Claims of 'indivisibility' or of an isomorphic relationship between language and culture have almost become a cliché in languages education, leading to claims that language and culture are 'inseparable', or are 'inextricably linked', or the most frequent that 'language is culture and culture is language'. Significantly, as Fantini pointed out more than a decade ago, although most language educators acknowledge that language and culture are interrelated, '... they often lack explicit understanding of this interrelationship' (Fantini, 1991: 115). This widespread but over-simplified description of the relationship between language and culture is thus highly problematic. It can lead to the assumption that, if targeted effectively, language learning per se will lead to culture learning. Robinson poetically refers to this assumption as the 'magic-carpet-ride-to-another-culture syndrome' (Robinson-Stuart & Nocon, 1996; Robinson, 1978), and it has been challenged by several researchers (Byram et al., 1990; Hall & Ramírez, 1993; McMeniman & Evans, 1997; Risager, 2006b; inter al.). Yet, it is an assumption that continues to be part of the collective subconscious in languages education, not only for teachers, but also for learners (Gieve & Cunico, 2012; Pauk, 2007) and other academics outside the languages field.

Thus, in spite of both espousing IC on paper and being 'favourably disposed' to its integration in practice, teaching curricula and actual teaching practices still reveal a relationship between language and culture largely disjointed (Piasecka, 2011; Sercu, 2007). This is evident in the predominant features of two areas of the curriculum: linguistically oriented learning goals and linguistically oriented assessment tasks and evaluation criteria. Predominance of linguistically oriented practices can be attributed to the field's historical focus on the study of languages as systems of grammatical categories[2] and on their corresponding assessment (Agar, 1994; Risager, 2006b).

Assessment raises another concern about how ICC is conceptualised. Use of the term 'competence' evokes positivist, assessment-driven agendas underlining communicative competence models and associated iterations such as Bachman's model of 'communicative language ability' (Bachman, 1990). Here some observers have suggested that the term 'competence' is itself one of the most controversial and confusing terms in the field. Many have attributed this confusion and conceptual discrepancies to the 'genealogy' of the term (Coperías Aguilar, 2007; Harden, 2011; Rathje, 2007, *inter alia*). In Byram's ICC model, IC is conceptualised as including *cognitive*, *behavioural* and *affective* dimensions – attributions commonly found in the field of education (Taylor, 1988; Wiemann & Backlund, 1980). However, this conceptualisation of 'competence' is not coherent with the conceptualisation of 'competence' that underlines the rest of ICC's sub-components: linguistic, sociolinguistic and discourse competences. Indeed, although Byram and Zarate developed their model specifically in the context of foreign language teaching, its influential notion of 'intercultural competence' does not specifically deal with the interrelationship of these *savoirs* and the linguistically oriented sub-components of the CC model they aimed to complement. These sub-components were conceived within predominantly cognitive and psycholinguistic dimensions. The internal conceptual discrepancies thus create confusion over how to approach development of the two competing conceptualisations of 'competence'.

Relational

As a direct corollary of these conceptual limitations, relational weaknesses also emerge among the components of ICC. Byram's model assumes, but does not clearly explain, how each of ICC's components – linguistic, sociolinguistic, discourse and intercultural competence – relates to, or influences, the others (Liddicoat *et al.*, 2003: 15–16; Rathje, 2007; Scarino, 2009). While Byram's description makes clear that the model does not 'attempt to represent in two dimensions the complexity of the relationships among all the factors' (Byram, 1997: 72), the model's diagram uses double-sided arrows to join these four components, thus *suggesting* rather than *articulating* their interdependent relationships (Byram, 1997: 73). As a result, these relationships are never explicitly addressed in the mechanics of the model.

Byram himself has recently acknowledged this shortcoming: 'the model does not, however, represent links of dependency or interdependency among the competences; it is a "list model", not a "structural model"' (Byram, 2009b: 325). He complemented this acknowledgement with a new visual representation of the ICC model (Byram, 2009b: 323) in which the doubled-sided arrows are not included. This acknowledgement notwithstanding, a list-model perpetuates an 'add-on' approach rather than an integrative approach to incorporating intercultural competence into teaching practices. The list-like nature of the model therefore perpetuates a 'disconnect' between linguistic and intercultural elements and their articulation into learning objectives and activities. As a result, the place of 'culture' within the more language-oriented domains of ICC is obscured, thus largely hindering the overall level of intended curricular integration.

Furthermore, another crucial issue for language educators in trying to help learners become effective intercultural communicators is how to address the components of IC – knowledge, skills and attitudes – in a coherent way. 'Knowledge', 'skills' and 'attitudes' have been listed and articulated as learning objectives in various sources (especially Byram, 1997). Yet how they interact with and complement each other, and how they interact with and complement the linguistic-oriented elements of the ICC model remain unclear. As a result, how to appropriately develop all such dimensions in conjunction with linguistic-oriented competences also remains unclear.

Developmental

This category raises concerns about the overall development of ICC. These concerns can be considered from a pedagogical/curricular perspective, but above all, from a holistic developmental perspective. From the pedagogical/curricular perspective, the limitations are clear. As Byram suggests in his critical review of ICC, the model does not provide a 'didactic ordering of which aspects of which competences should be taught prior to others' (Byram, 2009b: 325). This shortcoming is highly problematical, as such ordering is essential in formulating specific instructional objectives that may be mapped across levels within courses and within programmes of study, as well as in designing coherent assessment tasks and evaluation criteria.

From a more holistic developmental perspective, the ICC model lacks a clear outline of the potential progression touchstones to describe its overall development. Indeed, Coperías-Aguilar points out that Byram's conceptualisation of ICC fails to indicate whether there are *degrees* or *levels* of competence development that can be identified to provide teachers with useful progression touchstones (Coperías Aguilar, 2002). The body of work by Byram *et al.* addresses this issue only partially. Byram and Morgan (1994) and Byram (1997), for instance, contemplate psychological theories in relation to learners' cognitive and moral development *vis-à-vis* culture learning. Yet these considerations refer mainly to children and young adults within the compulsory education system, which means that adult cognitive processes remain unexplored. This is particularly significant given IC's focal concern on its affective dimension, and a 'perspective shift' in learners' attitudes (Byram, 1997) that becomes attainable only in late adolescence. We are able to theorise about alternative paradigms of thought or 'frames of reference' in this life period as sets of assumptions that significantly influence our interpretations of experiences and events (Mezirow, 1981).

Developmental models of 'intercultural competence' are presented in the literature (*cf.* Spitzberg & Changnon, 2009). The most prominent and extensively used model is Bennett's Developmental Model of Intercultural Sensitivity (DMIS) (1986, 1993). However, this model and its application have been focused largely on study abroad research rather than classroom situations (Shaules, 2007). This leaves language educators in the dark, without a clear path on how they may contribute to the continuing, long-term development of interculturally competent language learners.

Byram (1997) considers the individual development of IC's 'knowledge, skills and attitudes' towards a *threshold* level that may indicate learners' overall effectiveness in intercultural communication. Yet these considerations remain problematic. Concentrating on the development of the 'knowledge dimension' of IC may be feasible in terms of input and assessment, but knowledge of the target language and culture *per se* does not guarantee effective intercultural communication. The 'skills dimension' of IC assumes a relationship with the 'knowledge dimension', but because this relationship is not operationalised in the model, its development is also problematic.

Finally, the 'attitudinal dimension' of IC also presents a number of challenges. This dimension, described as 'openness', 'respect', 'curiosity', 'tolerance' and 'valuing all cultures,' is certainly a desirable objective. However, these are highly abstract constructs, and language instruction *per se*, or any other type of instruction on its own can only provide the appropriate context to develop such attitudes; it cannot guarantee their development (Ingram *et al.*, 2004). Additionally, such 'attitudes' are embedded in a Western view of intercultural communication that aspires to cultural relativism. Indeed, Byram acknowledges that because his model was developed in the European (British, French, German) context, it incorporates skills laden with values dominant in the West that are deemed important in cross-cultural encounters within the Western world. In other words, IC is itself a product of Western cultural views of languages education.

It can therefore be argued that teachers from non-Western cultural backgrounds may find this 'attitudinal' dimension very difficult to conceptualise and integrate into their teaching practice. The underlying concern about this model is thus, paradoxically, its potentially ethnocentric view of cultural relativity and its notion of effectiveness in communication. Appreciation of other cultures, for instance, may be considered a Western value. Notions of 'effectiveness' in intercultural encounters are not completely congruent across, perhaps even within, Eastern–Western contexts. As Spitzberg and Changnon (2009) observe 'most of the models and related assessments have been developed in Western or Anglo contexts. It is difficult to ascertain at present the extent to which such contexts may bias or shift emphasis' (Spitzberg & Changnon, 2009: 43).

As mentioned earlier, Byram (1997) argues that the key factor in assessing the attitudinal dimension of IC is 'the existence or absence of a *perspective shift*' (Byram, 1997: 108). However, attempts to explicate the processes involved in such perspective shifts, as well as their monitoring and assessment, remain largely unaddressed (Henerson *et al.*, 1987; Schneider & North, 2000; Vogt, 2006). Because assessment of 'attitudes' uses observable data, such as a learner's words or actions in specific contexts, identifying potential attitudinal qualities or changes that might occur through exposure to a particular teaching approach is highly subjective. This assessment would also require language teachers to be conscious of their own prejudices and acquired stereotypes about other cultures and peoples. Although Byram *et al.* (2002) emphasise teachers should ensure that only the ideas behind a learner's attitudes are challenged and not the learner personally, they do not explain how to identify ideas behind a learner's attitudes, particularly with adult learners at university.

We see, then, that the lack of clear understanding about the language/culture nexus coupled with the lack of a clear articulation of ICC's subcomponents and of an indicative outline of its development serve to limit the design and implementation of syllabi, assessment tasks and strategies that may demonstrate actual realisation of ICC in practice. As such, despite the breadth of advice on the overall formulation of goals and objectives, foreign language teachers 'are left without a clear vision of the different ways in which they could organise teaching activities and of how their students could or should develop' (Houghton, 2010: 198).

In theory, the intercultural shift driven by Byram's work in language pedagogy has led to enhancing significantly the cultural dimension of this field. In practice, however, the impact of this shift on the micro-level of syllabi, materials and assessment design, as well as on classroom practices, remains problematic. This is particularly so in the context of higher education. Research in this area is yet to acknowledge the limitations discussed in this section or the imperfect nature of the university language classroom, largely underpinned by structural and logistical limitations inherent to the higher education sector. This is an inconvenient truth that theorists and practitioners, as well as university administrators, need to acknowledge in order to come to terms with the nub of the problems. Only then can they move forward to promote sustainable curriculum innovation towards developing interculturally competent graduates.

Languages in the Higher Education Context: The State of Play in the International Scene

As foreshadowed in the Introduction, the current higher education context needs to be conceived in relation to the international scene (*cf.* Maringe *et al.*, 2013). This scene is characterised by emerging processes of globalisation, from the unprecedented rise in population mobility to the ubiquitous availability of instant international communication and the ever-increasing frequency of intercultural encounters in everyday life. All of these make the pursuit of internationalisation an unavoidable task for HEIs. Here, internationalisation is widely understood as a complex process 'integrating an international and/or global dimension into the purpose, function (teaching, research and service) and delivery of higher education' (Knight, 2006).

Internationalisation processes are largely focused on preparing graduates for an increasingly globalised world (Egron-Polak & Hudson, 2010). As such, most HEIs' mission statements and policy documents articulate this rationale, albeit under many guises, as specific graduate attributes. Descriptors of these attributes refer to graduates as 'global citizens' with awareness of and sensitivity to other cultures, and the ability to function in global, multicultural environments (Bourn, 2010). However, these descriptors do not provide evidence of a clear connection between intercultural graduate attributes and the crucial role of foreign language learning in the development of intercultural skills. Moreover, as Pauwels points out, 'there is greater tension or even disjuncture between rhetoric about the importance and relevance of learning another "foreign" language and its practice' (Pauwels, 2011: 248). Given the discussion presented in the first part of this chapter, we must surely wonder how 'prepared for a globalised world' are graduates who have not been exposed to learning other cultures through other languages.

The availability of national, government and intergovernmental reports from around the world as well as numerous academic publications concerning the state of languages education in HEIs provide ample data for international comparison. The data presented in these sources vary in terms of focus, breadth and depth. However, they provide a suitable starting point to begin articulating structural and logistical stumbling blocks standing in the way of developing 'interculturally competent' graduates through language education. There is evidence to suggest that notwithstanding substantial efforts in some institutions around the world, and at risk of generalising, the overall underlying thread connecting these stumbling blocks seems to be a lack of coherence between espoused goals at macro-policy levels and practices to support their achievement at the micro-level of curriculum development.

Structural 'stumbling blocks'

Examination of international reports and academic publications reveals at least three largely interrelated 'stumbling blocks' to creating linkages between internationalisation strategies, foreign language education and their espoused vision of interculturally aware graduates. The first stumbling block concerns the global state of language studies in higher education and the associated implications for upholding benchmarking of graduate outcomes. The second concerns the restrictive structure of degree programmes. The third concerns the common trends or strategies for integrating an '(inter) cultural dimension' in the curricula of university language programmes. Let us explore these stumbling blocks in detail.

The latest Global Survey conducted by the International Association of Universities polled 745 universities across 115 nations (Egron-Polak & Hudson, 2010). This survey revealed that 'internationalisation' features in the strategic plans of 87% of HEIs around the world and that the two top rationales driving internationalisation processes are 'improving student preparedness for a globalised world' and 'the internationalisation of the curriculum' (Egron-Polak & Hudson, 2010: 64). Yet few HEIs make it a priority for graduates to be multilingual. Only 52% expect their undergraduate students to fulfil some requirements in terms of course credits in foreign language in order to graduate (Egron-Polak & Hudson, 2010: 125). This figure, however, includes English as a 'foreign language'. Closer examination of HEIs in English-speaking countries, such as the United States, the United Kingdom and Australia, paints a particularly unsettling picture in this regard.

According to the study *Mapping Internationalization on U.S. Campuses*, released in June 2012 by the American Council on Education (ACE), only 37% of American HEIs require undergraduate students to complete some study of any language other than English to graduate, down from nearly 53% in 2001 (CIGE, 2012: 11). Among these HEIs, the most commonly reported requirement is one year of foreign language study. These figures are complemented by the 2009 survey *Enrolments in Languages Other Than English in United States Institutions of Higher Education*, carried out by the United States Modern Language Association (MLA), with support of the United States Department of Education. This survey reports that an annual average of 8% of undergraduates enrol in foreign language studies (Furman *et al.*, 2010).

This situation is not dissimilar from the United Kingdom or Australia, where government-commissioned reports have shown similar, but even more alarming declining trends in the study of languages (*cf.* Bawden, 2007; Gallagher-Brett & Broady, 2012). In England, for instance, the *Review of Modern Foreign Languages Provision in Higher Education in England* indicated that while in the 2002/03 academic year 3.3% of all full-time students were studying languages as part of their degree, in 2007/08 this figure had decreased to 2.9% (Worton, 2009: 17). In Australia, 'none of the 38 doctorate-granting Australian universities has compulsory language study requirements' (Martín, 2005: 54). According to Lo Bianco, 'fewer than 5 percent of students exit university with at least a minor study in a language other than English' (Lo Bianco, 2009: 56). This trend is substantiated by numerous reports (*cf.* Lo Bianco, 2009; Nettelbeck *et al.*, 2007; White & Baldauf, 2006). Given Australia's multilingual potential – and the United States and United Kingdom's, for that matter – this pattern of decline and erosion in the provision of languages education at university has been described as not only a national tragedy, but also an 'international embarrassment' (Clyne *et al.*, 2007).

The advocated 'interculturally aware' vision for the future of university graduates appears to be a poor competitor against the multitude of other claims on university teaching budgets. It largely neglects the crucial role of foreign language learning in the development of intercultural skills and, therefore, in advancing espoused internationalisation processes. This is happening at a time when the need to rationalise and substantiate the quality of such graduate outcomes is ever more momentous. Indeed, the international higher education scene is currently characterised by the need to establish accountability and, in so doing, to explicitly rationalise learning outcomes and academic achievement standards so they can be subject to comparison for quality assurance (QA) purposes.

The preoccupation with QA that currently drives policy is set to intensify in the future (Egron-Polak & Hudson, 2010: 137). Trends in QA efforts, however, have not reached the language studies field, or at least they have done so with inconsistencies at national and institutional level. In some cases, this has resulted in leaving the establishment of benchmarking up to professional associations. This means that the overall articulation of students' intercultural competence through language education is still at a rudimentary stage, reflecting the almost glacial pace at which substantive curricular reform occurs at professional and institutional levels.

In the United Kingdom, the *Languages and Related Studies* subject benchmark statement prepared by the Quality Assurance Agency (QAA) for Higher Education (QAA, 2007) provides explicit but quite general directives for standards in providing language education. This means that at the planning stage, institutions must take account of these nationally recognised standards and consider their specific application according to their own institutional context. This benchmark statement makes specific reference to the development of *intercultural awareness, understanding and competence* through the study of languages as a set of *skills*, indicating that:

> Through their studies, their contact with the target language and associated cultures and their related studies, all students of languages will develop sensitivity to, and awareness of, the similarities and dissimilarities between other cultures and societies, and their own. In particular, their competence in the target language means that they will have an appreciation of internal diversity and transcultural connectedness, and an attitude of curiosity and openness towards other cultures. The skills and attributes they develop will include: a critical understanding of a culture and practices other than one's own; an ability to function in another culture; an appreciation of the uniqueness of the other culture(s); an ability to articulate to others the contribution that the culture has made at a regional and global level; an ability and willingness to engage with other cultures; an ability to appreciate and evaluate critically one's own culture. (QAA, 2007: 8)

The formulation of this statement evokes Byram's conceptualisation of IC with a strong emphasis on the attitudinal dimension (sensitivity, appreciation, attitude of curiosity, openness, willingness to engage) and to a lesser extent on the more cognitive dimension of criticality (critical understanding, evaluating critically). This statement does not, however, articulate key indicators of students' achievement of these intercultural skills, nor does it suggest ways of establishing how to evaluate these skills in practice. As a result, compliance with these benchmarks remains the responsibility of teachers.

In the United States, there is currently no single QA entity. Rather, QA is primarily within the responsibility of a group of independent accreditation agencies which, in turn, are organised under the approval of the government

(Bernhard, 2012a, 2012b). For language studies, policymakers and practitioners have to refer to the Modern Language Association (MLA) and, in particular, to its affiliated Association of Departments of Foreign Languages (ADFL, 2012). The latter articulates field-wide consensus on standards of good practice on such topics as class size and workload, evaluation of teaching and scholarship, the employment of adjunct faculty members and procedures for departmental review. It does not, however, provide explicit guidance as to the overall objectives or curriculum strategies for integrating language and culture pedagogies.

In 2004, the MLA convened an *ad hoc* committee in charge of examining and analysing foreign language education in the United States and in so doing, working to 'identify problem areas, prioritise these, and make recommendations for improvement of language education and reform of departments and programmes' (Levine, 2011: 135). The committee subsequently released a report: *Foreign languages and higher education: New structures for a changed world* (Modern Language Association, 2007), which identifies several problem areas. One of the report's most significant contributions was the articulation of a new overarching objective for language education in the United States: 'translingual and transcultural competence' (Modern Language Association, 2007: 3–4), defined as:

> The ability to operate between languages. Students are educated to function as informed and capable interlocutors with educated native speakers in the target language. They are also trained to reflect on the world and themselves through the lens of another language and culture. They learn to comprehend speakers of the target language as members of foreign societies and to grasp themselves as Americans – that is, as members of a society that is foreign to others. They also learn to relate to fellow members of their own society who speak languages other than English. (Modern Language Association, 2007: 4)

This newly avowed goal provided a much needed focal point to language teachers in tackling reform of the language and culture curriculum. Levine (2011) offers a careful review of the numerous published academic responses to the report, and in so doing highlights both its contribution and its shortcomings, for instance, its lack of articulation with the National Standards in Foreign Language Education Learning in the 21st century (ACTFL, 2006) prepared by the American Council on the Teaching of Foreign Languages (ACTFL). This and other shortcomings were addressed in the edited volume: *Critical and Intercultural Theory and Language Pedagogy* (Levine & Phipps, 2012). All chapters in this volume present provocative ideas that challenge the theory/practice (research) tensions in the field and collectively shape the overall argument that this perceived dichotomy should be reframed into a move towards practice-driven theoretical change. Yet, much empirical research is needed to support this move.

In Australia, the Tertiary Education Quality and Standards Agency (TEQSA) is the new national regulatory and quality agency that promotes, audits and reports on QA in Australian higher education. This regulatory role was formerly the responsibility of the Australian Universities Quality Agency (AUQA). Currently, the only available language-related guidelines provided by AUQA and TEQSA focus on the development of English language education for international students. The AUQA report on *Good Practice Principles for English Language Proficiency for International Students in Australian Universities*, funded by the Department of Education, Employment and Workplace Relations (DEEWR), acknowledged that 'there is also an increased recognition within universities of the fundamental nature of language in learning and academic achievement for all students' (AUQA, 2009: 2). Yet efforts continue in areas of direct economic relevance to universities, that is, the satisfaction of full fee-paying overseas students. While ensuring the development of English language proficiency for international students is certainly an imperative, giving it such priority at the expense of other areas of language teaching is a clear indication of the often narrow, one-dimensional conceptualisation of internationalisation processes held not only by many institutions, but also by the national government (Crichton & Scarino, 2007; Eisenchlas *et al.*, 2003). This type of one-dimensional perspective perpetuates the monolingual mindset embedded in Australian society (Clyne, 2005; Clyne *et al.*, 2007).

Deliberate efforts have also been made to provide guidelines for the delivery of language studies at transnational levels. In the European context, the Language Network for Quality Assurance (LanQua) is the only current initiative devoted to QA in foreign language education. This three-year project (October 2007–September 2010) was funded by the Commission of the European Communities Lifelong Learning Erasmus Network programme and involved 60 partners from 29 countries across Europe. The final product consists of a set of toolkits available online. The toolkits include a Quality Model and a Frame of Reference that provides valuable information to map the current landscape of languages in European HEIs.

The field of languages is described in five areas: language learning, intercultural communication, literature and culture, content and language integrated learning (CLIL) and language teacher education. The overarching aim of these toolkits, which include several case studies of good practice in each of these five areas, is to promote reflection on how a subject–practitioner approach to quality assurance can inform quality assurance processes and enhance the quality of the learning experience for students (LanQua, 2010). The LanQua initiative was coordinated by the Centre for Languages, Linguistics and Area Studies (LLAS) hosted by the University of Southampton in the United Kingdom. LLAS is currently leading on a new EU-funded project that will use the LanQua Toolkit to support greater sharing of practice in QA across disciplines and institutions. The toolkit is also to enhance understanding of the ways in which quality is experienced and interpreted within the university by students, teachers and support staff working in QA roles. From October 2011 to September 2013, the project will concentrate on investigating implementation of the QA toolkits with nine partners across Europe.

Currently, efforts at the international level are being led by the Assessment of Higher Education Learning Outcomes (AHELO), which will test what students in higher education know and can do upon graduation across 15 OECD countries. The research currently being conducted by AHELO will provide data on the relevance and quality of teaching and learning in higher education diverse cultures, languages and different types of institutions. The study, expected to be completed by 2013, concentrates on graduate outcomes in relation to generic skills and, for strategic reasons, only two discipline-specific areas: economics and engineering (OECD, 2012). Data yielded by this study will, however, provide useful pathways for the future alignment of learning outcomes *vis-à-vis* foreign language education.

The discussion above provides evidence to suggest a lack of articulation between internationalisation processes committed to the development of intercultural graduates and the provision of languages education that also espouses this goal. There is also a lack of articulation between this espoused goal and current regulatory actions. HEIs around the world are expected to have a structured system to develop, monitor and validate existing programmes, but the lack of attention paid to this subject area largely results in relaxed accountability for the sector. This does not mean that individual institutions do not apply internal QA measures such as reviews and evaluations of programmes and subjects. But it does suggest that: (1) there is currently no way to compare or externally validate outcomes related to language and culture learning across countries, at a global level; and (2) it is up to individual language faculties, departments and, ultimately, language teachers themselves to rationalise, articulate and monitor the achievement of intercultural graduate outcomes. Some may argue that the latter has always been – and perhaps, *should be* – the case. Even so, given the limitations explored in the first part of this chapter, it is clearly not an easy task.

Ensuring learners' achievements, in terms of 'intercultural' goals, is exacerbated by the structural features of university degrees *vis-à-vis* language programmes and their provision. Given the individual histories and current imperatives driven by specific national contexts, it is difficult to establish commonalities in a degree's integration of an (inter)cultural dimension across countries. However, national, government and intergovernmental reports from around the world, as well as numerous academic publications, provide suitable data for international comparison in this regard.

Structurally speaking, foreign language programmes of study around the world share many similarities with regard to the sequence and range of subjects for specialist learners (Cañado, 2010; Dlaska, 2012; Gieve & Cunico, 2012; Nettelbeck et al., 2007; Pauwels, 2011). They also share a similar bottom-heavy enrolment structure, that is, a pyramid-like shape in terms of enrolments, with a high number of enrolments in the elementary subjects and a high attrition rate in the advanced, third-year subjects (Klapper, 2006; Nettelbeck et al., 2007). This trend of high attrition at advanced levels points to why very few graduates actually gain advanced proficiency levels in the target language (Pauwels, 2002).

Despite this ostensible lack of alignment between graduate attributes and comprehensive curriculum development, research reveals at least three common trends or strategies towards the integration of an '(inter)cultural dimension' in the curricula of most university undergraduate language programmes. The first and most traditional strategy has been to create language 'content subjects' dedicated to the study of specific areas such as literature, film and other 'cultural traditions' through the target language. These subjects require intermediate to advanced levels of language proficiency, which makes them accessible only to specialist learners, mostly students who are enrolled in the more advanced subjects of these programmes.

The syllabi of these subjects reveal that their approach to the study of 'culture' may be limited to acquiring what Crichton and Scarino describe as the content approach to 'the intercultural', that is: 'a body of knowledge to be analysed and acquired by the learner' (Crichton & Scarino, 2007: 4, 6). This presents 'culture' textualised as '"issues", "case studies", "examples", "values' perspectives", and "aspects", and "practices", which students are required to "analyse", "explore", "compare", "consider", and "examine"' (Crichton & Scarino, 2007). The content approach is evident in the type and focus of assessment items. Students are generally assessed on their knowledge of the subject matter (literature, film and so forth), and more specifically on their development of the four macro-linguistic skills (listening, speaking, reading and writing). Limiting the cultural dimension to this 'content' typically results in a separation 'from how learners are themselves situated in relation to, and potentially transformed by, their understanding of, and engagement with that content within and across cultures' (Crichton & Scarino, 2007: 4, 7).

The second strategy has focused on integrating non-language subject components. In addition to the core language subject components, language programmes may also include so-called 'cultural context' subjects, typically offered at beginners' level. 'Cultural context' subjects are usually open to students across faculties since they are taught in the students' *lingua franca*, which in the case of Australia and many other Anglophone countries, would be English. Generally, these subjects present an introduction to a potpourri of 'cultural' aspects about the target language and the countries where it is spoken. These 'cultural' aspects typically include historical and political developments, as well as literary, film and other salient representations of the country or countries where the target language is spoken from a variety of standpoints. This strategy is also underpinned by a 'content' approach to the integration of the cultural. As such, the focus of these subjects becomes acquisition of knowledge isolated from language, rather than examination of sociolinguistic and pragmatic aspects of the target language for critically exploring both native and target cultures.

The third strategy to address the '(inter)cultural' dimension entails incorporating an in-country exchange component (Godsland, 2010), which Crichton and Scarino described as the relocation approach, conceived 'as a matter of moving between culturally defined locations' (Crichton & Scarino, 2007: 4, 9). Some university language programmes offer such a component, usually at intermediate and advanced levels. Here the university offers some financial assistance to support students who want to pursue their language studies at an overseas university with which their university has a formal exchange agreement. The opportunity to pursue language courses overseas is generally identified as a motivating factor for students taking up language studies. Nevertheless, the number of students who take advantage of this opportunity is relatively low.

In the United Kingdom, for instance, when studying languages as a single, major or joint programme, students are normally required to take a year abroad in one or two locations. They usually spend this year in at least one of three ways: studying at a university (generally as part of a Socrates/Erasmus scheme), as a language assistant in the target community or in a work placement scheme (Lillie, 2003: 3). This requirement notwithstanding, the latest statistical data indicates that United Kingdom students abroad represent only about 1.6% (around 33,000) of the total population of United Kingdom students in higher education (King et al., 2010: 4). This figure mirrors trends in the Australian context (Nettelbeck et al., 2007) where undertaking an exchange abroad is not compulsory for completing their degree in language studies. Moreover, in many cases, it is often seen by cash-strapped university students as an expensive move that is not warranted and can easily be forsaken.

In the United States, according to the 2011 *Open Doors 2011: Report on International Educational Exchange*, the number of students choosing to study abroad has increased, with around 270,000 students reporting they studied abroad in the 2009/10 academic year (Chow & Bhandari, 2011). However, this is only 1.3% of all university students enrolled at any one time in the United States. Furthermore, this report revealed that only 6% of these students reported going abroad for language-related studies, compared with 22% in social sciences and 21% in business and management. This means roughly only one in 100 American students takes advantage of the opportunity to experience another culture or setting. This is despite data presented in the report, *Open Doors, Secure Borders: Advantages of Education Abroad for Public Policy*, which suggests that students who study abroad have higher average grades and degree completion rates than those who do not take advantage of this opportunity (Johnson & Mullholland, 2006) to say nothing of the rich opportunities for future work and life experiences that the study abroad opportunity opens. As a result, the United States does not produce enough graduates with advanced foreign-language skills to fill the needs of its defence, foreign relations and law enforcement agencies.

Despite these bleak figures, according to the Global Survey conducted by the IAU, 'outgoing mobility for students' (e.g. through exchange opportunities and internships) remains the top priority in internationalisation policies with a 44% aggregate result for HEIs around the world. On the other hand, 'foreign language teaching as part of the curriculum' is far behind at 14% (Egron-Polak & Hudson, 2010: 89). Many universities claim incorporating such exchange components as a key aspect in their commitment to the internationalisation process. But periods of sojourn abroad for students do not automatically guarantee the development of their intercultural competences. Indeed, as Crichton and Scarino suggest, limiting the integration of a cultural dimension to a relocation type of approach may reduce students' experiences to 'a matter of co-presence' with diversity, which may not necessarily prompt students to engage in critical reflection on their own cultural identity/identities in relation to others, or on the reciprocal nature of interaction between languages and cultures (Crichton & Scarino, 2007: 4, 10; see also Kinginger (2009) for an in-depth review of research on university students' foreign language study abroad).

The first two of these three strategies reveal two extreme versions of the integration of a cultural dimension in language teaching (*cf.* Gieve & Cunico, 2012). At one end is 'culture teaching' in the target language relegated to advanced levels for 'specialist' learners; at the other is 'culture teaching' in the students' *lingua franca* at beginners' levels for both specialist and non-specialist learners. However, both extremes seem to share two potential shortcomings: (1) their apparent disconnect with other subjects within the programme in terms of sequential development of cultural and linguistic competence; and (2) their focus on a rather static, one-dimensional view of 'culture' isolated from its pragmatic and sociolinguistic dimensions. This is apparent in some of the universities' language subject descriptions and in outlines of their programmes.

This disconnect is exacerbated at subject-level, where most subject descriptions include all-encompassing 'cultural' goals and objectives that appear to merely pay lip-service to university policy statements and graduate profiles. In addition to development of the four macro-skills, subject objectives typically refer to the acquisition of 'cultural knowledge' and 'awareness of differences and similarities with the target culture'. Yet subject syllabi fail to indicate how these objectives are addressed in terms of content, or how their achievement is evaluated or monitored in terms of assessment. This observation supports the claim that cultural goals continue to be subordinated to linguistic goals in most language subjects (Piasecka, 2011), casting further doubt upon their feasibility.

The bleak picture that these stumbling blocks present, however, is being increasingly offset at curricular level by language teachers' resilient commitment to their educational mission (Levine, 2011; Li et al., 2012). This commitment is evident in their continuing search for innovative practices and ideas to increase the chances that the language they teach will survive in the current slippery state of play. Grassroots movements by language teachers associations around the world are now responding to this call for action, triggering deep fractures in the 'conceptual plates' of the field. This is evident most notably in the United States, with the MLA's report: *Foreign Languages and Higher Education: New Structures for a Changed World* (Modern Language Association, 2007) and Levine and Phipps' edited volume: *Critical and Intercultural Theory and Language Pedagogy* (Levine & Phipps, 2012). The latter in particular has addressed head-on the 'perennial cycle' (Levine & Phipps, 2012: 3) of the theory/practice dichotomy in language pedagogy. Levine and Phipps' overall argument is that this perceived dichotomy should be reframed into an understanding that 'theory is practice is theory' (Levine & Phipps, 2012: 4) emerging in the myriad everyday practices and personal reflections manifested inside and outside the classroom. This position is gaining strength in the language teaching community. However, for the most part it remains the philosophy and action of individual departments and teachers willing to tackle these rapidly changing conditions.

The academic literature reveals countless studies that have attempted to address the development of 'intercultural competence' in university language programmes. In the Australian context, these range from specific course designs to the design of subject modules, from syllabus selection to development of specific assessment items (Crichton *et al.*, 2004; Eisenchlas & Hortiguera, 1999; Eisenchlas & Trevaskes, 2003; Eisenchlas & Trevaskes, 2007; Liddicoat & Crozet, 2001; Mrowa-Hopkins & Strambi, 2005; Visocnik-Murray & Laura, 2001, to name but a few). These studies provide ample evidence of good practice toward integrating an intercultural dimension in the higher education language curriculum. However, the parameters of these studies are relatively narrow and focus on isolated instances of innovation, as such, they do not bespeak – or offer – a comprehensive, programmatic view of curriculum innovation. Relying on this type of innovation supports 'a tendency to produce "islands of innovation" where the cumulative effect is a piecemeal approach' that attempts to address the development of intercultural competent learners 'but does embed it in a foundational way' (Lee *et al.*, 2012: 11) within the field or the institutional context as a whole. Indeed, except for few exceptions (*cf.* Crichton *et al.*, 2004; Davies & Devlin, 2007), for the most part, curriculum innovation tends to focus on specific languages and levels of proficiency and concern specific subject contexts that do not provide the field and language educators themselves, with an overall, clear conceptualisation of how language and culture are linked, and how to use this conceptualisation for selecting specific content across languages and proficiency levels within a programme.

Overall, an increasing sense of uncertainty and identity crisis pervades the sector. Even so, many language educators remain committed to their educational mission, as evident in their continuing search for innovative practices and ideas to survive or even to thrive through strategies that implant new understandings and practices into the currently transitioning field (Levine, 2011; Nettelbeck *et al.*, 2012). This constructive attitude, however, is undermined by the lack of continuing professional development opportunities (Klapper, 2006) that could help language teachers respond effectively to the changing nature of their discipline while addressing the universities' vision for the future of university graduates.

Conclusion

In this chapter we have explored the discrepancies between an interculturally aware vision for foreign language programmes in higher education and the practices in place to realise it. We have conceptualised these discrepancies as obstacles or 'stumbling blocks' in the way of achieving the highly desirable, but seldom carefully rationalised, goal of preparing graduates for an increasingly globalised world. In exploring the complex connections within this web of stumbling blocks we have identified two dimensions: conceptual/pedagogical and structural/logistical. Our critical interrogation of these dimensions reveals that their interconnection requires a holistic approach to reconceptualising teaching practices at programme and degree structure levels in order to build the interculturally aware vision that universities claim to seek for their graduates.

Exploration of the conceptual/pedagogical dimension has revealed several limitations embedded within the current conceptualisation of IC in language education; limitations that ultimately cast doubt upon its feasibility in practice. Exploration of the structural/logistical dimension suggests that, on paper at least, policy documents and university mission statements endorse an intercultural approach to internationalisation and languages education with a view to developing interculturally competent graduates. In practice, however, the reality for HEIs around the world reveals a serious absence of correlation between this espoused view and actual practises in place to achieve it.

If HEIs are to prepare graduates who can communicate confidently in culturally appropriate ways in a variety of contexts and settings, these institutions need to re-evaluate their commitment to this vision. Progress toward achieving this goal thus hinges on a shift in the organisational philosophy of the higher education sector (Eisenchlas et al., 2003). This shift should play a key role in creating structural alignment between, on the one hand universities' mission statements and curriculum goals, and on the other hand everyday teaching practices and actual learning. Such a shift will entail reconceptualising the values underlying what it actually means to be an interculturally competent speaker in today's globalised world.

The crux of the issue thus becomes how to turn these limitations and constraints into opportunities to generate innovation, underpinned by a coherent alignment of theory and practice. This means turning 'stumbling blocks' into 'building blocks'. For universities and policymakers it is a leap from rhetoric to reality. For language teachers and their students it is an exciting opportunity to learn and grow through ongoing action, reflection and creative innovation.

In the following chapter I start by articulating these building blocks on principles informed by theory from various fields as they converge to explain and support language and culture learning processes in the higher education context. Critical analysis of the framework's implementation is explored in Part 2 of this book.

Notes

(1) Deardorff's methodology was underpinned by the use of the Delphi technique: an iterative process used to achieve consensus among a panel of experts (Deardorff, 2011: 66).
(2) Here 'grammar' or 'grammatical categories' refer to syntax, morphology, lexis, phonetics and phonology.

2 From Stumbling Blocks into Building Blocks

Building Blocks for Sustainable Pedagogical Innovation

Challenges confront university language teachers as they try to develop in students the interculturally aware vision upheld at both discipline and institutional levels. In Chapter 1 we conceptualised these challenges as 'stumbling blocks' standing in the way of realising this vision in practice. At discipline level, these stumbling blocks concern the limitations embedded in how 'intercultural competence' is conceived in the field of language education. At institutional level, they are the product of incongruence between stated goals and practices in place to achieve them. I argue that these 'stumbling blocks' ultimately compromise the development of interculturally competent graduates in practice and without carefully informed remedial attention, these blockages will stay in place, or perhaps widen the existing theory/practice gap with deleterious consequences for the culturally aware vision of graduates.

These circumstances compel the need to generate organisational changes and pedagogical innovation from within; to undertake a centrifugal type of innovation driven by clear understanding of the limitations – and opportunities – imposed by the convergence of theory and practice. I conceptualise pedagogical innovation as any planned changes introduced to improve the curriculum and its elements – including learning objectives, materials, activities and assessment tasks – conceptually and in practice. The crux of the issue now becomes how to turn these 'stumbling blocks' into the 'building blocks' that support coherent alignment of theory and practice in pedagogical innovation. In this chapter I aim to articulate this transformation in detail to start mapping the way towards a new *guide to practice*.

I consider how each 'stumbling block' may be transformed into the 'building blocks' of a comprehensive curriculum development framework that acknowledges and embraces the complexities of language and culture teaching in the current educational landscape. Each building block thus rests on principles informed by multiple streams of literature from the field of language education as they converge to explain and support coherent language and culture learning processes in the higher education context. In so doing, I aim to reign in and synthesise the potential of these streams of literature to generate complementary principles that can support a comprehensive curriculum development framework conceived with the language teacher in mind. Given the role of teachers as catalysts for innovation, this framework seeks to guide teachers in unravelling the various elements that can lead to the development of interculturally competent speakers. This framework therefore aims to offer concrete suggestions for micro-level curriculum planning to help teachers make informed and deliberate choices that best enable them to address the demands of their broadened educational mission in a coordinated and sustainable way.

Conceptualising a Framework for Sustainable Pedagogical Innovation

The framework I offer in this book is the result of ongoing work I started in 2006. I present the empirical realisations of this framework in Part 2 of this book; in this chapter I describe the principles that underpin the design of the framework. These principles are based on the limitations identified in Chapter 1. As I revealed there, when I began this investigation these limitations were only slowly starting to emerge, but they became increasingly evident over time, thus strengthening the need to formalise this framework.

At no stage in conceptualising this framework have I envisaged providing a ready-made solution for the theory/practice divide in language and culture pedagogy. Rather, I have developed the framework to provide a systematic account of the elements that can support the meeting of theory with practice through curriculum innovation. In the context of this investigation, the curriculum is defined as 'a complex whole of philosophical, social, administrative factors which contribute to the planning of educational programmes and include processes of design, development, implementation and evaluation' (Allen, 1984: 61). My focus on curriculum stems from its potential to map students' development in a study programme.

Because frameworks are conceptual representations of reality or possibility, they will always remain simplified, abstract reductions of the more complex, multi-faceted reality they strive to represent. As such, they are rife with potential limitations. Yet the advantages of carefully conceived frameworks far outweigh their limitations.

Conceptualising a framework provides a frame of reference to consider a problem, in this case the lack of a cohesive, comprehensive approach to realising espoused goals in practice. Striving to conceptualise this particular framework forced me to identify and think through as many theoretical and real-world attributes as possible, attributes that would otherwise continue to be camouflaged or pass unnoticed in the complex web of interrelated elements. Rather than prescriptive guidelines, the framework aims to offer its users informed *choice*. Its strategy is for users to consider critically the complex relationships between the various building blocks as the basis for choosing what is the most appropriate action to bridge the theory/practice gap in a systematic way, fully cognisant of their complex interdependence within a given educational context.

Foundation 'building blocks'

This framework is underpinned by three sets of foundation building blocks: theoretical, pedagogical and institutional. Each of these building blocks is made up of internal elements or sets of tenets that we may conceive as the 'raw materials' that bind together each block. The idea behind the 'building blocks' metaphor is that weaknesses in the internal elements or sets of tenets binding the building blocks may cause the 'structure' of the framework to yield substantially, and in the worst case scenario, to collapse altogether. 'Weaknesses' may range from lack, to complete absence, of coherence among the tenets and building blocks.

Theoretical foundations: A critical languaculture approach

The first foundation stone in this framework aims to address the theoretical limitations discussed in Chapter 1. These limitations – conceptual, relational and developmental – were largely rooted in users' over-reliance on tacit connections between language and culture in interaction. This building block is therefore conceptualised on the basis of three main features or tenets that render the tacit explicit: (1) having an explicit conceptualisation (or, at the very least, working definition) of the language and culture nexus; (2) articulating this conceptualisation for language teaching; and, in turn, (3) mapping the progressive study of this conceptualisation against a curricular sequence of study. I discuss each of these three below.

Explicit conceptualisation of the language and culture nexus

The first tenet in this building block is concerned with having a clear, explicit conceptualisation of the relationship between language and culture. The discussion presented in Chapter 1 revealed that the lack of a clear conceptualisation of the language and culture nexus not only results in inconsistent, *ad hoc* culture-teaching practices, but also perpetuates the magic-carpet-ride-to-another-culture syndrome (Robinson-Stuart & Nocon, 1996; Robinson, 1978).

In considering how to define this relationship, I also consider how to 'name' it. In the literature, we find a number of widely used hyphenated terms such as 'culture-in-language' (Liddicoat & Crozet, 2000; Murphy, 1988) and 'language-and-culture' (Byram & Morgan, 1994; Papademetre & Scarino, 2000). The portmanteau term *linguaculture*, introduced by Friedrich (1989) and later adapted by Michael Agar, an American (cognitive) linguistic anthropologist (Agar, 1994), has been used less widely in the literature than these hyphenated terms – perhaps because of its portmanteau nature, slightly uncomfortable for some. Agar employs the term *languaculture* to speak of the interface between culture and those aspects of language that are 'culture bound'. The term *languaculture*, therefore stresses two relations: 'the *langua* in *languaculture* is about discourse, not just about words and sentences. And the culture in *languaculture* is about meanings that include, but go well beyond, what the dictionary and the grammar offer' (Agar, 1994: 96) (italics in the original).

Languaculture was later adopted by post-structuralist sociolinguist Karen Risager who took it into more useful territory by offering a comprehensively descriptive representation of the language/culture nexus. In *Language and Culture: Global Flows and Local Complexities* (Risager, 2006b), Risager proposes a comprehensive and theoretically encompassing, highly systematic definition of the *languaculture* concept that reaches beyond Friedrich's semantic-poetic and Agar's semantic-pragmatic foci to encompass a sociolinguistic dimension to the reflection of culture in language. Risager identifies three interrelated perspectives or loci for *languaculture*. The first is sociological or *languaculture* in linguistic practice; the second is psychological or *languaculture* in linguistic resources; and the third is system-oriented or *languaculture* in the 'linguistic system'.

- *Languaculture* in linguistic practices refers to oral and written behaviour in interaction, which covers verbal language, paralanguage and kinesics.
- *Languaculture* in linguistic resources refers to the socially constituted knowledge of language, developed as part of the life history of the person who is communicating, including an 'idiolectical repertoire' of productive,

receptive and interpretative, paralinguistic and kinesic skills unique to the individual (Risager, 2005).

- *Languaculture* in linguistic systems refers to language as a system, separated from culture. As such, it is a construct, a family of historically and discursively constructed notions of language ('English', 'French', etc.) that interacts with linguistic practice and resources as a kind of – more or less conscious – normative factor.

Risager identifies three dimensions in each of these loci. The first is the semantic and pragmatic dimension, which corresponds to Agar's interests. This dimension is concerned with the constancy and variability in the semantics and pragmatics of specific languages and the social and personal variability found in concrete situations (e.g. the choice of *'tu'* and *'vous'* in French). The second is the poetic dimension, which relates to Friedrich's definition of *languaculture*. This dimension refers to the specific kinds of meaning created in exploiting the phonological and syllabic structure of the language in question, its rhymes and its relationships between speech and writing. The third is the identity dimension, which some sociolinguists call 'social meaning' (Hymes, 1972, 1974). This dimension is concerned with the social variation of a given language, whereby its users project their own understanding of the world onto the interlocutors and consciously or unconsciously invite them to react. Works by Le Page and Tabouret-Keller (1985) further substantiate this particular view, recognising language use as identity construction.

> In using the language in a specific way, with a specific accent for instance, you identify yourself and make it possible for others to identify you according to their background knowledge and attitudes. Linguistic practice is a continuing series of 'acts of identity'. (Le Page & Tabouret-Keller, 1985: 14)

Risager argues that by introducing the term *languaculture* in this way 'one gains a way out of the all far too reaching claim concerning the inseparability of language and culture' (Risager, 2006b: 119). She stresses that 'not everything cultural is linguistic' (Risager, 2006a: 37); some 'culture' is not bound to any specific language (e.g. foods, musical traditions or architectural types). But 'language' cannot be separated from *languaculture*: the meanings carried and produced by language in any of the above-mentioned dimensions. Conceptualising the language and culture nexus in this way, 'offers the opportunity of seeing foreign or second language learners, especially adults, as people who exploit their first language *languaculture* in the process of learning a new language' (Risager, 2006a: 37). Thus, Risager distinguishes between *languaculture* in its function as first language (which includes early second language) and foreign language (which includes late second language).

Languaculture in all its dimensions is characterised as both relatively constant and relatively variable. Relative constancy is maintained by 'constant' aspects of the structure of language and relative variability is maintained by 'variable' social, individual and situational aspects of communication. As to the idea of first and foreign *languaculture*, these features become particularly relevant as they suggest individuals may select from their *languaculture* blueprint to act appropriately, but not reductively, in different social contexts within the same culture. This notion of 'constant' and 'variable' *languaculture* behaviour concurs with observations by Liddicoat *et al.* (2003) that, 'although an individual's use of language is to a certain extent "bound" by his/her native cultural blueprint, he/she is also capable of creating a personal unique expression in communication' (Liddicoat *et al.*, 2003: 10).

Risager offers one practical example throughout her 2006b book to illustrate the different aspects of *languaculture* that may emerge through a given language classroom exercise. In the counterpart book, *Language and Culture Pedagogy: From a National to a Transnational Paradigm* (Risager, 2007), she examines the notion of *languaculture* in relation to specific language and culture teaching approaches through 'a critical analysis of the international culture pedagogy discourse concerning language, culture and nations since the 1980s' (Risager, 2007: 2) and provides a number of useful suggestions for practical application. Notwithstanding the value of her comprehensive critical review and useful recommendations, Risager does not provide specific examples of how *languaculture* as a theoretical framework can be translated into the design of language courses or programmes across language levels from beginners to advanced, and more importantly, into everyday practice. As a result, although Risager's notion of *languaculture* addresses the complexities of the language and culture nexus, the question remains as to how language teachers can explore the various dimensions she identifies through specific pedagogical approaches and activities. This leads me to the second building block on which to continue designing this framework.

Articulating languaculture for language teaching purposes

The second building block requires that, in addition to the notion of *languaculture*, teachers have a conceptual framework that operationalises the specific points of articulation between language and culture. This means having what Byrnes defines as 'a principled and comprehensive, rather than an *ad hoc* and compartmentalised, way of linking the culture or content of a second language/cultural area with second language learning' (Byrnes, 2008: 105). In addition, I argue that such a conceptual framework should also be vertically and horizontally amenable to, and adjustable within, diverse educational settings – both language and cultural context subjects; subjects that involve fieldwork, and so forth. Such a framework should also be applicable across languages.

Here, I turn to a conceptual framework proposed by Crozet (2003), which may serve as a touchstone for both teachers and learners as 'they explore together ... the complexity of the links between language and culture' (Crozet, 2003: 40). This conceptual framework is underpinned by Kerbrat-Orecchioni's approach for describing what she refers to as 'the communicative profile' of speech communities. Crozet clarifies that here, 'speech community' follows Hyme's definition:

> [A] community sharing knowledge of rules for the conduct and interpretation of speech. Such sharing comprises knowledge of at least one form of speech, and knowledge also of its patterns of use. (Hymes, 1974: 51)

Here, Kerbrat-Orecchioni, whose seminal works on pragmatics and discourse analysis and interaction have focused mainly on French *languaculture* (Kerbrat-Orecchioni, 1994, 2000), draws on different sources of cross-cultural communication research to describe an approach that Crozet (2003) claims can be extrapolated and 'used by language teachers to help them structure their research on the typology of cultural traits in the languages they teach' (Crozet, 2003: 40). Crozet identifies this approach as a conceptual framework that can help teachers and learners identify where culture is located in language use. This framework consists of what Kerbrat-Orecchioni identifies as five 'axes' or principles, along which the communicative profile of a given speech community can be described. The first axis refers to 'the importance placed on speaking in the functioning of a society' or its 'levels of verbosity'.[1] This axis refers to how much or how little time people spend talking to each other and the importance they give to silence. The second axis, 'approaches to inter-personal relationships', refers to the way different societies conceive and express interpersonal relationships. Based on this axis, speech communities can be split into three groups according to the type of tendencies they express through their handling of human relationships, that is, societies valuing: proximity and/or distance between individuals; hierarchy versus equality; and consensus versus conflict.

The third axis, 'rules of politeness', refers to the conventions that pervade all verbal interactions and that can lead to serious communication breakdown when transgressed. The fourth axis refers to 'levels of ritualisation', whereby in some speech communities the socio-cultural behaviour of interactants strictly observes rituals and routines, as opposed to speech communities where the conversational rules are not so strictly adhered to, giving more room to the individual to accommodate common rules to his/her personal taste. Finally, the fifth axis, 'level of expressivity/emotionology' refers to the level of expressivity generally regarded as desirable in a given culture. Crozet exemplifies the use of this framework with the communicative profile of French conversational ethnolects living in France (Figure 2.1).

Crozet suggests that teachers can use this communicative profile as a sum of the dominant culture traits that are relevant to the understanding of culture in verbal interaction. Teachers may also want to contemplate the non-verbal realisation of each of these axes in communication. Indeed, the non-verbal dimension can provide a more holistic picture of *languaculture*.

In sum, Crozet's framework aims to 'make the intangible cultural features of spoken language tangible' (Crozet, 2003: 39) by describing specific aspects of culture that are reflected in language use, or, in Agar's and Risager's terms, aspects of *languaculture*. I have visually interpreted this framework in Figure 2.1. In this graphic interpretation of Crozet's framework we find a horizontal axis '*X*' where we can locate *languacultures* under discussion, and five vertical axes that represent five levels of *languaculture* features of the culture '*X*', which emerge, or are reflected, in interaction.

The rationale behind this graphic interpretation is that the vertical 'axes' (levels and approaches) can be studied cross-sectionally. This representation

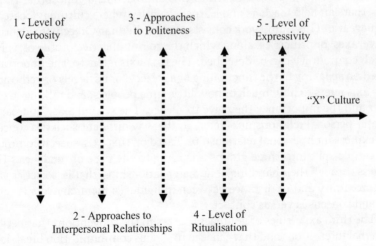

Figure 2.1 Graphic interpretation of Crozet's conceptual framework

of the vertical axes also serves to illustrate that the *languaculture(s)* under study (horizontal axis) may have a high degree (above the culture axis) or low degree (below the culture axis) of acceptance or emphasis in that particular axis in comparison with the native *languaculture*. This is particularly useful, as Crozet suggests, for describing these traits 'in terms of degree rather than absolute truths' (Crozet, 2003: 48).

Crozet's framework thus provides a *typology* of *languaculture* traits that can be used as a touchstone for teachers to explore aspects of both native and target *languaculture*. Yet, as she explains, this should not be read as a 'rigid framework', since these traits may 'fluctuate with time, space and social class [and] variables such as age, sex and personality can distort or cancel the culture-specificity of a particular form of behaviour' (Crozet, 2003: 47–48). Crozet also cautions teachers not to interpret this conceptual framework as simplifying or reducing a given *languaculture* to a number of salient traits. Instead, this framework utilises a typology of *languaculture* traits as a 'tool for students to unravel the complex webs which structure verbal interaction and culture' (Crozet, 2003: 48).

Crozet's framework is presented in Lo Bianco's and Crozet's edited volume *Teaching Invisible Culture: Classroom Practice and Theory* (Lo Bianco & Crozet, 2003). This volume provides practical suggestions and examples of operationalising Crozet's conceptual framework in several language classrooms: Australian English, Chinese, French, German, Italian and Japanese. These suggestions are mainly for 'inside-the-classroom' activities, such as case analysis, case comparison, role-play, film strip analysis and so forth. Yet, as noted by Luk (2004: 30) 'none of the chapters reports empirical and systematic data-collection methods', to exemplify the articulation of the framework in practice. Rather, the practical suggestions and activity examples arise from the authors' experiences as language teachers. Nonetheless, Crozet's conceptual framework represents a useful touchstone for teachers to explore *languaculture*.

In contrast with other available frameworks generally used by interculturalists (e.g. collectivism versus individualism, etc.), Crozet's framework specifically focuses on the systematic exploration of the relationship between language and culture in written and oral communication. Despite lacking empirical data, the volume's contributions on operationalising this framework in several languages are quite timely in a field searching for an explicit approach to defining the relationship between language and culture that can be applied across languages. That is why I adopted this conceptual framework and took it a step further by adding an empirical dimension, which I present in Chapter 3, and which provides empirical data for implementing this framework in the university language curriculum.

The notion of *languaculture* can therefore help language teachers to understand that while some aspects of language can be explored in isolation (pronunciation, morphology, etc.), many aspects are culture bound. Similarly, while many aspects of culture can be explored in isolation from language (historical matters, artefacts, etc.), many of these are realised through language. The key underlying issue from these building blocks is thus to have a clear notion of the language and culture nexus, which can serve as a touchstone in the language classroom, the cultural context classroom and in a language programme as a whole. Crozet's conceptual framework (Crozet, 2003), on the other hand, presents the key points of articulation that reflect linguistically mediated cultural behaviour in interaction. I use Risager's notion of *languaculture* and Crozet's conceptual framework as touchstones to systematically explore the relationship between language and culture underpinning this curriculum development framework.

Mapping the languaculture learning process

In most programmes, the notion of an underlying learning sequence is taken for granted when it comes to linguistic development. Yet, this is often ignored in the case of the language and culture nexus. Indeed, translating the language and culture nexus, or in this case, *languaculture*, into an incremental learning progression is challenging. The lack of developmental notions of *languaculture* learning make it difficult to map a coherent, progressive path from *ab initio,* beginning levels – the largest in most language programmes – to advanced levels. And because university language learning is generally given limited time within most degree programmes, language teachers cannot assume learners' formal long-term engagement with language study; learners may end their engagement as abruptly as they began it, depending on their circumstances. This emphasises the need to ensure continued exploration of *languaculture* through carefully articulated curricula – learning objectives, activities, materials and assessment – within a given language programme.

Here, cognitive approaches to adult learning have honed in on the concept of 'awareness' in relation to cultural – or *languaculture* – learning as an alternative to the concept of 'competence' and complementing the longstanding concept of 'language awareness' in the field of language education. Awareness-raising processes, and in particular critical awareness or meta-awareness, have been seen increasingly as the cornerstones of both language learning and ensuring sophisticated access to higher forms of cognition and consciousness mediated through language (Lantolf & Thorne, 2006).

In fact, the notion of language awareness (LA) has been present in the field of languages pedagogy for a number of decades. LA was initially defined as 'a person's sensitivity to and conscious awareness of the nature of language and its role in human life' (Donmall, 1985, cited in Donmall-Hicks, 1997: 21) and was later extended to include 'explicit knowledge about language, ... conscious perception and sensitivity in language learning, language teaching, and language use' (Donmall-Hicks, 1997). Raising levels of LA was considered to facilitate language development. Leow concluded that: (1) meta-awareness apparently correlated with an increased usage of hypothesis testing and morphological rule formation (conceptually driven processing); and (2) learners demonstrating a higher level of awareness performed significantly better than those with a lower level of awareness on both the recognition and written production of the targeted forms (Leow, 1997: 560 in Gabrys, 2002). Learners were also seen to develop a better appreciation of targeted forms and greater understanding of their complexity, and were more likely to transfer that understanding to structure and use of their mother tongue (Leow, 1997, in Gabrys, 2002).

Fairclough (1992) added a critical dimension through seeking to integrate critical discourse analysis into the language classroom as a pedagogical tool to help develop learners' 'Critical Language Awareness' (CLA). For Fairclough:

> People cannot be effective citizens in a democratic society if their education cuts them off from critical consciousness of key elements within their physical environment. If we are committed to establishing resources for citizenship, critical awareness of the language practices of one's speech community is an entitlement. (Fairclough, 1992: 6)

Similarly, many so-called interculturalists (Tomalin & Nicks, 2007; Tomalin & Stempleski, 1993; Tomlinson & Masuhara, 2004; *inter al.*) see 'cultural awareness' as the *keystone* on which effective and appropriate interactions depend. Byram, *inter al.*, cites '(critical) cultural awareness' as the most dominant dimension of the available models of intercultural communicative competence (ICC) (Byram, 1997, 2008, 2009b, 2012a). But despite widespread acknowledgement that development of 'cultural awareness' is at the core of the culture learning process, definitions of what learners need to be 'aware' of are neither clear nor consistent. Nor are there clear outlines about the processes through which teachers may go to raise learners' awareness, or how to map out these processes in a sequential programme of studies.

Two interrelated questions thus remain to be answered: (1) *what* do learners need to be aware of?, and (2) *how* can they become increasingly aware of this? In other words, in order to develop intercultural speakers, what should teachers guide students to notice about language and culture in communication (written or spoken), and how can teachers present this in a way that leads to incrementally advancing learners' levels of awareness.

On the first question, one must examine the mechanics involved in intercultural exchanges, and in particular in instances of miscommunication. The literature reveals widespread agreement that intercultural misunderstandings are more likely when interactants lack a basic level of awareness of their own 'cultural schema' in interpreting the interlocutor's message. Here, 'cultural schema' refers to the cognitive framework of unconsciously acquired assumptions, beliefs and value systems of a given culture. This cognitive framework is maintained and sanctioned largely through the very use of language, which is arguably the most observable and available expression of culture in communication (Brown, 1980).

The idea of raising one's awareness of our 'hidden cultural programming' is not new. Edward T. Hall was first to recognise the 'hidden' dimension of culture in interaction in 1959. However, as Shaules noted, 'the implications of [Hall's] fundamental insight are seldom focused on' (Shaules, 2007: 13), particularly in the field of language education. This field has focussed on study of the 'sociolinguistic transfer' phenomenon as a trigger for miscommunication. This type of 'transfer' refers to the learner's attempts to apply rules and forms of the native language into the target language.

Richards and Sukwiwat, for instance, provided a taxonomy of 'how culturally specific assumptions and strategies for conversation surface in cross-cultural encounters' (Richards & Sukwiwat, 1983: 113) owing to this type of transfer. They divided this taxonomy into two macro-categories: 'conventional usage in conversation' and 'interactional dimensions of conversation' (Richards & Sukwiwat, 1983: 125). The former refers to speech events and their conversational routines, that is, the systematically organised, socially significant communicative events where the interactants' communicative behaviour is prescribed by the setting, which also reflects the values and beliefs about the event. Some examples are meetings, conferences, weddings, funerals, elections, parties and the like. These communicative events also include specific speech acts as well as formulaic and idiomatic expressions that can be understood only through exploring their function, not their direct translation, e.g. 'how was your weekend?' (Béal, 1992) and the 'tall poppy syndrome' (Peeters, 2004) in the Australian context.

Interactional dimensions of conversation, on the other hand, refer to interactants 'marking dimensions of social distance, status and politeness, and the effects that different linguistic conventions for marking such dimensions have on the interlanguage of second language learners' (Richards & Sukwiwat, 1983: 117). These dimensions coincide with the notion of *languaculture* (Agar, 1994; Risager, 2006b) and the aspects identified in Crozet's conceptual framework (Crozet, 2003) discussed in earlier paragraphs. Approaches to interpersonal relationships and levels of ritualisation reflect some of these, while the potential triggers may be considered, in Agar's term, 'rich points'.

Transgression of these *languaculture* rules may thus be attributed to learners' low level of language proficiency, but most importantly, it may be owing to culturally based differences about what is expected during communication (Gudykunst, 1991; Gumperz & Hymes, 1986). Instances of these transgressions have been labelled 'pragmatic *failures*' (Thomas, 1983), and more recently, moving away from the word 'failure', 'pragmatic *dissonances*' (Zamborlin, 2007). Zamborlin has borrowed the term 'dissonance' from an essay by the sociologist Erving Goffman (1967) who did not use it with cases of miscommunication in intercultural encounters *per se*, but with the latent range of feelings in conversation that may range from uneasiness and discomfiture to embarrassment.

In this context, '*languaculture* dissonance' refers to any aspect of 'linguistic practice' that originates either intentionally or unintentionally, and which, on the part of the interlocutor(s), comes across as unexpected within an array of evaluation that may range from the slightly incongruous to the extremely out of place. Depending on the type and range, '*languaculture* dissonance' may not only cause break-down in communication, but also establish – and possibly perpetuate – negative stereotypes (Blum-Kulka, 1982). For instance, 'where are you going?' is a polite greeting form among Chinese-speaking people, but if used to show friendliness to native English speakers, it may be potentially regarded as intrusive.

Concurrently, as Hewstone and Giles (1986) point out, establishment of negative stereotypes is one of the causes for communication breakdown in intercultural encounters. Hewstone and Giles identify four essential aspects of the way stereotypes are created and perpetuated through communication:

> Stereotyping is the result of cognitive biases stemming from illusory correlations between group membership and psychological attributes; stereotypes influence the way information is processed, that is, more favourable information is remembered about in-groups and more unfavourable information is remembered about out-groups; stereotypes create expectancies (hypotheses) about others and individuals try to confirm those expectancies; stereotypes constrain others' patterns of communication and engender stereotype-confirming communication, that is, they create self-fulfilling prophecies. (Hewstone & Giles, 1986: 11)

It could thus be argued that teachers need to raise students' awareness of their own '*languaculture* schemas' and the effect of these schemas in communication for students to learn to function effectively in intercultural encounters. I define becoming cognisant of the 'hidden dimension' of intercultural communication and the underlying *languaculture* schemas as developing *'languaculture* awareness' and this is what I propose as an alternative to IC. Here awareness moves away from the 'intercultural competence' paradigm, which largely focuses on the development of desired 'attitudes' such as 'openness' and 'tolerance', to deal with difference. Instead, *languaculture* awareness focuses on the learners' cognitive processes and their development of relevant cognitive skills that can help them to deal with expected and unexpected *'languaculture* dissonances' in intercultural interaction.

Yet in adult education, according to Mezirow (2000), informed interpretations require not only awareness of one's *languaculture* schemas, 'but also *critical* reflection on the *validity* of their assumptions and premises' (Mezirow, 2000: 7, emphasis added). In other words, in the context of higher education, teachers should help learners in 'becoming *critically* aware of [their] own tacit assumptions and expectations and those of others and assessing their relevance for making an interpretation' (Mezirow, 2007: 4, emphasis added). This critical aspect of awareness is certainly not new. The concept of 'criticality', like 'awareness', abounds in the language and culture teaching literature but is seldom problematised. Byram claims, 'criticality should be a crucial element of all intercultural training and education' (Byram, 2009a: 213; and more recently, Byram, 2012a). Here he refers to the 'criticality' dimension included in his intercultural competence (IC) model's subcomponent 'critical cultural awareness' or *savoir s'engager*. This is defined as the 'ability to evaluate, critically and on the basis of explicit criteria, perspectives, practices and products in one's own and other cultures and countries' (Byram *et al.*, 2002: 9). Yet this definition seems to assume 'criticality' is somehow embedded in the analysis and evaluation of specific practices and products, without explaining the mechanisms behind it. This definition also infers that fostering learners' *savoir s'engager* leads to what Byram called 'perspective shift' (Byram, 1997: 108), but as I discussed earlier, Byram *et al.* (2002) do not articulate the mechanics of such 'perspective shifts', particularly in the context of adult education.

On the other hand, Mezirow (1981, 1991) provides a strong conceptual framework for his theory of 'perspective shifts', or as he calls it, 'perspective transformation'. According to Mezirow, 'perspective transformation' refers to:

> The emancipatory process of becoming critically aware of how and why the structure of psycho-cultural assumptions has come to constrain the way we see ourselves and our relationships, reconstituting this structure to permit a more inclusive and discriminating integration of experience and acting upon these new understandings. (Mezirow, 1981: 6)

Mezirow (2000) extends his notion of 'perspective transformation' into Transformative Learning, a theory of adult learning underpinned by philosophical (Socrates, Marx, Hegel, Habermas), as well psycho-developmental and educational (Freud, Piaget, Vygotsky, Bruner, Freire), approaches to learning.

Research conducted in the field of intercultural communication has long acknowledged this theory's contribution to intercultural learning processes (*cf.* Taylor, 1994). Similarly, research in language education underpinned by the IC model of Byram *et al.* (2002) has increasingly acknowledged being informed by Mezirow's 'transformative learning' theory (*cf.* Guilherme *et al.*, 2009; Jackson, 2011; Korhonen, 2010). However, neither field offers explicit articulation of this theory in the language and culture learning classroom. Moreover, despite ample research into its evolution and redefinition since its inception (*cf.* Kitchenham, 2008; Taylor, 1997, 2007), for the most part, reference to this learning theory in intercultural language teaching has been largely reified. The time is ripe, then, to bring together the insights from this theory *vis-à-vis languaculture* awareness.

By transformative learning (TL) Mezirow refers to:

> ... the processes by which we transform our taken-for-granted frames of reference (meaning perspectives, habits of mind, mind-sets) to make them more inclusive, discriminating, open, emotionally capable of change and reflective so that they may generate beliefs and opinions that will prove more true or justified to guide action. (Mezirow, 2000: 7–8)

In this context, we may tackle the second question posed earlier in this section. It concerns *how* to identify the awareness-raising processes involved in helping learners to become increasingly aware of the pervasive effect of culture when they interpret a given exchange, to transform the frames of reference that the learners otherwise take for granted. Mezirow classifies 'frames of reference' under three categories: meaning perspectives, habits of mind and points of view (Mezirow, 2000: 16–19). Perspectives refer to the assumptions and expectations through which we filter sense impressions. These include one's worldview – both cultural learning that is unintention-ally assimilated, and intentionally learned philosophical, sociological and psychological orientations. Habits of mind refer to sets of assumptions and predispositions that act as a filter for *interpreting* the meaning of experience. These include preference to work alone or with others; tendency to respect or challenge authority; approaching a problem analytically or intuitively; and judgements about aesthetics, such as the ugly, the beautiful and so forth. Points of view are the expressions of habits of mind, comprising sets of beliefs, expectations, values, attitudes and judgements that 'tacitly direct and shape a specific interpretation and determine how we judge, typify objects and attribute causality' (Mezirow, 2000: 18).

Mezirow argues in that study that our frames of reference provide us with 'a sense of stability, coherence, community and identity. Consequently they are often emotionally charged and strongly defended' (*Ibid.*). This means that when other frames of reference call into question our own, we tend to dismiss them by using our own 'frame of reference' criteria to judge them. Adult education should thus focus on fostering critical reflectivity, that is, raising learners' awareness of *why* they view and interpret experiences and events through a particular uncritically assimilated frame of reference.

In an earlier study, Mezirow (1981) observed that transforming these frames of reference by questioning their validity becomes a distinguishing characteristic of adult learning. Here Mezirow referred to the work of developmental psychologist John Broughton, who argued that only in adulthood are we able to develop a 'theoretical self-consciousness', which allows us to recognise the paradigmatic assumptions in our thinking. Broughton (1977) explained:

> What emerges at adolescence is not self-consciousness but theoretical self-consciousness, an intellectual competence that enables us to articulate and communicate systematic justifications for the felt necessities of our ideas. Such legitimising activities require epistemological reasoning about how we know, about how the self knows reality. (Broughton, 1997: 95)

The notion of reflectivity is central to perspective transformation. Mezirow has graphically represented the different levels of reflectivity in a useful model (Figure 2.2).

In this set of concentric squares we find three sub-levels of reflectivity, with the most complex level on the outer-squares increasingly incorporating the less complex ones. At the most basic level, we can see that an act of *reflectivity* entails becoming aware of specific perceptions, thoughts or behaviours, and habits of seeing, thinking or acting. At the next level we find *consciousness*, which has three components. *Affective reflectivity* entails becoming aware of *how we feel* about our perceptions, thoughts or behaviours. *Discriminant reflectivity* enables us to assess the efficacy of our perceptions, thoughts or behaviours. *Judgemental reflectivity* entails making and becoming aware of our value judgements about our perceptions, thoughts or behaviours.

In the third level of reflectivity we find *critical consciousness*, which entails becoming aware of the previous levels of reflectivity and being able to critique

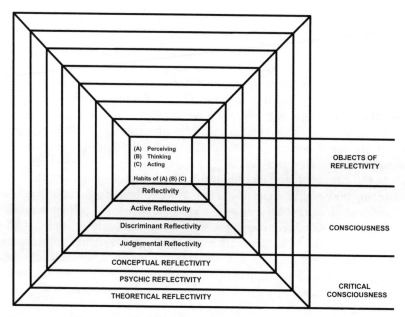

(A) Perceiving
(B) Thinking
(C) Acting

Habits of (A) (B) (C)

Reflectivity

Active Reflectivity

Discriminant Reflectivity

Judgemental Reflectivity

CONCEPTUAL REFLECTIVITY

PSYCHIC REFLECTIVITY

THEORETICAL REFLECTIVITY

OBJECTS OF REFLECTIVITY

CONSCIOUSNESS

CRITICAL CONSCIOUSNESS

Figure 2.2 Mezirow's levels of reflectivity
Source: Mezirow, 1981: 12.

them. Critical consciousness has three components. (1) *Conceptual reflectivity* refers to the concepts we use to critique our perceptions, thoughts or behaviours. (2) *Psychic reflectivity* entails recognising the habit of making precipitant judgments about people on the basis of limited information about them. (3) *Theoretical reflectivity* entails becoming aware that this precipitant judgment or conceptual inadequacy in our interpretations is caused by a set of taken-for-granted cultural or psychological assumptions that explain personal experience less effectively than another perspective with more functional criteria for seeing, thinking and acting. This last level of 'consciousness' can also be conceived as 'meta-awareness', which entails becoming aware and increasingly in control of one's own internalised frames of reference and their effect in filtering experiences and events. In this transformative theory of learning, Mezirow explains that even though there is uncertainty about the degree to which these levels of consciousness are age-related, the highest level, critical consciousness and within it theoretical reflectivity in particular, are a uniquely adult capacity (Mezirow, 1981).

Mezirow's theory of adult learning and critical consciousness is underpinned by both the philosophical work of Jürgen Habermas (1971) and his notion of 'critical awareness' or '*kritisches Bewußtsein*', and the seminal works of Paulo Freire (Freire, 1970, 1973, 1998). In Freire's radical pedagogic approach, 'critical awareness' or *conscientização* is made possible through *praxis*, which Freire defines as 'reflection and action upon the world in order to transform it' (Freire, 1973). In this way, Freire connects reflection with action as part of the process of coming to recognise and transform social, economic and political contradictions. According to Freire, the development of *conscientização* is the most important task of education as it concerns the awareness of the self and the other in a social situation, which in turn can lead to the transformation of the self and of one's relations to others, and to dealing critically and creatively with reality (and fantasy).

At the core of these tasks lie Bruner's reflections on awareness. When discussing how reality is construed in narrative, Bruner observed three classic antidotes for 'unconsciousness': *contrast, confrontation* and *metacognition* (Bruner, 1996: 147). According to Bruner, learning about the relativity of knowing by contrast and confrontation may work as 'medicine for unawareness' (Bruner, 1996: 148). But it is *metacognition* (where the object of thought is thought itself or, for example, turning around to see what one has learnt) that provides a base for negotiating meanings in interaction (Bruner, 1996: 88, 148).

Bruner's reflections on awareness are complemented by Vygotsky's considerations about the development of awareness. He argues that this takes place within the zone of proximal development (ZPD), which he defines as:

> The distance between the actual developmental level as determined by independent problem solving and the level of potential development as determined through problem solving under adult guidance or collaboration with more capable peers. (Vygotsky, 1978: 86)

Bruner defined Vygotsky's notion of 'adult guidance' or the help received from 'more capable peers' as 'scaffolding' (Bruner, 1996: 20–22). By providing adequate guidance and instructions in the context of a given activity or class discussion, teachers can build a 'scaffolding' structure to support the learners' problem solving. In turn, the learners' guided participation fosters an active role in their own learning and contribution to the successful solution of problems. In this way teachers' effective guidance involves transferring the learning responsibility to the learner. Effective 'scaffolding' generally entails dialogic guidance. In the Second Language Acquisition (SLA) context, Donato (2000) defines scaffolding more explicitly as a kind of dialogue that is:

> ... conversational in its attention to coherence, distributed turn taking, spontaneity and unpredictability and its focus on new information ...

[and also] instructional because teachers shape the discussion toward a curricular goal, build or activate background knowledge in students, engage at times in direct instruction or modelling, and promote more complex language expressions by using questions to help students expand, elaborate or restate. (Donato, 2000: 34)

Therefore, the task of the university teachers, Mezirow (1981) argues, is to promote an educational experience that challenges the taken-for-granted, uncritically acquired frames of reference, to call them into critical consciousness. Here Mezirow integrates the work done by Freire in demonstrating how adult educators can trigger, as well as facilitate and reinforce, 'perspective transformation'. He explains that teachers should start by considering the problems and perspectives of the learner in order to develop instructional material – contrasting pictures, comic strips or stories – 'posing hypothetical dilemmas with contradicting rules and assumptions rooted in areas of crucial concern to learners' (Mezirow, 1981: 19). These dilemmas may include representations of cultural discrepancies that the teacher may perceive learners take for granted. Here, Socratic dialogue may then be used in small group settings to engage learners in solving the dilemma (Morgan, 2008).

Socratic dialogue is a type of educational strategy that encourages cooperative reflection in a dialogue setting (Saran & Neisser, 2004: 3). Reflection is triggered by questioning tacit knowledge, fixed perspectives or points of view. This problem-solving task aims to elicit and challenge the psycho-cultural assumptions behind the frames of reference, ways of perceiving, thinking, feeling and behaving represented in the dilemma. Here Mezirow emphasises that 'an ethos of support, encouragement, non-judgmental acceptance, mutual help and individual responsibility' (Saran & Neisser, 2004) should be created. It is important to emphasise that participants 'may not reach definitive outcomes in the form of agreed answers' (Saran & Neisser, 2004: 3).

In addition, Bruner (1996: 92–93) sees that human beings take an agentive approach to problem-solving, to the world around us. But a person cannot deploy her or his mind unassisted or unscaffolded. It is the dialogue between the agentive mind and its context that builds the scaffold. The aim of scaffolding in collaboration is 'to achieve not unanimity, but more consciousness. And more consciousness always implies more diversity' (Bruner, 1996: 97).

To sum up, in this section, I have used the notion of 'critical *languaculture* awareness' to address the lack of clarity about the learning processes involved in IC, that is, how IC is acquired or developed. Critical theories of adult education and transformative learning theories help to underpin awareness-raising processes involved in de-stabilising learners' assumptions about the target *languaculture* and their own *languaculture* schemata. Presenting learners with instances of 'cognitive dissonance' can provide an adequate starting point for subsequently developing IC's avowed attitudes as a by-product. The issue remains of how to integrate the development of 'critical *languaculture* awareness' to the language learning classroom.

Pedagogical foundations: A post-method stance

The second founding 'building block' is concerned with the alignment of pedagogical aspects involved in development of a *languaculture* dimension in language programmes. Here, pedagogical alignment refers to the integral articulation and enactment of critical *languaculture* awareness in the curriculum: its *goals*, its *syllabi* and the *methods* underlying our teaching practices as they relate to our specific educational context. Indeed, one of the key 'stumbling blocks' we identified in the previous chapter to traversing the theory/practice divide is the ubiquitous discrepancies between avowed intercultural teaching principles and their absence in enactment of the language curriculum. The pedagogical foundations of this framework are, therefore, underpinned by three interrelated principles. These principles are: (1) formulating learning objectives coherent with the overall conceptualisation of 'critical *languaculture* awareness' and corresponding awareness raising processes; (2) purposefully selecting *languaculture* aspects to be explored; and (3) embedding these goals and syllabi within a post-method paradigm.

Formulating coherent learning objectives

The first principle, formulating specific educational goals and instructional objectives related to the notion of *languaculture*, operationalises a dimension that is usually incidental, *ad hoc*, and as a result, not assessed. If teachers are to formulate specific goals in relation to *languaculture* and its conceptual framework, then they are bound to monitor its development among learners in their classes. Choosing how to do so will be guided by the context and characteristics of the teaching programme.

The literature discussed earlier reveals that it is by raising the levels of critical awareness about their taken-for-granted frames of cultural reference that teachers can help learners develop a transformative stance towards both linguistic and cultural (or *languaculture*) frames of reference (Mezirow, 1981, 2000). Specific tasks that promote cognitive dissonance and conflict, as well as consensus and compromise (Guilherme, 2002: 219), have been identified as catalysts for the learners' 'perspective transformation' (Mezirow, 1981, 2000). In this model each level of awareness builds upon the previous one(s). Each level also implies the development of a number of skills. Table 2.1 presents the skills involved in the different levels of cognitive involvement and draws parallels between Mezirow's levels of reflectivity and Bloom's taxonomy of cognitive development (Bloom, 1956). Interest in the latter has been renewed at university level, where academics are increasingly required to refine the formulation of the specific objectives in their subject descriptions (McAlpine & Harris, 2002; Young, 2008). Table 2.1 may therefore be useful for curriculum design in formulating goals and objectives that reflect a sequential progression of cognitive skills, from basic to more advanced, that can be mapped out against the curricular progression of linguistic proficiency levels. Table 2.1 may also be used as a tool in creating criteria for assessment items, helping to enhance accountability by making the intercultural learning goals explicit.

In Table 2.1, the first level of awareness is 'noticing', which Schmidt argues is nearly isomorphic with 'attention', and seems to be associated with all types of learning (Schmidt, 1995: 1). This basic level would thus include 'noticing' patterns in communication and be followed by a more complex level of awareness that integrates Bruner's 'contrast' and 'confrontation' skills. Becoming aware of our own *languaculture* schemata may be challenging because we are not conscious of it. Thus, misunderstandings or misinterpretations are more likely when we lack this basic level of awareness of our own *languaculture* behaviour. At this basic level, learners need to be guided into becoming conscious of their native *languaculture* schemata. This consciousness-raising process could be triggered by tasks whereby learners observe, identify and compare elements of their own *languaculture* schemata *vis-à-vis* the target *languaculture* schemata.

Learners identifying, observing and contrasting the *languaculture* dimensions through which they become 'conscious' of their *languaculture* schema should, in turn, encourage them to question and challenge their *languaculture* schema. This takes us to the next level of critical consciousness or 'metacognitive awareness' whereby comparative practices may lead to processes of 'cognitive dissonance', i.e. the cognitive, mental conflict that people experience when they are presented with evidence that their beliefs or assumptions are limited or misplaced (Montier, 2002). The theory of 'cognitive dissonance' (Festinger, 1957) essentially argues that contradicting cognitions serve as a driving force that compels the mind to acquire or create new thoughts or beliefs, or to modify existing beliefs, to reduce the amount of dissonance (conflict) between cognitions.

The skills related to this level include being able to identify and question stereotypes or stereotypical portrayals by putting into perspective the similarities and differences identified in level one. Being able to identify stereotypical portrayals of target *languaculture* behaviours is indeed an underrated skill that requires learners to be critical, that is, to critically analyse

Table 2.1 Taxonomy of awareness levels and related skills

Levels of Reflectivity (Mezirow)	Critical Languaculture Levels of Awareness	Levels	Related Skills (Bloom)
Reflectivity: an awareness of a specific perception, meaning, behaviour, or habit.	**Basic Level of Awareness**	**Noticing**	Observe Describe Identify Recognise
Affective reflectivity: awareness of how the individual feels about what is being perceived, thought, or acted upon.		**Analysis**	Compare Classify Arrange Outline Explain Illustrate
Discriminant reflectivity: the assessment of the efficacy of perception, thought, action or habit.	**Complex Level of Awareness**	**Synthesis**	Summarise Synthesise
Judgmental reflectivity: making and becoming aware of value judgments about perception, thought, action or habit.		**Evaluation**	Assess Convince Measure Criticise Judge Support Justify Validate

CONSCIOUSNESS

CRITICAL CONSCIOUSNESS	**Conceptual reflectivity:** self-reflection which might lead to questioning of whether good, bad or adequate concepts were employed for understanding or judgment.	**Meta-cognitive Level of Awareness**	Combine Reframe Reorganise Substitute Negotiate Adapt Generalise Plan Anticipate Speculate
	Psychic reflectivity: recognition of the habit of making percipient judgments on the basis of limited information.		
	Theoretical reflectivity: awareness that the habit for percipient judgment or for conceptual inadequacy lies in a set of taken-for-granted cultural or psychological assumptions that explain personal experience less satisfactorily than another perspective with more functional criteria for seeing, thinking or acting.	**Epistemological Level of Awareness** **(Re)framing**	

languaculture information presented in textbooks, advertising and the media in general.

This level also includes the ability to use the cues or hypotheses about what goes on during interaction from the observations made in level one, in order to interpret the interlocutor's behaviour and negotiate meaning. For instance, if learners are aware that answers to negative propositions in questions, such as 'Don't you want me to come?', may trigger an unexpected response in some non-English speakers such as Chinese owing to their *languaculture* system, they can understand their interlocutor's response or follow with questions to clarify if necessary.

The last level within 'critical consciousness' concerns the development of theoretical reflectivity, a more dynamic type of awareness. This entails the ability to accept that *languaculture* behaviour may be negotiable among interactants and that, ultimately, the outcome of intercultural encounters is open to interpretation, which requires the ability to suspend interpretation and judgement of *'languaculture* dissonances'. This term couples the concept of *languaculture* as I have presented so far, with 'dissonance', which suggests a less dramatic meaning than 'failure' or 'breakdown' that tend to infer some personal shortcoming or responsibility in the communication. In fact, 'dissonance' can denote different degrees of intensity and can have rather unpredictable consequences, being strictly bound to contextual conditions.

This level can also be linked to the concept of 'dynamic-in-betweenness' (Yoshikawa, 1987) where speakers can consciously manage their alternative frames of *languaculture* reference in intercultural encounters. At this level, learners may become 'aware' of the fluidity and dynamic nature of culture in interaction, and that their identities are not pre-destined by the differences and similarities in their native *languaculture* schemata; multiple factors may affect their own *languaculture* behaviour and that of their interlocutor. While the first two levels of *'languaculture* awareness' may be developed through a number of tasks inside and outside the classroom, within a certain period of time the third level requires learners to have more personal experience in intercultural encounters. Some of the skills concerned with this level may be developed only over time.

Thus we can conclude that 'critical *languaculture* awareness' is multi-dimensional, entailing language and culture learning and use in communication. This involves learners using language in interaction to interpret and construct meaning, and analysing and reflecting upon this experience and continuing to learn from the use of language in intercultural interactions. Learners therefore develop this awareness over time. As such, awareness of the *languaculture* dimensions of cross-cultural encounters, that is, the interactants' language-mediated cultural behaviours, may be more conducive to processes of 'cognitive dissonance', which, in turn, may help learners in developing the sought after attitudinal dimension of IC.

A final aspect in the development of critical *languaculture* awareness is taking into account learners' awareness-raising processes. Native speakers realise the process of becoming a competent member of society through exchanges of language in particular social situations. Every society orchestrates the ways in which children participate in particular situations, which in turn affect the form, function and content of children's utterances. Caregivers' primary concern is not grammatical input, but the transmission of lexical input and sociocultural knowledge (Buttjes & Byram, 1991). Adult foreign language (L2) learning is clearly different. To begin, adult learners already have a rich knowledge of their own mother tongue (L1) and perhaps other languages they have learned, as well as sociocultural knowledge. Bialystok (1993) emphasises this sociocultural knowledge may be used as a foundation for building language instruction.

The process of sociocultural acquisition in foreign and second language (L2) contexts can be conceptualised in ways analogous to the L1 language acquisition processes. The learner begins with a knowledge of the practices of their own first culture and gradually acquires an 'approximative' system of practices (*cf.* Nemser, 1971) that vary from the starting position as a result of exposure to new input. Liddicoat (2003) compares this 'approximative' system with the concept of interlanguage (Selinker, 1972) using the term *intercultures*. In this context, different stages of *interculture* can contain rules that are identical to those of the first culture and are derived from the target culture or belong to neither culture, but are learners' accommodations to their noticing of, and reflection on, the input. In this case, each stage of *interculture* represents a new step in developing a set of intercultural practices, as shown in Figure 2.3.

However, language learners may not be aware of their own cultural knowledge or how to apply it in an L2 context, which leaves a clear role for pedagogical intervention (Rose & Kasper, 2001). Schmidt (1993) emphasises the absence of evidence for implicit learning of L2 sociocultural rules and thus he highlights the importance of the role of consciousness as a precondition for developing L2 pragmatic competence. He argues that to acquire ability in pragmatic norms, for instance, learners must 'attend to both the linguistic forms of utterances and the relevant social and contextual features with which they are associated' (Schmidt, 2001: 30).

Schmidt's proposition argues that language learners acquire pragmatic competence by consciously paying attention to linguistic form, pragmalinguistic function and sociopragmatic constraints. However, Schmidt argues

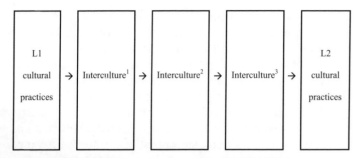

Figure 2.3 Progression in development of intercultural practices
Source: Liddicoat *et al., 2003: 21.*

that learners do not have to consciously attempt to notice gaps since it is 'awareness' of pragmatic features rather than the 'intention' to notice them that matters. This means learners may benefit more from noticing specific aspects in their input with the initial help of a teacher (Schmidt, 1993).

Swain's and Long's ideas on the functions of output and interaction in second language learning can be adapted to the acquisition of *critical langua-culture awareness*. Swain (1995) identified three main functions of output. These are *consciousness-raising*, in that learners are forced to notice non-L2-like elements of their output; *hypothesis-testing*; and a *reflective* function, whereby learners can reflect on L2 forms. On the other hand, Long's (1996) research emphasised both input and output and integrated them in his 'interaction hypothesis', which views communication as a platform for language acquisition. In this context, negotiating meaning plays a key role in interaction, while negative evidence and modified output are the main learning channels (Long, 1996).

From these observations, Liddicoat (2002, 2003) proposes a more process-oriented acquisitional model of sociocultural learning for the field of foreign language teaching. This cyclical model (Figure 2.4) conceives the development of sociocultural knowledge as an on-going process of acquisition where the primary stimulating tool is a reflection on the linguistic behaviour of oneself and one's interlocutors.

Yet an observation by Schmidt (1993) raises an important qualifier: for any acquisition to take place, particular elements of the input have to be 'noticed'. As mentioned above, our cultural conventions are often 'invisible' to us, making it more difficult for us to notice cultural differences. Thus, Liddicoat (2002, 2003) highlights promoting 'noticing' as one of the key tasks of the teacher. Once learners have noticed input, it is available to them for reflection and experimentation.

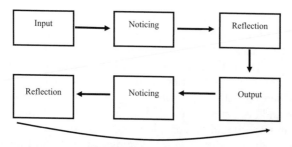

Figure 2.4 Cyclical model of the acquisition of sociocultural knowledge
Source: Liddicoat, 2002: 11.

For Liddicoat (2003), it is important for the learner who has noticed a difference in input to reflect on the nature of the difference and decide how to respond to that difference; that is, whether and how far the learner will modify his/her practices to accommodate this new input. But this initial modification is not the final stage of the output. Swain (1995) argues that output itself provides opportunities for new noticing and reflection. This noticing may be the learner's positive or negative evaluation of the new modified practices, which may feel comfortable or uncomfortable. Or it may be of a native speaker's response to the learner's modified practices, which the learner may construe as indicating whether their modification has been successful. These 'noticings' can become the target of further reflection, which the learner again effects in their output, creating a (potentially) continuous cycle of acquisition (Liddicoat, 2003). This cyclical model supports the critical *languaculture* awareness raising process under discussion here.

Finally, to actually embed critical *languaculture* awareness, learning objectives should be mapped sequentially throughout a language study programme. Critical *languaculture* awareness-raising should be integrated from the beginning stages of language learning in both language and cultural context subjects, from the lowest most basic levels, to higher more complex levels of critical awareness. It should not be delayed until learners have acquired a certain level of proficiency in the target language. Delaying input about *languaculture* may not delay culture learning as such, but may lead to the learner practising a prescriptive approach to culture as a result. At beginners' levels this may involve providing students with the terminology to categorise points of articulation in language–culture interaction through the learners' *lingua franca*. At more advanced levels this may involve exploring the points of articulation by using the target language outside the classroom through fieldwork and other guided ethnographic research tasks.

Selecting and developing material for languaculture exploration

Although beginner language learners can be considered 'blank slates' in many ways, their lack of familiarity with the target language should not be confused with that of the target culture. Particularly in the case of adult beginners in the higher education context, they already have some background knowledge of the target culture, which may include attitudes, presuppositions and even stereotypical ideas. This is why cultural information and representation should be considered crucial when evaluating teaching resources such as textbooks, videos and audio-tapes. According to Ros i Solé (2003), 'the treatment of culture [in FL teaching materials] should entail a process where the individual not only absorbs, but also interprets and becomes critical about the information presented' (Ros i Solé, 2003: 142).

When selecting suitable input for *languaculture* awareness-raising tasks, teachers may resort to available 'cultural assimilators', 'mini-dramas' or 'critical incidents', or even create their own. However, teachers should be aware of the 'edited' features of some materials specifically designed for language learners, which may try to 'nativise' cultural information in an attempt to focus on language, thus giving students a distorted picture of the target culture (*cf.* Kramsch, 1987). Teachers may also use authentic material from films, television or radio shows, cartoons (cultoons) and stories. The input embedded in these tasks may include authentic instances of dissonance between the native and target *languaculture* or instances of failure in interaction. This type of tasks may be more conducive to 'cognitive dissonance', that is, the cognitive, mental conflict that people experience when they are presented with evidence that their beliefs or assumptions are wrong (Montier, 2002).

Situating the framework within a post-method paradigm

Acknowledgement of the complexity and diversity of the educational contexts, particularly evident in higher education, has prompted some to claim that languages education has moved 'beyond methods' to what has been defined as a 'postmethod condition' (Kumaravadivelu, 2003). In this context, Savignon (2007) has suggested that 'the quest for a better method has been or should be abandoned in favour of the identification of practices or strategies of teaching designed to reflect local needs and experiences' (Savignon, 2007: 207). Such a 'postmethod' era may lead to recognition of teachers as 'professional decision-makers' (Savignon, 2007: 218).

In this vein, and also in line with recent discussions in the field (*cf.* Liddicoat & Scarino, 2013), I argue that those attempting to embed a *languacultural* dimension into their curricula are best placed by adopting a 'postmethod' view. Language teachers should not have to decide on one specific teaching 'methodology' or 'approach' in order to integrate *languaculture* aspects of communication. They should be able to make pedagogical decisions based on principles that are informed by understanding of the complex relationship between language and culture and the development of intercultural competences, or as argued in this book, critical *languaculture* awareness. I therefore argue that language educators at university level need to consider a 'beyond-methods' approach. When grounded on relevant theoretical principles, a 'beyond-methods' approach enables the language educator to incorporate an intercultural (or *languaculture*) dimension tailored to the specific conditions of a given subject or programme. These include the medium of instruction used in the subject, the proficiency level of the students from beginners to advanced, the amount of contact hours and so forth.

I also argue that conceptualising critical *languaculture* awareness as 'teaching' is inappropriate and should be reconsidered carefully. Conceptualising in this way implies a static viewpoint. Use of the term 'culture teaching' throughout the literature suggests that culture can be 'taught' by presenting 'facts', and concrete answers to questions such as 'why, what, how'. As I have argued earlier, this view can easily lead to stereotyping and leave students with static sets of generalised and inaccurate features of the target culture. Crawford and Lange (1984) present a cogent argument that conceptualising 'culture teaching' is misleading since the acquisition and dissemination of cultural information puts severe limits on learning about culture.

> An information-centred, culture teaching strategy implies that the culture under study is closed, final, complete... [It also] eliminates consideration of culture at the personal level, where the individual interacts with and acts upon the culture... Although culture contains knowable facts, these facts are in constant flux. More important to an understanding of culture than the collection of facts is an appreciation of culture as a constellation of phenomena in a continual process of change, brought about by the participants in the culture as they live and work. To study culture as a body of facts is to study the characteristics of culture; to study culture as a process is to study its essence. (Crawford & Lange, 1948: 141–142)

On an epistemological level, these issues raise the important question of whether culture teaching and the development of IC, which involve affective and attitudinal dimensions, can actually be achieved through language education. Some have argued the impossibility of teaching culture in its complexity and totality in the classroom (Byram, 1989; Kramsch, 1993). Sauvé raises the valid question about teaching culture: 'how possible is it to teach something when we cannot even be fully conscious of it?' (Sauvé, 1996: 17), which is particularly relevant for native language teachers.

This view is relevant for all foreign language learners, including adults in higher education, who arrive in the language classroom with a set of acquired cultural practices of their own background. Teachers need to assume that these learners, and indeed the teachers themselves, are not fully cognisant of their own cultural behaviours. Because we become generally inured to our cultural practices through habit and familiarity, they are largely invisible to us; we do not usually see them as cultural and constructed. Therefore, to explore the target *languaculture*, learners need to be given the opportunity and encouraged to develop the appreciative capacity to 'explore' their own cultural behaviour at the same time they explore the target one. In other words, learners must first recognise that they see the world through their own '*languaculture* lenses' and therefore need to learn as a generic skill how these lenses work in the trans-cultural context of foreign language learning.

In this context, 'exploration' primarily involves learning how to gain new insights into the native and target *languacultures*, while engaging with the target language and culture. 'Exploration' involves comparison and reflection processes that can be integrated into any classroom activity and transferred to authentic situations. These claims echo the awareness-raising processes described earlier, thus I argue that within the 'beyond-methods' paradigm, '*languaculture* exploration' can be conceptualised and integrated into different teaching approaches and techniques inside and outside the classroom, in interactions with fellow classmates, international students and native speakers in the community. Importantly, a *languaculture* exploration approach can be integrated into both language-specific subjects and cultural-context subjects taught in the students' *lingua franca*. The latter are particularly relevant as they offer beginner-level learners the opportunity to discuss pragmatic issues early in their language learning journey. Hence, exploring, comparing and reflecting on the effects of the pragmatic dimension in intercultural communication can help create a propitious environment to productively de-stabilise students' beliefs about their own culture and the target culture. After all, we are talking here about the cognisance of difference and similarity between ourselves and others, whose views of themselves and us are through lenses different from our own.

As suggested in Chapter 1, the language and culture teaching literature is rife with clear examples of curricular innovation. However, in the field there is a tendency to produce islands of innovation rather than comprehensively integrating or embedding it. The articulated embedding of critical *languaculture* awareness in the curriculum is surely at the crux of bridging the gap between expected goals and practices in place to achieve them, between 'ends' and 'means'. These pedagogical principles may help language teachers start to purposefully engage in curriculum innovation through systematic embedding of critical *languaculture* awareness raising processes.

Institutional foundations: A programmatic approach

The third and final foundation stone is concerned with the role of higher education institutions (HEIs) in the processes of curriculum innovation. When I began the process of conceptualising this curriculum development framework, it became increasingly obvious to me that if HEIs are to prepare graduates, who can communicate confidently in culturally appropriate ways, in a variety of contexts and settings, HEIs need to re-evaluate their commitment to this vision. The critique presented in the previous chapter illustrates clearly the glaring lack of coherence, not only between 'ends' and 'means' in the field of language and culture pedagogy, but also within the inherent organisational structure of HEIs. When we talk about language education, the internationalisation rhetoric and lip-service paid by policy documents and university mission statements to the development of global, interculturally competent graduates is seemingly nullified in practice.

Curriculum innovation for the development of a *languaculture* dimension clearly requires a high level of institutional commitment and support. As revealed in Chapter 1, institutional commitment and support are no longer considered to simply be a desirable aspiration. On the contrary, there is a pressing need for HEIs around the world to rationalise and substantiate the quality of graduate outcomes. This founding building block is therefore supported by three main principles aimed to weave in critical *languaculture* awareness as a vital aspect of, and contribution to, what universities and national policies aspire to produce: globally minded, prepared and capable international citizens.

The first principle addresses the issue of graduate profile goal alignment; the second concerns the existing structural constraints in university degrees, and the third refers to the underlying programmatic constraints in developing and implementing innovative curricula.

Graduate profile goal alignment

Universities need to revisit their mission statements to ensure that their notion of 'interculturally sensitive graduates' includes a *languaculture* dimension. In the Australian context in which I began conceptualising this framework, HEIs have been increasingly concerned with preparing graduates for an ever more globalised academic and employment market, and have embarked upon a number of initiatives to promote internationalisation and the development of interculturally sensitive graduates. However, these initiatives have been largely bereft of a linguistic dimension, or at least, one that goes beyond the focus on English language.

At national level, the latest Review of Australian Higher Education specifically referred to the importance of language education in the development of 'interculturally competent graduates', emphasising that 'knowledge of other cultures and their languages is an essential life skill for future graduates if they are to engage effectively in global professional practice' (Department of Education, Employment and Workplace Relations (DEEWR), 2008: 104). At institutional level, examination of mission statements and policy documents indicates that 63% of the 38 Australian universities articulate this rationale, albeit under many guises, as specific graduate attributes (Pitman & Broomhall, 2009: 445–446). Descriptors of such attributes largely conceptualise (inter)cultural awareness as both a value (respect, civic responsibility, appreciation of diversity) and a skill (ability to function in global/multicultural environments) (ITL, 2012; Pitman & Broomhall, 2009). However, these descriptors do not provide evidence of a clear connection between 'intercultural graduate attributes' and the crucial role of foreign language learning in the development of intercultural skills and, therefore, in advancing espoused internationalisation processes (Crichton & Scarino, 2007; Liddicoat, Eisenchlas & Trevaskes, 2003).

If HEIs are to prepare graduates who can communicate confidently in culturally appropriate ways in a variety of contexts and settings, the universities need to re-evaluate their commitment to this vision. Progress toward the achievement of this goal thus hinges on a shift in the organisational philosophy of the higher educational sector (Eisenchlas *et al.*, 2003). This shift should play a key role in creating structural alignment between universities' mission statements, curriculum goals and everyday teaching practices. Here it is important to note that processes for raising critical *languaculture* awareness should not be reified (that is, objectified, assumed to have a fixed, static form) – as several intercultural competence models largely have been – nor can critical *languaculture* awareness be conceived as a static notion. The preceding building blocks emphasise the dynamic, on-going, long-term nature of these processes, which can be targeted through various educational contexts. Therefore, a shift in HEIs' organisational philosophies would ideally entail reconceptualising the values underlying what it actually means to be an interculturally competent speaker in today's globalised world. This reconceptualisation may be informed by the theoretical building blocks described earlier in this chapter, and may be further supported by the remaining two principles, which are deeply interrelated.

Degree structure requirements

This principle concerning degree structure is closely related to the first one as it entails ensuring that degree programme structures are flexible enough to enable the study of languages across faculties. This requires universities to revisit the place of language learning within the structure of degree programmes, while developing and implementing international and nationwide collaborative arrangements to enhance maintenance and capacity of university language programmes. The literature examined in Chapter 1 reveals that much work has been done to attend to this principle in HEIs around the world. In the Australian context, much work remains to be done in this respect (Díaz, 2012).

Language programmes in the Australian higher education sector are not a compulsory element in most undergraduate degrees, except for those specialising in linguistics or applied linguistics. As Martín indicates, 'none of the 38 doctorate-granting Australian universities has compulsory language study requirements (compared with 90 per cent of similar institutions in the United States)' (Martín, 2005: 54). Most faculties, other than those in which languages are taught, allow students to undertake language studies as an elective subject (Nettlebeck et al., 2007), but the structure of their degree programmes often allows for only a limited number of elective language subjects. In most degree programmes, the elective language subject/s allowed are 'usually limited to one year of instruction, which is sufficient for no more than a superficial introduction to the foreign language' (Eisenchlas et al., 2003: 145). Currently, most degree programmes in specific professional areas, including engineering, business, information technology, medicine and law, have a prescribed curriculum that largely prevents students from taking on 'elective' subjects such as language studies. Australian HEIs should encourage collaboration among faculties and language departments to ensure that while language study may remain an optional component, it nevertheless becomes an integral part of degree programmes.

A programmatic approach

This third principle is concerned with one of the arguments that emerged from the limitations identified in Chapter 1, that is, the need for a programmatic approach to developing a *languaculture* agenda. Articulating the study of *languaculture* against a curricular sequence is a key aspect to bridging the theory/practice gap. At university level, this entails an articulation of a curricular sequence that may be done both horizontally, that is, across subjects and degree programmes, or vertically, throughout a given language programme. While much attention has been given to horizontal approaches, my concern in designing this framework was the vertical sequence. A sequence that could be translatable into different curricular progressions that recognise the idiosyncrasies of teachers' programmatic needs.

Approaching this task at programme level would ensure genuine integration and development of a coherent *languaculture* thread interweaving language and non-language subject components. The contention behind this argument is that the development of intercultural competences, or in this context, 'critical *languaculture* awareness', cannot be expected solely within one subject, whether language or content, but rather within a programme that includes a variety of learning contexts inside and outside the formal classroom environment. A 'programme approach' to curriculum innovation thus provides a coherent starting point for the subjects involved and ensures alignment with overarching graduate outcomes from first to third year subjects.

Another tenet binding together this building block relates back to the developmental nature of raising learners' levels of 'critical *languaculture* awareness'. It may be developed through a combination of formal and experiential learning. Indeed, formal learning that promotes reflection, together with individual and group experiential learning tasks, may be more conducive to processes of 'perspective transformation' than exclusively formal learning (Mezirow, 1991, 2000). Here, 'perspective transformation' for *languaculture* learning takes place through interaction, not simply through exposure and analysis (McMeniman & Evans, 1997). If learning a culture means learning the 'system of symbols in the minds of the members of a society by which they interpret their experiences and predict the behaviour of their fellows' (Taylor & Sorenson, 1961: 350), then *languaculture* exploration must include more than imparting factual information. It should not be conceived as passive reception of 'facts' about language and culture, but rather as active involvement in communicative events. This means that language programmes should consider a variety of contexts within their subjects, integrating learning events inside and outside the classroom, in the learners' *lingua franca* and in the target language (Liddicoat, 2008), across both language and non-language subject components.

Conclusion

In this chapter I have argued for the need to formalise a curriculum development framework supported by three founding 'building blocks' – theoretical, pedagogical and institutional – which aim to address the limitations identified in Chapter 1. These founding building blocks are bound by principles that can serve to guide integration of a *languaculture* dimension in university language programmes. In this context, *languaculture* functions as an alternative way of conceptualising the relationship between language and culture. The notion is complemented by a conceptual framework showing specific points of articulation between language and culture, which helps to formulate coherent learning objectives for developing 'critical *languaculture* awareness'. The framework also presents the specific pedagogical steps to developing relevant elements of the curriculum within language programmes. This *languaculture* curriculum development framework thus provides teachers with a flexible conceptualisation of culture learning that is not restricted by any given teaching methodology. It avoids notions of effectiveness and generalisability to focus on providing flexible descriptive guidelines as a blueprint for creating extended instructional sequences that may be suitable across languages and may help teachers in promoting sustainable curriculum innovation processes. The notion of 'critical *languaculture* awareness' and its potential to promote 'perspective transformation' in teachers and learners provide a compelling argument for universities to consider formalising this framework. Such a move would also signal genuine commitment to the process of 'internationalisation' that all HEIs now espouse.

In Part 2 of this book I explore the viability of this framework in promoting curriculum innovation in the Australian higher education context. In so doing, I present a bottom-up perspective of what is pedagogically achievable in the classroom through four case studies of curriculum innovation.

Note

(1) Crozet clarifies that the term 'verbosity' is used in this context as a technical term. In other words, it does not have a negative connotation and refers simply to the volume (amount) of speech considered acceptable in a given speech community.

Part 2

Theory Versus Practice and the Realm of Possibility

3 Case Studies of Curricular Innovation

Introduction – Moving From Theory to *Praxis* Through Everyday Classroom Activities

My motivation for conducting this study was a desire to help university teachers improve their *languaculture* teaching by revisiting their teaching philosophies and practices in light of a broadened educational mission. Therefore, while Part 1 of this book examined the theory/practice gap from a top-down perspective, Part 2 shifts the focus to the bottom-up perspective. This perspective represents the empirical dimension of this study: that is, implementing the 'critical *languaculture* awareness' curriculum development framework in practice. Problematising the principles underpinning this framework through collaborative critical reflection in practice was central to bridging this gap and supporting a praxis-driven approach to innovation. As Guilherme (2002) has highlighted, 'the articulation between reflection and action provides for the nullification of the dichotomy between theory and practice, thus changing the educational practice,... into a *praxis*...' (Guilherme, 2002: 37).

This implementation was informed strongly by the philosophical assumptions of two complementary paradigms or worldviews: the critical constructivist paradigm (Kincheloe, 2005) and the participatory inquiry paradigm (Denzin & Lincoln, 2005; Guba & Lincoln, 1994; Heron & Reason, 1997). Critical pedagogy (CP) (Freire, 1973; Giroux, 1988; Guilherme, 2002; Kincheloe, 2003) has also provided an ideal theoretical underlay to promote connection between theory and practice, between 'ends' and 'means'. This critical stance on pedagogy contends that teachers should embrace their role as researchers of their own teaching practices. In so doing, they 'can revolutionise professional practice by viewing themselves as potentially the most sophisticated research instrument available' (Kincheloe, 2003: 52).

Critical constructivism combines key elements of social constructivism (Bandura, 1986; Bruner, 1960; Piaget, 1970) and critical theory (Dewey, 1933, 1938; Habermas, 1971). Constructivism and critical theory provide unique and complementary epistemological perspectives. Constructivism emphasises individual cognitive activity, but acknowledges negotiation with others as a means of determining the viability of knowledge. Critical theory emphasises the socio-cultural legitimation of knowledge, but argues for emancipating the individual from repressive traditions that constitute the social reality of legitimating institutions.

Critical constructivism therefore provides a powerful theoretical framework for developing a *praxis*-driven language and culture curriculum and in so doing, promote the professional development of teacher–participants. The key philosophical assumptions of this paradigm are grounded in a constructivist set of beliefs about truth, or ontology, which claims that there is no single, tangible reality that can be reduced or approximated; there are only multiple, participative, co-created, subjective–objective realities. This paradigm is underpinned by an epistemology, or a set of beliefs about knowledge, which values the creation of knowledge through critical subjectivity and the co-creation of findings.

This is why the research I conducted included a component of participatory action research (PAR) (Kemmis & Wilkinson, 1998; Zuber-Skerritt, 1992b). Zuber-Skerritt (1992a: 12) and Kemmis and Wilkinson (1998: 23–24) identify features of PAR that make this approach particularly relevant for this investigation. PAR is participatory and collaborative. The researcher is not considered to be an 'outsider' expert conducting an investigation on subjects, but a 'co-worker' doing research with and for those concerned with the practical problem and its actual improvement. This collaborative PAR component thus enabled me as researcher, co-working with the teacher–participants, to embrace the roles of (a) reflective practitioners; (b) dialogue facilitators; and (c) transformative intellectuals (Kumaravadivelu, 2003). Teacher–participants could thus engage directly in innovation within the context of their own subjects through a scaffolded cycle of inquiry.

PAR is interpretative: Research participants understand that the inquiry will result, not in the researcher's positivist statements based on right and wrong answers to the research questions, but in solutions based on the views and interpretations of the participants involved in the investigation.

PAR is critical: The researcher seeks not only to bring practical improvements, but also to act as a critical and self-critical catalyst of 'change'. In this investigation, 'change' stemmed from contesting and problematising teacher–participant approaches to language and culture teaching.

PAR is reflexive: PAR researchers critically reflect on issues and processes within their own inquiry, making explicit their role in interpretation of the findings. In this way, the practical accounts can give rise to theoretical considerations.

PAR is emancipatory: PAR aims to help participants contest the constraints that limit their self-development. It is a process that encourages and supports participants to explore how their practices are shaped and constrained by wider structures. Participants are then able to decide whether they can and will intervene – to release themselves from these constraints, or to minimise the extent to which they themselves contribute to perpetuating those constraints.

PAR is cyclical or iterative: By changing their practices through a spiral of cycles of critical action and reflection, language teachers can learn more about their own practices, their knowledge of their practices and the context in which they realise their practices (Kemmis & McTaggart, 1988).

The ultimate aim of this study was to provide recommendations on how to develop and implement a curriculum that bridges the gap between the theoretical and practical aspects of language and culture teaching at university level. This aim was congruent with another feature of PAR: its practical nature. The results and insights gained from the research are not only of theoretical importance to advancing knowledge in the field, but also lead to practical improvements during and after the research process.

Finally, at the core of PAR is its bottom-up process of *praxis*-driven action with the potential to bring about positive change. As Flamini and Jiménez Raya (2007: 105) point out, research has shown that top-down professional development (PD) has been largely ineffective in bringing about substantial, sustainable change in classroom practice (*cf.* Fullan, 1982; Leithwood *et al.*, 1994). A bottom-up approach that incorporates a collaborative teacher–researcher inquiry is more likely to result in relevant, long-lasting improvement in teaching practices. In this investigation, my choice to use PAR as an alternative avenue for continuing PD stemmed from recognition that PAR is engaging and purposeful, which makes it particularly fitting to the higher education context.

Overview of the case studies

The curriculum innovation projects that inform these four case studies were underpinned by the critical *languaculture* awareness curriculum framework discussed in Chapter 2. I used these case studies to explore how teachers might address the challenges and limitations inherent in the programme structure and curriculum delivery of languages education in their everyday practices. The languages faculty in the Australian university where I conducted this study over four academic years (2006–2010) represented well the common salient features I have outlined in Chapter 1. This faculty offered a three-year undergraduate programme for specialist students and the option of additional specialisation through an Honours programme. In 2006 the faculty offered six language programmes: Chinese (Mandarin), Indonesian, Italian, Japanese, Korean and Spanish. Four years later, only two thirds (four language programmes) were still on offer; two of the four Asian language programmes had been closed. The four languages still on offer were two Asian languages – Japanese and Chinese – and two European languages – Italian and Spanish.

I chose two language programmes[1] for this investigation: Italian and Chinese, each representing different language and culture teaching approaches. In each programme I purposefully selected two subjects, in conjunction with the programme's coordinator: a language subject and a 'cultural context' subject. The latter had been designed specifically as adjunct to the programmes' language components and was therefore ideal to explore the integration of *languaculture*. Selecting these subjects was particularly relevant since they enabled me to explore curriculum innovation strategies in both language and non-language subject components within a specific programme. In addition, each of these four subjects had a different approach to construing and presenting the relationship between language and culture. They therefore provided an opportunity for my investigation to explore the teacher–participants' different conceptualisations of culture and their culture teaching rationales.

I then proceeded to contact directly the academic staff involved in these subjects to organise a brief preliminary interview. At the interview, I explained the aims of this investigation while explicitly discussing its collaborative, PAR nature. I stressed confidentiality issues, encouraged their participation and discussed a tentative research schedule for those interested in participating as volunteers in my research. Four of the academic staff I approached were willing and able to participate in this research project. Each of these academic staff members and the subjects they were involved in became a case study unit, making four case studies for this investigation. These four were heterogeneous, making this what qualitative researchers label a 'multiple case study' investigation.

I developed this multiple case study investigation in four phases: (1) operationalising the *languaculture* teaching framework; (2) designing and implementing specific pedagogic interventions for the various educational contexts; (3) selecting suitable data collection instruments to study the outcomes in each educational context; (4) the fourth and final phase entailed a two-pronged process: presenting study results to the teacher–participants and scaffolding their practices with a follow-up to observe the individual teacher–participants' curriculum development and implementation strategies. The flowchart in Figure 3.1 provides an 'at a glance' visual representation of these four phases.

The teachers in charge of each of the four selected subjects were all female and three were native speakers of the language they were teaching. In the Italian programme, Maria[2] – the only non-native speaker – was in charge of a first-year Italian 'cultural context' subject taught in English, while Valentina was in charge of a second-year intermediate Italian language subject focused on developing oral skills. In the Chinese programme, Lili was in charge of a first-year Chinese 'cultural context' subject taught in English, while Mei was in charge of a first-year elementary Chinese language subject.

The four teacher–participants were allocated a key role in the curriculum innovation process. This role involved reflecting on the subject's enacted

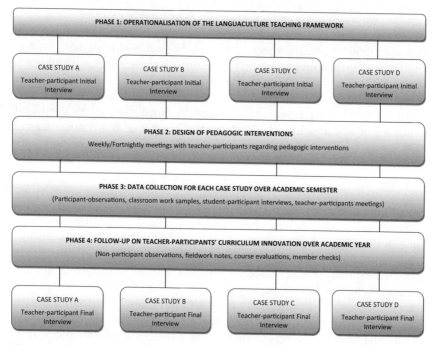

Figure 3.1 Flowchart of multiple case study development

curriculum, collaborating in development of the *languaculture* modules for pedagogic intervention in the subject, and reflecting on the outcomes of these interventions. In turn, this involved the collaborative design of an implementation schedule for each of the educational contexts, bearing in mind the syllabi and aims of the subjects. The intervention schedules are presented in tables and discussed later in this chapter. I selected these curriculum elements in collaboration with each of the teacher–participants after the initial introductory interview. The initial interview was followed by an introductory session on the *languaculture* conceptual framework and critical awareness-raising activities and, subsequently, by weekly/fortnightly meetings in which we discussed the implementation outcomes.

To explore the discrepancy between 'ends' and 'means' explained in earlier chapters, the underlying rationale for innovation required that we problematise the cultural goals and objectives of each of the four subjects and explore their realisation (or lack thereof) in practice. The teacher–participants revised, and in some cases reformulated, their subject goals and objectives to address the students' development of critical *languaculture* awareness and knowledge. Subsequently, I worked with the teacher–participants to focus on developing *languaculture* modules aimed at exploring if/how the subjects' newly formulated goals and objectives were realised in practice.

Development and implementation of these modules entailed addressing the questions behind the theoretical aspects discussed in earlier chapters, that is, the curriculum goals (why?), syllabus or content (what?) and teaching activities (how?). In terms of content, all four case studies were underpinned by Risager's conceptualisation of *languaculture*, as well as Crozet's (2003) conceptual framework of *languaculture* traits. They all included a relevant set of readings from Lo Bianco and Crozet's (2003) volume: Carroli *et al.* for the Italian subjects and Li for the Chinese. Other academic resources such as supplementary textbooks and readers, authentic material such as film excerpts and documentaries, and electronic sources such as blogs were also selected purposefully.

All interventions included a preliminary presentation of the *languaculture* concept and the *languaculture* conceptual framework for students to frame subsequent activities. In terms of activities, all *languaculture* modules included the integration of in-class presentations and discussions around specific *languaculture* aspects. These discussions aimed to promote 'transformative learning', the type of reflective learning I discussed in Chapter 2. This type of discussion sought to help students in questioning their 'uncritically acquired' frames of reference and in so doing, provide them with tools that promote an ongoing reflective process of 'perspective transformation' (Mezirow, 1991, 2000). The ultimate aim of these discussions was, therefore, to raise students' awareness of *languacultural* differences and similarities so that they may develop a dynamic view of *languaculture* behaviour(s) in intercultural encounters and thus may be able to manage contentiously their alternative frames of *languaculture* reference.

Each subject had an average of 20 students. Each of these cohorts was largely heterogeneous; they included domestic and international students from various backgrounds and disciplines as well as age groups. In addition, these cohorts included students who had travelled abroad – to Italy and China – to study and on holidays, as well as students who had very limited experience interacting with native speakers of the target languages.

Before analysing and discussing each of the four case studies, it is useful to consider the overall programme structure, its existing language and culture teaching rationale and the role of each subject within the programme. Each case study includes a detailed profile of the subject based on an initial in-depth interview with each of the teacher–participants. This is followed by explanation of how the underlying language and culture teaching rationale was (re)conceptualised and how the *languaculture* modules for pedagogic intervention were developed and implemented in conjunction with the teachers.

Finally, I analyse the outcomes of these interventions in relation to the various data collection tools. The primary data were obtained using the following data collection tools.

- An initial and a final semi-structured interview with each teacher–participant. (That is, a total of eight main interviews of approximately one and a half hours each.)
- Field notes on weekly/fortnightly meetings held with teacher–participants.
- Work samples produced by students during *languaculture* exploration class activities, as well as homework tasks such as reflective worksheets.
- Participant-observation field notes that I took during interventions and non-participant observation of subsequent classes.
- Semi-structured interviews at the end of the semester with student–participants (a minimum of four in one of the subjects and maximum of six in another, making a total of 20 student interviews of approximately 25 minutes each).
- A personal reflective journal that I completed throughout the investigation.

To identify good practice[3] and shortcomings in the pedagogic interventions, I used data from my interviews with teacher–participants as well as relevant class work samples, and data from both participant observation and my interviews with student–participants at the end of each subject. My analysis and discussion of these data highlight a fundamental predicament in meeting the discrepancies between 'ends' and 'means' in language and culture teaching. Despite teachers' ostensibly positive intentions and instances of good practice, curriculum innovation to develop critical *languaculture* awareness remains problematic in practice. The overall structure of university language teaching and a number of pedagogical variables seriously limit possibilities for successful innovation.

The Italian Language Programme

The Italian programme at this university mirrored the main structural features and enrolment patterns discussed earlier in Chapter 2. Table 3.1 below illustrates the three-year sequence of Italian language subjects aimed to develop learners' proficiency from elementary to advanced levels. This programme also offered a fourth-year subject for students wishing to continue their language studies into their Honours degree, a unique feature compared with other programmes available within the faculty. This programme also included two cultural context subjects taught in English, the first one in first year, second semester; and the second one in second year, first semester. Although the first cultural context subject was not a pre-requisite for enrolling in the second cultural context subject, both subjects were compulsory for specialist learners. The subjects highlighted in the table represent the ones selected for the curriculum innovation PAR projects.

In my interview with Valentina, the coordinator of the Italian language programme, she revealed that the Italian teaching team as a whole tried to

Table 3.1 Italian language programme structure

Year	Semester 1		Semester 2	
First year	Elementary language subject I		Elementary language subject II	Cultural context subject I – **Case study A**
Second year	Intermediate language subject	Cultural context subject II	Intermediate language subject (writing skills)	Intermediate language subject (oral skills) **Case study B**
Third year	Advanced language subjects (content-based)		Advanced language subjects (content-based)	
Fourth year	Advanced language subject for honours level learners			

work in consultation with one another to develop and implement their teaching curricula coherently and cohesively. This was substantiated by the team-teaching approach and documents that the team had produced to explicate the programme's overall teaching rationale. One of these documents provided to me by the programme coordinator specifically described the programme's rationale for language and culture teaching. This document revealed a seemingly coherent thread underlying the teaching team's approach, that is, presenting Italian language:

> ... not only as an object of study in itself, but also as a means by which to study Italian culture and society and the debates and discourses transmitted through the language. [...] *to develop students' awareness of Italian mentalità, or ways of thinking, and how these are reflected in language use.* (Emphasis added)

This rationale, included in several subject outlines[4] within the programme, appeared to be well thought out and mindfully integrated within the curriculum. However, when probed about how the team explicitly realised the development of such 'awareness' and evaluated or monitored its development, the coordinator admitted that activities for raising cultural awareness were rather *ad hoc* and incidental. This was particularly so in first-year language subjects, and there were no assessment items to monitor 'awareness' development within each subject or sequentially throughout the programme. This response substantiated literature examined in earlier chapters, suggesting that even where the place of culture within a programme is presented on paper as well established and deliberate, its realisation in practice falls short. Almost camouflaged by such descriptions in writing, in classroom practice (inter)cultural awareness remains unquestioned. Nevertheless, the teaching team's positive attitude on innovation provided a suitable starting point for developing and implementing our PAR projects.

Case Study A: Italian cultural context subject

This cultural context subject was purposefully selected. It represented a formal introduction to issues in language, society and culture in Italy for both specialist and non-specialist students wishing to learn essential concepts in Italy's linguistic history and sociolinguistic landscape, relations between popular culture and linguistic and societal developments, as well as some key issues in the historical development of Italy's language and culture. As outlined in the subject description, this subject was designed to complement the first-year elementary language subjects and lay the foundations upon which later courses in the Italian studies major are built. While it was a compulsory component for students specialising in Italian language, it was also recommended as an elective component for students undertaking Italian-related studies within any other degree programme. Class work was conducted in English, although activities were often based on material in Italian (with translations available where necessary).

The syllabus of the subject had three modules. Module 1 provided an introduction to the subject and an overview of Italian linguistic history. It examined the major influences on Italy's linguistic development from ancient times to unification in 1860 and then through to the present day, with particular attention to processes of modernisation and diversification of Italian society since World War 2. Module 2 looked at language and the arts in historical perspective, with respect to four areas in which Italians have made a major contribution to the arts in Europe: poetry, theatre, opera and cinema. Module 3 explored relationships between language, society and culture in contemporary Italy, through a survey of the variation in Italians' linguistic repertoires: territorial, social, by context of use and by medium of communication. It also briefly examined Italian language and culture in Australia as a component of the Italian *diaspora*. This third module explored links between language and culture in daily life and sought to develop familiarity with some Italian *mentalità* or ways of thinking, especially through the work on gestures and food.

The delivery mode consisted of three contact hours per week: a one-hour lecture followed by a two-hour workshop. In the workshops, the concepts introduced in the lecture were explored further and practised through examining Italian texts, usually with an English translation available. These texts included songs, scenes from films, extracts from novels and material from newspapers, television and websites. The assessment items required students to engage in a wide range of academic activities, including small-scale research, preparation and delivery of an oral presentation and writing a summary and a critical comment on specific texts. Students were also expected to keep abreast of the set of weekly readings and participate actively in class work throughout the semester.

Pedagogic interventions

The guiding thread in this subject was the study of Italian language and its historical evolution – from its origins in Latin vernacular forms to *dialetti*[5] and today's regional varieties, and their coexistence with other minority languages – in relation to societal changes. Specific factors influencing linguistic developments were explored, alongside identification of significant historical milestones, political events, and literary, musical and other artistic manifestations of language in use. Therefore, the sociolinguistic aspects of this subject were a 'static' object of study, viewed largely from a historical perspective. In other words, the subject did not set out to include *languaculture* aspects of Italian language: levels of politeness, verbosity or other paralinguistic features as expressions of the dynamic, *linguistically mediated* manifestations of Italian *mentalità*, out-of-awareness cultural values and beliefs.

The PAR project on curriculum innovation therefore set out to add a new significant thread: that of culture manifested in language in everyday communication. This entailed incorporating *languaculture* modules under the guise of 'intercultural reflection workshops' (or intercultural workshops). Five intercultural workshops were developed to explicitly introduce the *languaculture* conceptual framework and discuss its axes. The format of these workshops consisted of a 20–30 minute class discussion that I conducted at the end of the two-hour tutorial in five separate instances throughout the 13-week semester. The structure of the workshops consisted of a brief presentation of conceptual and/or theoretical points drawn from the set reading, followed by trigger questions aimed at raising students' awareness of their prior knowledge and specific discussion questions aimed to promote students' critical reflection on the *languaculture* aspects under examination.

The set reading was the interpretation by Carroli *et al.* (2003) of Crozet's conceptual framework for the Italian *languaculture* context, specifically in face-to-face communication. The paper illustrated Crozet's five *languaculture* axes and explicitly set out to help teachers, and ultimately, learners:

> … develop critical awareness of general cultural traits expressed in everyday conversation in Italy and at national level, whilst pointing out that there are geographical and social cultural differences. By 'critical' awareness we mean that both teachers and students, when reading materials on the subject, are able to discern between blatant stereotype and cultural trait, between regional trait or biased description. (Carroli *et al.*, 2003: 178)

In addition to the in-class discussions, students were also asked to continue reflecting on and discussing the *languaculture* aspects introduced during the workshops through the online discussion forum available in the subject's Blackboard webpage. Incorporating this element of participation had a twofold purpose: to complement the subject's in-class participation requirement and to give students who were not able to contribute to the class discussions time and space to formulate their ideas and share them with their classmates.

Table 3.2 illustrates the schedule of the presentations that were designed in conjunction with the teacher–participant, Maria. Each of the five presentations

Table 3.2 Case Study A: *Languaculture* modules intervention schedule

WEEK	TOPIC	LEVEL OF LANGUACULTURAL ANALYSIS	DISCUSSION QUESTIONS
WEEK 2	Introduction to cultural traits expressed in everyday Italian conversation	Introduction to the concept of *languaculture* Introduction to the *languaculture* analytical framework	
WEEK 5	Stereotypes of Italians and Australians	Deconstruction of the concept of stereotyping Concept of reverse ethnocentrism	What are some possible stereotypes about Italian people? (think about stereotypes based on *languaculture* differences identified in the reading and in your own experience). What about Australians? How can we demystify these stereotypical views?
WEEK 6	Expressing opinions and embracing/avoiding conflict	Approaches to interpersonal relationships Avoidance or love of conflict Levels of expressivity Levels of politeness	Have you ever experienced misunderstandings based on different approaches to interpersonal relationships/ degrees of expressivity? How did you react? Why? How do these levels of analysis help you conceptualise the *languacultural* differences between Italian *languaculture* and your own?

WEEK 10	Formal and informal modes of address	Levels of politeness/Approaches to interpersonal relationships Terms of address Formal and informal registers Levels of ritualisation (greetings, etc.)	What do you think about Sobrero's definition of "hypocritical informality" (Sobrero in Carroli et al., p. 183)? Have you ever experienced misunderstandings based on different "Approaches to interpersonal relationships"? How did you react? Why? How do these levels of analysis help you conceptualise differences and similarities between Italians' *languacultures* and your own?
WEEK 11	Pauses, interruptions and overlaps	Approaches to interpersonal relationships Kinesic behaviour (gestures, posture, etc.) Proxemics (use of personal space, physical contact) Paralinguistic aspects (tone of voice, speech rate, interjections) Levels of verbosity Importance placed on speaking Silence and pauses in conversation	Have you ever experienced misunderstandings based on different "Levels of verbosity" or "Approaches to interpersonal relationships"? How did you react? Why? How do these levels of analysis help you conceptualise differences and similarities between Italians' *languacultures* and your own?

was underpinned by a guiding topic and *languaculture* aspect(s). The last column includes the main questions used to trigger the in-class discussion and posted later on the online discussion forum. These questions served as catalysts for further discussion and sharing anecdotes and experiences. Here the goal was to raise students' awareness of their assumptions and their taken-for-granted frames of reference, and to reflect on their personal experiences in relation to interpreting salient Italian *languaculture* features.

Discussions were steered towards providing students with an analytical framework to understand, conceptualise and further examine these features and to scaffold their reflection on past and potential instances of *languaculture* dissonance, both generally and with specific relation to the target *languaculture*. This type of reflection aimed to encourage and provide a space for learners to become cognisant of their uncritically acquired frames of reference and in so doing, foster 'perspective transformation' processes.

The following vignette illustrates the development of a typical *languaculture* exploration workshop and is based on my participant observation field notes.

Languaculture exploration vignette
Fourth intervention: Formal and informal registers in Italian

The fourth intervention was designed to give the students the opportunity to reflect on Italian *languaculture* approaches to interpersonal relationships and the manifestation of these approaches in speakers' formal and informal registers. In particular, students were asked to discuss the rationale behind the use of *'lei'* (you-formal) and *'tu'* (you-informal) as well as other terms of address (titles: *dottore, signore*, etc.). Appendix 1 contains the slides used during the workshop.

To complement the discussion of these *languaculture* aspects, I also wanted to provide an Italian's point of view regarding Australian *languaculture* approaches to interpersonal relationships. I thus selected a blog entry published by a recently migrated Italian in Australia (slide 11). In this blog entry the author discussed what he defined as 'most beautiful Australian word: mate'. I provided students with a verbal translation of the text and asked language students to help me with the translation. Students were then asked to comment on the content of the blog entry and explain their use of the word 'mate'.

The trigger questions asked students to critically reflect on the concept of 'hypocritical informality' discussed in the set reading. This concept, which emerged through Italian sociolinguistic studies, referred to the generalised use of '*tu*' (you-informal) with anyone below 30–35 years of age even if the interactants do not know each other and may never see each other again.

Finally, students were asked to discuss any instances of *languaculture* dissonance they had experienced owing to interactants' differing expectations regarding the use of terms of address. Students' contributions to the discussion were varied. Not surprisingly, most of the discussion centred on two key points/issues: (a) the Italians' potential imagined views of Australians' *languaculture* behaviours and (b) the conflict that the Australian students perceived they would find themselves caught in when interacting with Italians – between the need to manifest the appropriate degree of formality that Italians might expect, and the appeal of 'hypocritical informality' that, according to the reading, many Italians subscribe to. This intervention is a clear example of a *languaculture* exploration that both incorporated and challenged 'etic' and 'emic', that is, both native and target, *languaculture* frames of reference.

Outcomes and limitations

Maria indicated that the intercultural workshops added a much needed component to the subject. They enhanced the subject's underlying notion of culture, which Maria conceptualised as the worldviews of Italian people, by integrating the *languaculture* dimension, as Italians' worldviews reflected in interaction. The students' in-class participation generated in-depth discussions and in the end-of-semester interviews students indicated that they had enjoyed learning and reflecting on the various *languaculture* aspects and their impact on everyday communication. Nonetheless, a number of concerns were identified in the process of integrating these elements into the subject. First was the lack of seamless integration of the intercultural workshops with the rest of the subject, second was the lack of readily available teaching resources such as intercultural sensitisers and third was the format of the discussions *vis-à-vis* Maria's teaching style and conceptualisation of *languaculture* for teaching purposes and several students' lack of experience of interaction with Italians.

While Maria and I tried to integrate the 'intercultural reflection workshops' into the subject structure and syllabus, we found it difficult to map out each of the *languaculture* aspects and match them to the topics discussed in the lectures and workshops of an already established subject. This meant that, while some of the *languaculture* aspects were explicitly related to the lecture and workshop content (e.g. formal and informal registers, aspects of non-verbal communication), most were not, and at times the connection was not apparent to the students. Holding the discussions at the end of the regular workshops created time constraints, which meant that the discussions sometimes had to be closed before reaching their full development. Students indicated that, while the discussion–debate format of the intercultural workshops was an interesting addition to the regular workshops, overall contribution of the former to the subject was undermined by the limited amount of time dedicated to these workshops. The opportunity to continue the discussions online, however, did not encourage many students to do so. Many students indicated that they chose not to participate in the online forum because they preferred the in-class exchange of ideas.

Thus, despite our efforts to ensure their seamless integration, overall, the 'intercultural reflection workshops' appeared to be an add-on component to the subject. Other variables may also have influenced this outcome. First, the apparent separation between Maria's part of the workshop and mine, that is, having two different teachers present information, may have contributed to the perception that the cultural workshops were not intrinsically part of the subject. Second, the discussion–debate format of the intercultural workshops involved teaching and learning strategies different from those of the regular class time. Here, one student indicated that this made the intercultural workshops seem 'quite disjointed' and that the transition to a different type of learning required students to suddenly change from one learning mode to another. A fourth variable was the frequency of the *languaculture* workshops. Because they were not conducted every week, a recapitulation was required at the beginning of each workshop to remind students of what had been discussed in the previous session. This also indicated that discussion of *languaculture* aspects was limited to these moments rather than integrally embedded in the rest of the subject. This was corroborated in my interviews with the students who indicated that 'it was up to [them] to make the connection' between the content of the lectures and the intercultural workshop discussions.

In terms of teaching resources and materials, the paper by Carroli et al. (2003) was considered a useful introductory reading for exploring *languaculture*. However, Maria expressed concern about the lack of readily available material for further analysis and discussion of *languaculture* aspects. This was particularly evident at the end of the semester in preparing the final written exam. Maria wanted to incorporate case studies or intercultural sensitisers into the exam to trigger students' written reflection on the *languaculture* aspects discussed in class, yet lack of available resources meant that in the end she had to abandon this aim.

As for the overall format of the discussions and the use of trigger questions, students indicated that they appreciated the incorporation of this type of content, and this type of personal-reflection approach, into their learning experience as it enabled them to share their ideas with others and to reflect on their own perceptions of Italians and Australians in everyday interaction. This substantiated the use of 'perspective transformation' techniques developed within the context of this subject. At the end of the semester, students were asked to reflect on the overall experience and indicate how the examination of various aspects of *languaculture* had helped them conceptualise differences and similarities between Italians' *languacultures* and their own. This question was posted on the online forum to give students time to reflect outside the classroom. Figure 3.2 shows one student's answer to the question. This post highlights several positive outcomes, including the idea of 'noticing' and raising students' levels of awareness. However, this was the only response from the class cohort.

In my final interview with Maria, we observed that the type of discussions conducted in the *languaculture* workshops was not without pitfalls. Leading intercultural discussions through trigger questions is a pedagogical skill that requires explicit attention and ongoing reflection and experimentation, and relies heavily on the individual teacher adapting her teaching style to incorporate such practices and being able to monitor both students' reactions to each other's comments and her own.

Maria explained that her own teaching style/philosophy did not normally rely on this type of open discussion using students' anecdotes as their basis. Her pedagogical concern had to do with inviting students to give first-person accounts that may potentially reflect personal prejudices and considerable lack of critical awareness of their own reactions. She saw this as possibly contributing to the perpetuation of stereotypical assumptions through stereotypically influenced interpretations of interactions with Italians and possibly involving remarks that could be interpreted as thoughtless or offensive by other students. Here, the lack of students' experience in

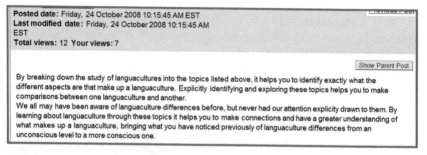

Figure 3.2 Discussion forum excerpt

interaction with Italians, particularly for those at first-year level, compounded the problem of generalisation and limited the bases on which students could critically engage with each other's claims. In this vein, Maria also pointed out that perhaps some student cohorts may have more first-hand experience in interactions with Italians than others and also be more predisposed to share this type of first-person anecdotal information and discuss different experiences, so she was not sure to what extent this type of discussion could be effectively implemented in different cohorts. For all these reasons, Maria preferred the use of accounts, such as the Italian blogger's post discussed in the vignette, as a more effective tool, in that it still allows for individual reactions and responses, but based on a shared experience/ encounter by all students of the same text. In other words, in this example, the whole class was able to engage personally with the same situation or description presented by the same Italian person, protagonist of this account, at the same time. From this common ground, everyone was able to provide their own responses, reactions and interpretations and potentially to challenge and/or critically engage with each other's views.

Maria's concerns raised two important issues for me in the implementation of *languaculture* discussions; first, the teachers' personal teaching style and philosophy as well as the specific characteristics of individual student cohorts *vis-à-vis* the type of learning experiences fostered by the *languaculture* framework to promote processes of 'perspective transformation'; and second, the lack of readily available material presenting first-person accounts that could be objectively discussed in the classroom. These are essential variables in the development and implementation of critical *languaculture* awareness raising strategies.

In terms of assessment, students' lack of participation in the online discussion forum meant that they could be assessed only on their contribution to in-class discussions. This contribution was particularly difficult to assess as the same students would take part in the debates each time, and there was never enough time to organise mini-group discussions to give everyone the opportunity to express their ideas. Some of the student interviewees suggested using written homework (instead of participation in the online forum) as an assessment item, in order to ensure the active participation of the class as a whole, and the monitoring of any students who did not feel comfortable contributing during the workshop.

Case Study B: Italian language subject

The language subject selected for the other Italian PAR project – a second-year, second-semester subject taught in Italian – focused on development of oral skills. This subject had two main aims, as specified in its subject outline. These were to (1) consolidate and extend students' proficiency and understanding of spoken colloquial Italian; and (2) enhance students' cultural understanding of, and familiarity with, Italy and Italian popular culture through work with texts drawn from a variety of media (in class and in private practice) and through interaction with native or near-native speakers of Italian in the community. Meeting with members of the community sought 'to further develop students' awareness of Italian mentalità' by creating opportunities to gain 'direct insight into Italian and Italo-Australian ways of life'. That feature gave this subject a particularly significant role within the programme as the only subject that required learners to meet with members of the Italian community. Valentina, the programme's coordinator and teacher of this subject, referred to this subject as particularly representative of the programme's language and culture teaching rationale discussed earlier.

Thus, students were required to meet with Italian native speakers or near-native community members of Italian heritage selected by the subject convenor, in addition to the subject's four contact hours each week. The group of Italian community members included recently migrated Italian native speakers, as well as Italian immigrants who had lived in Australia for a number of years but returned to Italy regularly or were in contact with the Italian community on a regular basis. Students were required to meet the community members (CM) at least four times (five meetings were recommended) during the semester, for a total of six hours. The meetings were to be organised by the students in agreement with the CM. Depending on the number of students enrolled and the number of community members available, some students were required to share their meetings with the CM.

These meetings were to be conducted in Italian and students were required to tape their conversations, or at least half an hour of each meeting, to help them complete a *scheda* (worksheet) that they had to submit as part as their assessment. The tape-recording requirement was to enable students to concentrate on their conversations without taking notes and to review the conversation after meetings so they could complete the *scheda* accurately and in detail. Students were also encouraged to pursue other activities with their allocated CM, including cooking an Italian meal, shopping, watching an Italian film or television programme and going to an Italian restaurant.

As such, this subject included both in-class and outside-the-classroom activities. In-class contact hours were divided into weekly two-hour workshops and one-hour tutorials. In the workshops, various types of activities were conducted, in pairs and groups, aimed at promoting development of both fluency and accuracy in speaking, and comprehension of spoken and written Italian. The tutorials were mainly concerned with preparing students for their meetings with the CM and exploring particular linguistic or cultural elements. Time was also dedicated to discussing the communication and interaction strategies that students may find useful during their conversations with the CM. During the tutorials, students were also required to complete the first section of the *scheda* before each meeting.

This *scheda* or worksheet had five sections. The first section encouraged students to list a series of questions, points of discussion, and words and expressions relevant to the topic of the meeting. After the meeting, students had to complete the rest of the *scheda* by writing comments and notes based on the recording or on their own notes. The second section focused on new words or expressions they encountered while listening to the recording; and the third section required them to provide a summary of the meeting in Italian. The fourth section, a process of self-reflection on the students' linguistic performance, was designed to give students the opportunity to reflect on grammatical difficulties or recurrent mistakes they could identify in their production during the meeting. The fifth section included general questions about the meeting that students could answer in English or in Italian. These questions included aspects such as the CM's use of English or simpler expressions in Italian, the CM's error correction strategies, the student's use of pictures and dictionary to convey their message, and examples of misunderstandings arising from cultural/social differences.

Suggested topics for each meeting as specified in the subject outline were personal – getting to know each other and describing their personal histories; reasons for coming to Australia; their family; their region or city of origin; their household, home life and life in the community; spare time activities; and impressions of Italy and Australia – and current issues such as immigration, the environment and political issues. In addition to submitting the *schede*, assessment of this subject consisted of a listening test, an oral presentation in class, an oral exam with the teaching team and regular tasks concerned with preparing for, and reporting back from, the conversations with the CM.

Pedagogic interventions

The main ways this subject sought to introduce key aspects of Italian culture involved the students' required interaction with members of the Italian community. My initial observations revealed that while exploration of specific cultural aspects, such as *campanilismo* (local patriotism) or *mammismo* (belief among sons that no one can ever love them as much as their mothers), was introduced explicitly in class, the students' worksheets focused largely on their reflection on linguistic and strategic competence. Cultural aspects were relegated to an open question at the end of the *scheda* where students were prompted to 'Give (if possible) a few examples of misunderstandings arising from cultural/social differences'.

The curriculum innovation for the PAR project in this subject therefore had two trajectories. One entailed systematic introduction of specific *languaculture* aspects in class, as part of preparing for the meetings with the CM. The other was a separate, more detailed, section on *languaculture* in the students' worksheets. Four interventions of 40 minutes each for presentations by me with Valentina's assistance, on specific *languaculture* aspects, were programmed into the class schedule throughout the semester. We conducted each intervention during the two-hour workshop in the target language, seeking to correlate with the topics suggested for the students' meetings with the CM. Table 3.3 illustrates distribution of the four presentations throughout the 13-week semester (after a brief introduction to *languaculture* in Week 1), and the main guiding topics and *languaculture* aspects introduced in each class. The last column on the right, which provides a brief description of materials and specific tasks during the workshops, indicates reformulation of the fifth section in the *scheda* to integrate: *'Riflessione sul contenuto linguistico-culturale'* (*Languaculture* reflection).

The fifth section in the *scheda* (*Languaculture* reflection) aimed to provide a space for students' written reflections on the particular *languaculture* aspect(s) presented in class. Table 3.4 presents the questions included in this section of the *schede vis-à-vis* the topics assigned to each meeting.

The following vignette illustrates the development of a typical *languaculture* exploration workshop in this subject, based on my participant observation field notes. See Appendix 2 for a lesson plan example.

Languaculture exploration vignette
Fourth intervention: Non-verbal communication
(gestures and silence)

This intervention was designed to give the students the opportunity to reflect on Italian *languaculture* levels of verbosity and how these are manifest in conversation. In particular, students were asked to discuss the use of gestures as well as turn-taking rules in interaction. Appendix 3 contains the slides used during the workshop.

To complement the discussion of these *languaculture* aspects, we included (a) pictures of common Italian gestures, and (b) contextualised use of gestures in excerpts of a film (*Il mio meglior nemico*, My Best Enemy). Students were asked to compare the use of gestures in their native and target *languaculture*(s). Next, to trigger additional discussion, students were asked to comment on the explanations of Italian *languaculture*(s) use of silence and turn-taking in conversation presented in the set reading. Finally, students were asked to discuss instances of turn-taking difficulties during their meetings with the CMs, for instance, whether they had noticed instances of *pause vuote*, (silent pauses), *pause piene* (pauses filled with hesitation fillers, or other strategies to hold the floor), and *accavallamenti* (overlapping) and whether they had experienced any discomfort owing to their interactant's differing expectations of these turn-taking strategies. Students' contributions to the discussion raised several interesting issues. They expressed how in their first few meetings with the CMs they found it difficult to follow these turn-taking rules, especially to interrupt their interlocutors to ask for clarification or simply to attempt to ask more questions. Similarly, they told of their difficulty in holding the floor while conversing, especially where there were two students per CM.

This class discussion led us as teacher/facilitator to formulate strategies for students to adapt their *languaculture* behaviour so that they felt comfortable interrupting their interlocutor or continuing to talk to hold the floor when necessary.

This vignette illustrates the complementary role of the *languaculture* exploration modules in this subject. Overall, the discussions helped students to share their frustrations as well as positive experiences in learning to interact with their CM. Additionally, these reflective processes were complemented by the *languaculture* section in their *schede* (see Table 3.4).

Outcomes and limitations

Valentina advised that one of the main contributions of the interventions to her culture teaching rationale was that they provided a more specific, systematic way of relating language with culture. She could share this with the students and use it to explicitly present and exemplify the points of articulation between the two. As well as this systematic description of the language/culture nexus, Valentina also found it extremely useful to have the terminology that the interventions provided to discuss their relationship: '*I learned the language to talk about this. It has broadened my theoretical*

Table 3.3 Case Study B: *Languaculture* modules intervention schedule

WEEK	TOPIC	LANGUACULTURE ASPECTS INTRODUCED IN CLASS	MATERIAL/ACTIVITY USED IN CLASS
WEEK 1	Introduction to *languaculture* discussions	Concept of *languaculture* and the conceptual framework proposed by Crozet (2003) and developed in the Italian context by Carroli et al. (2003).	PowerPoint presentation to illustrate cultural iceberg, *languaculture* and Crozet's framework. Presentation of the set reading to be analysed throughout the semester: Carroli et al. (2003).
WEEK 2	Intercultural reflection workshop: Introduction to cultural traits expressed in everyday Italian conversation.	• Levels of Politeness/Approaches to interpersonal relationships ○ Terms of address ○ Formal and informal • Levels of ritualisation ○ Pragmatic routines (greetings, etc.)	DVD – *Italia Contemporanea*: Conversations with native speakers (Lucas, 2000) used to explore native speakers' reflections on formal and informal registers. Handout with greetings for students to classify according to register.
WEEK 5	Family	• Levels of politeness/Verbosity ○ Turn-taking in conversation (fillers) ○ Speech acts (thanking, interrupting, complimenting, complaining, etc.) • Levels of ritualisation ○ Pragmatic routines among relatives (greetings, etc.)	PowerPoint presentation to trigger brainstorming session about Italian family as well as stereotypes regarding Australian and Italian family models. Reflection on statistical data and new family models in Italy. Distinction between *stereotipo* and *sociotipo*.
WEEK 7	City/Region of origin	• Identity formation – Importance of the city of origin • Levels of verbosity ○ Importance placed on speaking ○ Silence	PowerPoint presentation to present theoretical aspects of non-verbal communication. Two scenes from the film *Il mio meglior nemico* (My best enemy) were used to exemplify the use of kinesic behaviour, proxemics and other paralinguistic aspects.

(Continued)

Table 3.3 (*Continued*)

WEEK	TOPIC	LANGUACULTURE ASPECTS INTRODUCED IN CLASS	MATERIAL/ACTIVITY USED IN CLASS

		• Approaches to interpersonal relationships
		  ○ Kinesic behaviour (gestures, posture, etc.)
		  ○ Proxemics (use of personal space, physical contact)
		  ○ Paralinguistic aspects (tone of voice, speech rate, interjections)	

WEEK 11	Comparisons between Australia & Italy	• Poetic dimension – Sayings/proverbs • Approaches to interpersonal relationships – avoidance or love of conflict • Levels of expressivity – emotionology • Levels of politeness – speech acts (disagreeing) • Identity formation – maintaining one's identity away from home	Comic video presentation depicting the stereotypical view of Italians and rest of the European countries, used to trigger expressions of agreement and disagreement with this view. (http://www.youtube.com/watch?v = 1wvSSqiHCHE) Oral activity in pairs to discuss stereotypical views held about Italians by people from different nationalities. This activity was used to practice the present subjunctive to express opinions/ assumptions/beliefs, etc. *Source: Ricette per Parlare* – Unità 29 – "Italiani, sliana gente!" (Bailini, 2002: 93–95). Analysis of a mini-drama depicting a conflict and how interlocutors from Italy and from the United States handled and interpreted the encounter. *Source: Incontri Culturali* Unità 47 "Punti di Vista" (DAlleva, Bee & Synder, 199: 47).

Table 3.4 Case Study B: Schedule of intercultural reflection questions in *schede*

MEETING	TOPIC	
		Questions in the *Scheda* (Worksheet)
		PART 5: *Riflessione sul contenuto linguistico-culturale.* For each meeting you will be asked to reflect on specific *languacultural* **aspects** of the meeting. (*You can do this part in point form in English or Italian*).
		Give (if possible) a few examples of misunderstandings arising from cultural/social differences. Refer specifically to the following:
First Meeting	1. Getting to know each other (obtaining personal information)	• Approaches to Interpersonal Relationships – Terms of address – Formal and informal (Did you use *tu* or *lei*? Did you use name and surname, first name? Did you change these terms of address during the conversation? Why? How?) • Levels of Politeness and ritualisation (Did your meeting take place at lunch time? How did this affect the conversation? Did you interrupt each other in conversation? How?) • Pragmatic routines (greetings, leave-taking, etc.). (How did you greet the CM? How did s/he greet you? Did you shake hands? Did you kiss twice? Why? Why not?)
Second Meeting	2. Family	• Stereotypes regarding the family unit and interpersonal relationships within the family in the Italian and Australian *languacultures.* (Were you able to explore the notions of "*stereotipo*" and "*sociotipo*" in relation to the topic of the family? How? What did you discover?) • Level of verbosity: Did you notice difference in the loudness and liveliness of Italian *languaculture*? Are there "silent" moments in the conversation? What about "*pause vuote*" (silent pauses)? What about "*pause piene*" (hmmm, lengthening of vowels "dicoooo")? What about "*accavallamenti*" (overlapping)? Does turn-taking in conversation feel different in Italian *languaculture*? How do you manage turn-taking? Refer to pages 179 & 180 of the paper provided in WEEK 2 for a detailed description of "Levels of verbosity" in Italian *languaculture.*
Third Meeting	3. City & region of origin	• Identity dimension & city of origin: In this meeting you were asked to explore aspects of the CM's city of origin. Do you think the city of origin reflects an aspect of the CM's identity that goes beyond their national identity? Please elaborate.

(Continued)

Table 3.4   (*Continued*)

Meeting	Topic	
		• Non-verbal communication: Have you had the chance to overtly explore aspects of non-verbal communication with your CM? Have you been able to observe or attend to any of the following dimensions of non-verbal communication: o *Kinesic behaviour* (gestures, posture, etc.) – Has your CM used any of the gestures explored in class? Has your CM used gestures to clarify, add or emphasise aspects of the conversation? Have you noticed any other "kinesic behaviour" that is the same as or differs from your native *languaculture?* o *Proxemics* (use of personal space) – How close does your CM normally sit/stand? Have you ever felt they've invaded your "personal space"? Please elaborate. o *Haptics* (physical contact) – Is there any physical contact during die interviews? Do you kiss twice to greet each other hello and goodbye? How do you feel about this?
Fourth Meeting	4. The house/ Life at home and in the community 5. Free time and hobbies	• Poetic Dimension – Sayings/Proverbs: Did the you notice your CM using sayings or proverbs? Were you able to discuss specific proverbs or sayings similar to ones presented in class? • Approaches to interpersonal relationships: o Levels of Expressivity – Emotionology: Did you notice verbal/non-verbal ways in which your CM expressed his/her emotions? Were you able to discuss issues regarding the level of "emotional disclosure" in Italy and in Australia? o Levels of Politeness & Avoidance or love of conflict – Speech acts (disagreeing): Were there instances in which you and the CM disagreed on a specific issue? How did you express your disagreement? How did your CM express his/her disagreement? How did you manage this situation?
Fifth Meeting	6. Comparisons between Italy and Australia 7. Current affairs	• Identity Dimension – Maintaining one's identity away from home: Were you able to discuss with your CM issues about identity? What about when you compared aspects of their life in Italy and in Australia or differences, in general, between the two countries? What aspects did they compare? How did you feel about these comparisons? Did you agree? Why? Why not? Were any stereotypes/stereotypical views about Australians or Italians triggered by these comparisons?

understanding and seeing how it can be realised in practice'. Valentina thus acknowledged the importance of having such a 'blueprint' to describe *languaculture* and allocating time to present these aspects and promote in-class discussions. In a similar vein, Valentina observed that adding a fifth section to the *schede* provided *'more visible, tangible goals for the students'*. She felt that in the Italian programme the teaching team members *'always have the intention to teach culture through language, but to know how to do it is not easy'*.

While allocating specific moments for in-class *languaculture* discussions was a welcome addition to the subject, Valentina also acknowledged the issue of time constraints. She considered the time she spent outside the classroom in preparing the discussions as well as the time she dedicated to the discussions during the lesson. She indicated that allocating time for planning is essential: *'[the exploration of languaculture aspects] needs to be planned; some of it is incidental, but it has to be intentional'*. Time for in-class discussions was also scarce given the extent of work to be covered in the subject. Valentina explained that while she felt it was important to present the *languaculture* concepts in the target language, doing so took more time to provide examples and to check students' understanding than if done in the native language. She would have liked 'more time' for group or pair activities so that students could discuss the concepts among themselves. She felt that once the specific *languacultures* aspects were introduced to students, students needed time to reflect and revisit these aspects, particularly after their experiences meeting with the CM. For Valentina, *'recycling'* the concepts and discussions was important so that they did not remain isolated in the students' minds. However, she felt restrained by having to cover the rest of the subject content, particularly since other assessment items focused on linguistic aspects and the 'four macro-skills'.

Valentina offered two specific suggestions to address these issues. First, if the Italian programme incorporated the concept of *languaculture* and Crozet's conceptual framework at an earlier stage, perhaps in the first year, by the time students take her subject in the third year, less time would be needed for concepts and more time could be dedicated to discussions. This suggestion was particularly relevant as it revealed the need not only for a 'programmatic approach' to the development of critical *languaculture* awareness, but also to start raising students' *languaculture* awareness from an early stage in their language learning experience. Here the inconvenient truth remains that *languaculture* is still perceived by many as 'time away' from the rest of the curricula rather than as an intrinsic component of the curricula, and that efforts need to be coordinated among willing staff in different subjects across the study programme in a coherent, sequential manner.

Second, Valentina suggested that a way to complement the in-class discussion is to provide students with a social network forum so they can move from a teacher-centred discussion in the classroom to a learner-generated discussion online. She intends to look into this approach in the future, as computer-assisted language learning (CALL) is also one of her research interests. This suggestion was significant for highlighting several key issues in the critical reflexivity learning process. First is the need for students to discuss *languaculture* issues among themselves in an asynchronous mode, that is, giving themselves time to reflect before responding to other students' comments. Second, this approach would give students who may be too shy to express themselves 'on the spot' during in-class discussions the opportunity to express their views in another context. Third, social networks and online discussions are more appealing to younger people than classroom activity.

On the material used throughout the subject, Valentina indicated that students found the chapter by Carroli *et al.* (2003) useful for presenting the theoretical concepts in English as the students' *lingua franca*, with examples of the conceptual framework axes in relation to Australian and Italian *languacultures*. During in-class discussions students were encouraged to thoughtfully critique the claims and some of the examples and conclusions that seemed particularly dogmatic in this paper. Valentina acknowledged that the theoretical reading material on the topic is scant and mostly in English.

Valentina also pointed out that there is little material available in the target language that can be used to trigger *languaculture* discussion or exemplify *languaculture* aspects without reinforcing stereotypical views. In fact, she said, this is an issue she tried to challenge in class. In the last intervention, concerning the use of present subjunctive to express personal opinions, students were asked to complete phrases that expressed the stereotypes that people of many nationalities hold about Italian people; the students felt quite strongly that these stereotypes were not *'entirely true'* in their experience. Valentina felt it is important for students to understand that using stereotypes as departure points for discussion can be a way to engage critically with their experience, as well as with other people's points of view. For these reasons, she is continuously searching for authentic audio and written material in the target language that can be used or adapted for this purpose. Valentina indicated that the interventions made her more aware of topics that can promote *languaculture* discussions and as a result she has set out on a research project to collect material in Italy that she can use for this purpose in her subject.

Some of the main challenges in the format of this subject concern the very feature that sets it apart from other language subjects: the students' interaction with members of the Italian community. First, pairing up students with members of the community is extremely time consuming for the teacher. Second is the issue of how the students view their interactions with these community members, some of whom have resided in Australia for years and have a somewhat 'fossilised' view of Italian *languaculture*. During in-class discussions, students were encouraged to reflect on the role of the CM in providing both a linguistic and a cultural model. Here students were reminded to consider the CM's (*langua*)cultural behaviour in relation to the general descriptors used in class and in the set reading to describe Italian *languaculture*, as well as the CM's personal, idiosyncratic characteristics.

A student reflected on her CM and this CM's level of expressivity and emotional disclosure during their meetings in one of her *scheda*:

> [My CM] isn't an extremely expressive person in comparison to other Italians I have met. Once again, this could be to do with the fact that she has been living in Australia for quite a few years. [...] We didn't actually talk about levels of emotional disclosure at all. It never even entered my mind because to me she seems to be adapted to the Australian social way. I wonder though if this level of emotional disclosure has a lot to do with personality as well, and not just culture or region. Although she loves to talk and be around people, she isn't overwhelming at all, which is what I have felt from a few Italians I have met. (*Francis – Worksheet Number 4*)

This student's reflections reveal her level of awareness in relation to similarities and differences between Italian and Australian *languaculture* in relation to other Italian people she has met. But above all, her comments reveal her transition to a higher level of awareness in which she considers her CM's behaviour in relation to factors such as the amount of time living in Australia as well as her personality. Later in her *scheda*, Francis continues her reflection on another point of 'comparison between Italy and Australia', the topic of this last meeting with her CM. Here she presents the issue of clothing and self-representation as a key difference noticed by her CM. Although this issue is not part of the *languaculture* conceptual framework, Francis and her CM discuss how clothing can be a reflection of what and how people communicate in both countries. Francis then traces her reflective thinking process and openly discloses that she is not sure what to think – perhaps implying that she should decide which way is better – but concludes that there are positives and negatives in both:

> From what we have discussed, [my CM] mainly noticed the difference between Italy and Australia through the clothing/self-representation and the people's attitude. When she first arrived she was shocked at the way people dressed and thought that it was strange. However, now she sees

it as something positive, that people here are freer to express themselves without being judged, whereas in Italy there isn't so much social freedom. [...] Even if Italy is more sophisticated and Australia is less, Italy has less social freedom in terms of dressing and Australia has more. If Australia is sloppier, and Italy is less, which is actually better or worse and to whose perspective? If Australians seem more open, is it fake openness or is it real? [...] [does that mean that they are] being truthful about how they are [and how they] really feel? Just think that with every positive and negative there could be a downside and an upside so it is always really hard to make concrete decisions. (*Francis – Worksheet Number 4*)

The nuanced description of Francis' experience presented in her final worksheet clearly points to the issue of cultural relativity and thus highlights the complex level of self-reflexivity that can be made evident in this type of reflective task. Another issue highlighted by Francis' reflections was the need to consider the inclusion of non-verbal aspects, such as clothing (*dimensione vestemica – vestemic dimension*, described in Carroli et al., 2003) to the *languaculture* framework. Currently, the non-verbal dimension of the *languaculture* framework focuses largely on levels of verbosity and its paralinguistic features, such as use of silence and overlapping in conversation, as well as some features of kinesic behaviour, in particular, gestures, and some features of the haptic and proxemic dimensions of communication.

Adding in-class discussions and, in particular, a new section in the worksheets aimed at guiding the students' reflections on *languaculture* aspects introduced in class, significantly improved this continuous assessment item. They provided Valentina with a tool to explicitly integrate *languaculture* as part of the students' assessment and to observe the level of awareness evident in the students' comments. Valentina felt that by the end of semester students seemed '*more critical without being judgemental*'. However, the 'increased' level of critical reflexivity was difficult to gauge from some of the students' reflections.

This discussion reveals several limitations in using the worksheets as a type of reflective journal assessment. The first concerns the assumption that learners are equipped adequately to observe their interlocutors' behaviour in an ethnographic manner while focusing simultaneously on their own linguistic performance and making sure they follow the conversation. Second, this type of task assumes that students are capable of, and willing to, disclose their reflection processes that may include the range of questions they ask themselves, as in the case of Francis. A corollary to this, which reveals a third limitation, concerns evaluation of this type of reflections. Here teachers would be required to develop feedback strategies to help learners to move to higher levels of awareness. In the context of this study, for ethical reasons students were not given a numerical mark for this section of the *scheda*, which was used as a tool to document their reflections. A fourth limitation is that students need to feel confident and comfortable enough to discuss such personal questions, and similarly, tutors need to be ready to ask further questions and provide comments that can scaffold learners' reflective skills to take their learning further.

The Chinese Language Programme

The Chinese programme in my PAR projects had the main structural features shared by most language programmes in Australian universities. Table 3.5 illustrates the three-year sequence of language subjects that aimed to develop learners' proficiency from elementary to advanced levels. This programme also included one cultural context subject taught in English in the first year, second semester. The distinctive feature of this programme was its hourglass shape enrolments from a high number of enrolments in both the *ab initio* first-year subjects and the third year, advanced language subjects, whose cohort was mainly students with Chinese heritage and international students from China.

The subjects highlighted in the table represent those purposefully selected for the curriculum innovation PAR projects. The first year elementary Chinese language subject was selected in order to explore the integration of *languaculture* modules from early stages in the language learning process. The cultural context subject was selected as the only subject of its kind in the programme.

My interview with Mei, the coordinator of the Chinese language programme, suggested that while the Chinese teaching team as a whole did not

Table 3.5 Chinese language programme structure

Year	Semester 1	Semester 2	
First year	Elementary language subject I	Elementary language subject II **Case study C**	Cultural context subject **Case study D**
Second year	Intermediate language subject I	Intermediate language subject II	
Third year	Advanced language subjects (Including subjects for heritage and native-speakers)	Advanced language subjects (Including subjects for heritage and native-speakers)	

engage in team-teaching, team members shared similar pedagogical practices. The Chinese programme's language and culture teaching rationale seemed to be underpinned by two main types of strategies or approaches for introducing cultural content, particularly in the language subject components. The first strategy was to use the set textbook as the *de facto* syllabus upon which the teacher decides what cultural aspects are relevant as s/he introduces each unit's topic for the first two years of language subjects. For instance, if a chapter was centred on the topic of shopping, the teacher might discuss bargaining customs in China. The second strategy entailed addressing culture-specific concepts as teachers recognised their emergence through specific ideographic Chinese characters, that is, a lexical approach to culture.

However, both these strategies are problematical. They enable only an *ad hoc* approach to the inclusion of cultural content in a subject and rely on a teacher's knowledge and experiences of the target culture and his/her own point of view on the topic at hand. As noted in earlier chapters, the latter can be particularly detrimental if the teacher does not incorporate a critical dimension to his/her own perspective and encourage learners to apply this critical dimension to their experiences and perspectives. The first strategy in particular assumes the teacher's critical awareness and understanding of *languaculture* conceptually and in practice, or if it does not, it fails more fundamentally to recognise and appreciate the pedagogical benefits of using a *languaculture* approach to exploring the language–culture nexus. In the two Chinese case studies, both strategies appeared to be applied in an *ad hoc* manner, with no planning or coherence across subjects or proficiency levels. The teacher in charge was responsible for deciding whether, how and for how long to discuss culture aspects, and which aspects these would be.

Overall, the Chinese programme presented the archetypical features of university language programmes: a textbook as *de facto* syllabus, focus on linguistic aspects (particularly owing to the demands of a character-based language) and teacher responsibility for the incidental integration of cultural aspects in the classroom. It was thus important that the PAR projects addressed not only the discrepancies between what subject profiles claimed about subject content and what was actually enacted by the teachers, but also the shortcomings limiting this programme.

Case Study C: Chinese language subject

This first-year, second semester subject was conducted mainly in Chinese. It was a compulsory subject for students majoring in Chinese language. Although it belonged to the Languages and Applied Linguistics programme, students from other degree programmes were allowed to enrol. As stated in the subject outline, this subject aimed to provide students with a basic knowledge of Chinese language and culture through the study of prepared or selected texts structured around set topics. The subject objectives were further detailed in relation to students developing the four macro-skills: listening and speaking (through discussion, oral presentations and role plays on topics in Chinese and Australian contexts) and reading comprehension and basic writing skills.

This subject included five contact hours per week: (1) a two-hour lecture; (2) a two-hour practical workshop; and (3) a one-hour writing workshop. The two-hour lecture focused on presenting new vocabulary, linguistic features, grammar and its usage, introduction of ideographic characters and relevant cultural information. The two-hour practical workshop focused on vocabulary use, practice of linguistic functions and other aspects of language use encountered in the texts, including pronunciation and tone, through a variety of exercises and activities. This session entailed individual or group work to complete a set task, e.g. devising a questionnaire or an interview that may culminate in a group presentation, individual report to the class, a role play or other activities. The one-hour writing workshop focused on practising the writing of Chinese characters and used a textbook different from the one used in the practical workshop.

Assessment in this subject consisted of two oral tests and two written tests. Oral tests generally consisted of an interview between the assessor and the student, involving questions and topics discussed during the semester. The criteria used to assess students' performance in oral tests included evidence of ability to: (1) respond accurately to questions asked; (2) use a variety of linguistic structures; and (3) accurately use both tones, intonation and sounds, and linguistic structures, grammar and expressions. The two written tests included both writing and reading characters (sounds and meanings) and the assessment criteria included evidence of ability to read and understand simple narratives and to respond accurately to questions asked.

Pedagogic interventions

Of the four case-study subjects, this language subject was arguably the most challenging to tackle. I acknowledge here that my near fluency in Italian language and familiarity with aspects of Italian culture[s], and my virtual illiteracy in Chinese language and very limited exposure to Chinese culture[s] may have had a minimal influence upon my approach to the interventions. But as my explanation below reveals, the nature of this subject made it least amenable to the *languaculture* intervention. While description in the subject outline specifically referred to *'the acquisition of basic knowledge of Chinese language and culture through the study of selected texts around set topics'*, discussion of subject content did not mention any such texts nor did it indicate how such a goal would be assessed. When I discussed the subject with Mei, she acknowledged that the textbook did not include any cultural background information. She advised that her approach to remedy this situation was to introduce *'cultural aspects as they emerged in class'*. For instance, if a lesson focused on shopping, she would introduce not only the linguistic input presented in the textbook, but also additional cultural background details that were not included in the textbook, such as bargaining in China. Mei also acknowledged that this practice leaves it up to the teacher to decide whether to integrate any type of cultural information and *'what'* kind of cultural information is relevant in relation to the topic; that is, *'it depends on the teacher to bring that [cultural] knowledge with them'*.

Because this subject relied heavily on the textbook as the syllabus, and focussed firmly on the linguistic content of each lesson, the *languaculture* interventions consisted of 6, 15–20 minute presentations by me as facilitator and Mei as the teacher. These presentations focused on exploring speech acts that had a correlation with the linguistic aspects presented in the textbook and had been dealt with recently in class. Table 3.6 illustrates the correlation of topics and class activities in the semester. The discussion of speech acts was based on the set reading 'Chinese' (Li, 2003), which presented analysis of specific speech acts, such as complimenting, thanking, requesting and so forth, in relation to Crozet's conceptual framework to examine Chinese *languaculture* aspects. Students were also given a quiz prepared by their teacher to encourage them to reflect on the content of the presentations in Li's chapter in relation to their own experiences.

The following vignette illustrates the development of a typical *languaculture* exploration workshop in this subject. This vignette is based on my participant observation field notes.

Languaculture exploration vignette
Third intervention: Inviting to dinner, offering food and drinks, and paying for dinner

The third intervention was designed to give the students a chance to reflect on Chinese *languaculture* levels of ritualisation together with approaches to interpersonal relationships and politeness, and their manifestation in specific speech acts: inviting to dinner, offering food and drinks, and paying for dinner. Appendix 4 presents the slides used during the workshop together with the presenter's notes. The first part of the presentation invited students to critique the set reading's assertions and relate them to their own experience.

The trigger questions proposed in the final slide aimed to encourage students to both reflect on past experiences and anticipate potential behaviours. Students were thus asked to reflect on whether they had experienced instances of *languaculture* dissonance owing to their interactant's expectations differing from their own when making an invitation or offer. Students were also asked to consider whether they could see themselves adopting some of the *languaculture* behaviours discussed (e.g. insisting on acceptance when someone rejects an offer they have made or rejecting an offer the first time it is made to them even if they would like to accept it straight away).

In previous discussions, many of the students in the class had indicated that they had Chinese-speaking classmates in other classes, as well as language exchange partners with whom they practiced their 'foreign languages' outside the class (most partners were Chinese-speaking international students). As a result, students' contributions to the discussion raised the issues of individual idiosyncrasies, age and gender differences. In particular, students discussed the issues of drinking alcohol and avoiding both losing face themselves or causing their hosts to lose face. Students also questioned the *languaculture* behaviours of the Chinese international students with whom they interacted and commented on how and how far these students were being influenced by Australian *languaculture* when interacting with them, especially when extending invitations and paying for dinner or meals in general. The content of this discussion was particularly interesting as it pointed to a developing level of meta-awareness of *languaculture* frames of reference among the students in this subject.

Outcomes and limitations

Exploring speech acts through a *languaculture* lens presented a complementary component to the subject, but poor overall integration of the *languaculture* modules with the rest of the subject became evident from the start of the project. This appeared to stem from Mei's underlying resistance to including the *languaculture* component, a position that seemed to be related to Mei's belief that a language subject should focus solely on developing linguistic competence.

This belief is not uncommon among both language teachers and language learners alike. It reflects underlying assumptions, for instance, that languages

Table 3.6 Case Study C: *Languaculture* modules intervention schedule

WEEK	BOOK LESSON	RELATED TOPIC	LANGUACULTURE CONTENT	CLASS ACTIVITY
WEEK 2	LESSON 12 Buying things Comparing things		INTRODUCTION	Presentation to introduce the "intercultural/ *languaculture*" teaching framework Distribute Li Kaining's chapter
WEEK 3	LESSON 13 Shopping	Asking/giving advice Making a request Bargaining	RULES OF POLITENESS	Differences between Chinese & Western politeness strategies Linguistic strategies Asking and giving advice (p. 91) Greetings – hello & goodbye Thanking and apologising (p. 90) 客气 *keqi* (politeness) – insider & outsider strategic uses
WEEK 4	LESSON 14 Dining out and ordering food	Inviting to dinner Ordering food Paying for the meal		Making an invitation (pp. 86–88) Paying after dinner (p. 88) Banquet at home? 客气 *keqi* (politeness) Guest-host interaction 场面 *chang mian* (visual presentation of food & aural atmosphere) Cooling down
WEEK 5	LESSON 15 Asking for directions	Modes of transport Manners when taking public transport		QUIZ – ACTIVITY

Case Studies of Curricular Innovation 99

WEEK 7	LESSON 16 Talking about present activities	Men's and women's roles Freedom to find a job	LEVEL OF INTERPERSONAL RELATIONSHIPS	TERMS OF ADDRESS (pp. 67–76) 关系 guanxi (connections)
WEEK 8	LESSON 17 Talking about past activities	How to be a visitor and treat guests		
WEEK 9	LESSON 18 Weather	Some traditional Chinese festivals in different seasons. Chinese people make direct comments on people's appearance.	LEVEL OF VERBOSITY	Appropriateness of Topics that can be discussed (weather, food, traffic, pollution, age and family background) (pp. 55–58) Topics that should not be discussed (sex, personal health, religion, political dissent) (p. 58)
WEEK 10	LESSON 19 Hobbies/free time How well you do something/ sports	BEIJING OLYMPICS		
WEEK 11	LESSON 20 Leaving after learning at a lang. school in China	Compliments	LEVELS OF EXPRESSIVITY & RITUALISATION	Experiences in China (pp. 93–97)

can be learnt in isolation from culture or that language and culture are some-what related but only linguistic accuracy is important for communication. A corollary of these assumptions is its 'backwash' on assessment. In other words, if a subject focuses on learning linguistic aspects, then it should assess only these aspects. As a result, one of Mei's main concerns was time con-straints in relation to being able to cover the rest of the linguistic content that she needed to assess. I responded to this situation by carrying out only three of the above-mentioned presentations and left the other three for her to incor-porate into her lessons. I attended these lessons as a participant-observer to follow up on completion of the curriculum innovation project.

Other limitations in this case study entailed the textbook: both its con-tent and how it was used. First, the chosen textbook presented isolated and decontextualised speech acts. Second, in a style that appears to be common in many language subjects around the world, Mei followed a textbook-based syllabus guided by the grammatical progression of linguistic content and the discussion of related thematic aspects. Although the set reading provided an additional source of examples and material for discussion, Mei objected to using it. She felt the reading was inappropriate for the subject and an imposi-tion on learners since as she saw it, the content was highly technical and therefore unnecessary for language learners at this level. Student-interviewees, however, found the reading very useful. They did not object to its integration in this subject, but had difficulty relating it to the rest of the subject content.

As for assessment, because the *languaculture* presentations were quite brief, the in-class discussions were also brief. Nevertheless, Mei indicated she felt that the presentations were *'time-consuming'* and that students were *'car-ried away by the excitement of discussion and it took some efforts to get them back to the learning* [of the language]'. Mei's assessment takes us to the perspective that the *languaculture* exploration represented 'time away' from the core learning component in the subject, and to an informed counterpoint under-standing that the type of *'learning mode'* necessary to promote 'perspective transformation' is likely to be quite different from that involved in learning grammatical structures.

As well as participating in class discussions, students were asked to com-plete a quiz after the third presentation to help them review the *languaculture* aspects explored so far in class. The quiz was not an assessable item, but all students completed it. It was also planned that students be given the oppor-tunity to write a brief reflective piece on their experience. Nevertheless, Mei found this reflective task unnecessary. She also objected to the reflective line of questioning that involved learners considering whether, when speaking Chinese, they would choose to adopt certain *languaculture* behaviours, such as self-deprecating compliments and so forth. Mei advised her belief that this is a personal choice – by implication, not associated with *languaculture* influences – and that the questions seemed to be biased, as if forcing students to think they had to adopt such behaviours.

Overall, even though Mei and I held several meetings to discuss these issues, at times we both found it difficult to communicate with each other. In particular, I was unable to alter Mei's perspective about the benefit of including *languaculture* in language subjects. This pointed to the difficulty, or impossibility, of changing some teachers' beliefs about language, its relationship to culture, and most importantly, the teacher's role in the process of language and culture learning. Mei appeared to be particularly concerned with the students' expectations of the subject, which she assumed were mainly linguistic. In our final interview Mei and I discussed these issues and when probed about her resistance, Mei indicated that in this first-year subject, she saw the curriculum as simply linguistically driven and in which she may integrate 'culture' but only when she considered it relevant to do so:

> I guess because culture is a very broad word [...] and also for the teacher to decide which aspects [are] to be included into a syllabus or the curriculum is a little bit difficult. [Students to ask maybe the linguistic aspect is more solid, is more concrete.] It's there, you have to teach them that stuff otherwise they can't express their ideas. But with the cultural part, we just feel sometimes maybe we can put it off a little bit, or the students can acquire, afterwards or after class or sometimes maybe, yeah. Not sure. It's not a resistant, I wouldn't say because if there is opportunity, you know, if the content is relevant, then we would try to put this culture element there. But to me it's not like cultural-guided kind of curriculum. It's more like linguistically guided one.

While this case study was particularly challenging and resulted in what I consider to be a largely unsuccessful innovation project, it drew attention to several limitations that provide constructive guidance for other similar contexts. First are the teacher and learners' beliefs about language subjects, particularly beginners' subjects, and their focus on acquiring grammatical structures. Second, and a direct result of these beliefs, is the 'backwash' effect on assessment. These beliefs may stem from specific assumptions about not only the relationship between language and culture, but also the teacher's role in the language and culture learning process. Third is use of the textbook as the syllabus for the subject, which seems to be particularly common. This poses challenging limitations if the textbook does not contemplate a cultural dimension, especially if the teacher is not willing to supplement the text with additional resources.

Case Study D: Chinese cultural context subject

The final case study was based on a first-year, second semester subject, conducted in English. It was a compulsory subject for students majoring in Chinese language, but students from different degree programmes were also allowed to take it as an elective subject. As specified in its subject outline, this subject had two goals: to give students of Chinese language an introduction to key pragmatic features of Chinese language in social interaction as a complement to their language learning, and to provide students with a critical knowledge of the important political, social and cultural trends and issues in contemporary China.

The subject syllabus had three modules. *Module 1* provided an overview of the subject and an introduction to contemporary Chinese society, politics and history. *Module 2* focused on the nexus between language and culture in everyday social interaction. This included concepts of face and politeness, language use in interpersonal relationships, *guanxi* (human connections and networking) and key areas in Chinese pragmatics. *Module 3* explored the relationships between language, society and culture through a survey of Chinese media, examining how social change is interpreted by Western scholars and the Chinese media.

This subject involved three contact hours per week: a one-hour lecture followed by a two-hour workshop. Class work was conducted in English as no Chinese language knowledge was required. In the workshops, the concepts introduced in the lecture were further explored and practised through work with texts and activities. Some fostered students' intercultural communicative competence by giving them the opportunity to perform problem-solving tasks, role-plays, interpreting scenarios, and vignettes and other materials. The assessment items required students to engage in a wide range of academic activities, including small-scale research, preparation and delivery of an oral presentation, and writing a summary and a critical comment on specific texts.

Pedagogic interventions

This subject sought to introduce key aspects of Chinese culture mainly through exploring set readings (journal articles and oral history accounts). However, these readings focused mainly on historical and political aspects of Chinese culture and did not present an underlying coherent thread for exploring culture in relation to language. During our pre-intervention meetings, the teacher of this subject, Lili, indicated that she was particularly interested in helping students understand the nature of miscommunication based on aspects of *languaculture*. The pedagogic interventions therefore centred on exploring specific instances of miscommunication caused by various types of *languaculture* dissonance. Lili and I decided to concentrate in particular on three specific areas through which *languaculture* dissonance may be explored.

The first area concerned core Chinese culture concepts and their meaning in social interaction. Here, particular attention was paid to the distinctions between 'self/other', 'insider/outsider': 生人 *shengren*; 熟人 *shuren*, vis-à-vis 外人 *wairen*; 自己人 *zijiren*; and corresponding linguistic behaviours in relation to 关系 *guanxi* (networking and social capital), 客气 *keqi* (politeness) and 面子 *mianzi*, 脸 *lian* (face) as well as other *languaculture* dimensions explored in key readings (Li, 2003; Ye, 2004). I present more examples in Table 3.7. The second area entailed examining stories of people's lives, exploring manifestations and potential instances of *languaculture* dissonance. These stories ranged from intercultural sensitisers in textbooks to autobiographical accounts (Ye, 2007) and oral history interviews (Ye, 2006). The third area consisted of examples of authentic oral and written text portraying China as a rapidly transforming society. These included film excerpts, documentary excerpts, intercultural sensitisers and oral history interviews.

This was a newly established subject developed in concert with the PAR component of this investigation. As such, the *languaculture* modules and their implementation schedule were developed with relative flexibility. As a result, eight interventions were developed and scheduled in correlation with the topics planned for each of those weeks. The interventions, conducted in English during the two-hour workshop, were implemented jointly by myself and Lili, who, as a native Chinese speaker, was able to provide the linguistic input on the *languaculture* aspects under examination.

The format of the interventions included a theoretical segment based on analysis of the reading(s) proposed for each week, and a practical activity underpinned by analysis of a given text featuring a 'rich point' of *languaculture* dissonance. Analysis of the readings was guided by a 'Study Guide' designed to help students identify the *languaculture* dimensions to be explored before coming to class. The practical activities were designed to raise students' awareness of their assumptions and taken-for-granted frames of reference, and encourage students to reflect on their personal experiences in relation to interpreting the given concept, situation or story. The following vignette illustrates the development of a typical *languaculture* exploration workshop and is based on my participant observation field notes.

Languaculture exploration vignette
Fifth intervention: Interacting in society

This intervention was designed to give the students the opportunity to synthesise the theories and concepts hitherto presented in the lectures and workshops and covered in the readings (Brick, 2005; Li, 2003; Pratt, 1991; Ye, 2007). In particular, as the theme of the intervention suggests, students were to focus on the notions of self/other, insider/outsider, how to interact within those categories and how to potentially traverse those categories.

Students worked in small groups with an overhead transparency and different colour markers to design a concept map explaining the relationships between the theories and concepts on Chinese interaction discussed in earlier sessions. A nominated speaker for each group then presented their concept map to the rest of the class using the overhead projector. The class members were thus able to ask for clarification on the concept maps and provide feedback to each other. In addition Lili and I also provided feedback and probed the groups when needed. The concept map in Figure 3.3 is one of those produced in class with the feedback from students and teachers.

This concept map illustrates the Chinese levels of interpersonal relationships as well as the approaches to politeness and levels of verbosity associated with them. With the various arrows, students explained the relationships between the key concepts of *zijiren* 自己人 ('one of us') and *shuren* 熟人 (acquaintance); *vis-à-vis: shengren* 生人(stranger) and *wairen* 外人 (outsider). The differentiated ways of acting with *shengren* and *shuren* means that a great deal of investment goes into moving from *shengren* and *shuren* and ultimately to 'one of us'. This is done using linguistic strategies and pragmatic acts through: (1) specific 打招呼 *da zhaohu* (greetings); (2) ways of addressing people using the prefixes同 *tong* and 老 *lao*; and (3) rules of 客气 *keqi* (politeness).

One of the most interesting issues raised by the students was that while the concepts of 'insider' and 'outsider' are not limited to Chinese *languaculture*, the rules of politeness and strategies to traverse those categories are vastly different from Australian *languacultures*. The final activity consisted of discussion about one of Brick's intercultural 'case studies' or 'intercultural sensitisers' (Brick, 2005: 47). This activity invited students to reflect on two stereotypical views of friendship from the Chinese and the Australian points of view, that is applying both 'emic' and 'etic' points of *languaculture* reference. Lili and I thus invited students to put on the cultural 'eyeglasses' and answer the questions and the answers were discussed in a centralised manner.

Table 3.7 Case Study D: *Languaculture* modules intervention schedule

WEEK	TOPIC	LECTURE – THEORY/CONCEPTS	WORKSHOP ACTIVITIES
WEEK 2	China – Politics, Society & History	Structures of power in China Contemporary Chinese history	Analysis of assigned reading: Ye Zhengdao – cross-Cultural & cross-linguistic autobiographical accounts, experiences in Australian – Chinese identity
WEEK 3	Chinese Language in Use	Features of Chinese communication Level of verbosity and approaches to interpersonal relationships: 含蓄 *han xu* (implicit communication) 听话 *ting hua* (listening-centeredness) 客气 *keqi* (politeness) Power-distance Difference between 外人 *wairen* (outsider) & 自己人 *zijiren* (one of us)	Analysis of assigned reading – Presentation of Crozet's conceptual framework:
WEEK 4	Defining "Self" in Society	Approaches to interpersonal relationships: Relational self: "self" and "other" 外人 *wairen* (outsider) & 自己人 *zijiren* (one of us) 生人 *shengren* (stranger) & 熟人 *shuren* (acquaintance) 打招呼 *da zhaohu* (Greetings) Prefixes 同 *tong* (fellow) & 老 *lao* (old) Strategic use of 客气 *keqi* (politeness)	Analysis of case studies (intercultural sensitisers) from Brick's book

(Continued)

Table 3.7 (*Continued*)

WEEK	TOPIC	LECTURE – THEORY/CONCEPTS	WORKSHOP ACTIVITIES
WEEK 5	Interacting in Society	Approaches to interpersonal relationships and approaches to politeness: 感情 *ganqing* (measure of the emotional commitment between people) 人情 *renqing* (human feeling) 报, *bao* (reciprocity) Filial piety Speech acts	Getting together all the concepts and ideas. Group mind-map activity
WEEK 6	Face & Politeness	Approaches to interpersonal relationships and levels of expressivity: Face – emic & etic perspective 面子 *mianzi* 脸 *lian* Face and identity Face and politeness Loosing/enhancing face	*Languaculture* Dissonance Analysis of film excerpt – "Joy Luck Club" (dinner with the family scene) Analysis of intercultural sensitiser from *Turning Bricks into Jade* (Are you mad at me?)
WEEK 7	*Guanxi* in Business settings	关系 *guanxi* – Networking and social capital Relational self Kinship Approaches to interpersonal relationship building Confucius – Five relationships axes	Analysis of assigned reading Case study: Chinese vs American & French business practices

WEEK	TOPIC	LECTURE – THEORY/CONCEPTS	WORKSHOP ACTIVITIES
		感情 ganqing (measure of the emotional commitment between people) 信用 xinyong (trustworthiness) 关系 guanxi & corruption/legitimacy	
WEEK 8	Social relationships "around the table"	Approaches to interpersonal relationships, levels of ritualisation and expressivity: Food and 面子 mianzi 客气 keqi – Politeness in guest-host interaction 场面 chang mian (visual presentation of food & aural atmosphere) "Cooling down" Positive and negative face Face-threatening acts Face, 客气 keqi and sincerity	Analysis of assigned reading: "Mianzi at the Chinese Dinner table"
WEEK 9	Chinese Education	Nature and purpose of education Roles of teachers, parents and learners Approaches to teaching and learning Significance of examinations Chinese education system	Analysis of the film "The mobile phone" scene (face & drinking) Analysis of "A Great Wall" scene (University-entrance examination in China – role of parents) Analysis of intercultural sensitiser from Turning Bricks into Jade (The best way to learn)

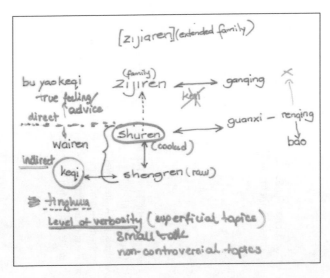

Figure 3.3 Chinese insider/outsider *languaculture* concept map

Students were also required to submit a 'Discovery Page' after each intervention (see Appendix 5). This 'Discovery Page' contained questions to help them reflect further on the particular *languaculture* aspect(s) discussed in class. This worksheet had three sections. The first asked students to reflect on both what they learned during the class discussion and how studying a particular *languaculture* aspect helped them to understand differences and similarities between the target and the native *languaculture*. The second section focused on applying that knowledge outside the classroom, asking students to provide examples of miscommunication. The third section asked students to identify other *languaculture* aspects they would like to explore in the future. This last section was very useful for Lili and me as it helped us keep the content of the discussions relevant to the students' needs and interests and to the syllabus we had planned for the subject. Overall, the aim of these worksheets was to ensure that students who may not feel comfortable contributing during the workshop would still be able to express their ideas and reflections in written form.

Outcomes and limitations

Since this was a newly established subject, the pedagogic interventions became an integral part of the curriculum. The *languaculture* conceptual framework provided Lili with a '*map to play with*', a map that she found '*broad enough*' and flexible enough to adapt to all her lessons and bring specific areas to the foreground in the discussions. The *languaculture* modules thus served as a backbone to addressing the goals Lili had set for the subject, particularly in relation to the salient pragmatic features of Chinese language.

With regard to the material used in this subject, Lili explained that she found Li Kaining's chapter (Li, 2003) on *languaculture* contained aspects that may be considered '*old fashioned*' and as such, she invited students to add their own point of view to the article and add information they thought was missing. While we were able to use several resources for in-class discussion (biographical accounts, documentaries, film excerpts), Lili also highlighted the difficulty in finding readily available authentic material for analysis.

The process of reflectivity in this subject took place both during class discussions and through 'Discovery Page' worksheets. With regard to in-class activities, Lili felt that use of personal experiences proved particularly useful as catalysts for discussion. She explained '*you always have to let them reflect on the experience, and "puzzles", any experiences of miscommunication, anything that they do not understand, and use them as a starting point to bring about discussion and the exploration of stereotypes,* [which can be] *a very rewarding fruitful discussion on something that they never understood*'. She felt that through some of these discussions she had 'saved a few relationships' as many students revealed their frustration and perplexity about certain *languaculture* behaviours in their Chinese friends and partners.

The 'Discovery Page' worksheets provided students with an opportunity to further reflect on the content of the class discussions. The *languaculture* module centred on perpetuating stereotypes based on *languaculture* dissonances, for instance, generated particularly interesting reflections from the students. Here Christian, a Fijian-Indian student, reflected on how learning about possible areas of *languaculture* dissonance helped him reflect and interpret misunderstandings he may have experienced in the past:

... realising I was unconsciously transposing my cultural norms and values on the other interlocutors during interactions or while evaluating pragmatic failures. I was restricted to a biased view of a situation owing to a limited intrinsic understanding of Chinese cultural norms and values. (Christian – Discovery Page – WEEK 6)

Ted, a mature age student who had travelled throughout Southeast Asia reflected:

[It] made me consider more the perpetuation of stereotypes about Westerners and how my behaviour in overseas contexts might have reinforced and perpetuated such beliefs.

Despite positive evidence such as this about the value of the 'Discovery Page' as a useful tool to promote students' reflection, two issues became evident at the end of the subject. One was that some students used the 'Discovery Page' not as an opportunity to reflect on their learning, but rather to summarise the main ideas discussed in class. The second issue concerned students failing to submit these reflections as they were not a compulsory assessment item. Only five students out of the class cohort (20 students) submitted the 'Discovery Page' every week. The rest of the class submitted them after two or three sessions and others all at once at the end of the intervention period. Lili felt that asking students to complete the 'Discovery Page' from one week to the next meant that most students would write *'what the teacher wants to hear'*, rendering these reflections *'less real'*. Lili suggested to instead initiate every lesson with a brief discussion on whether students experienced any instance of miscommunication during the week and use that as a starting point for the discussion.

The relatively large number of interventions implemented in this subject entailed Lili's engagement in the PAR project over an extended period of time. This enabled Lili to reflect on her experiences from a viewpoint different from those of the other teacher–participants. When discussing the use of PAR as a strategy for sustainable curricular innovation and professional development, Lili observed that participating in the project brought her professional practice *'to a different level'*. She felt that she had a *'consultant'*, someone in the capacity of a *'personal trainer'*, which made her feel *'privileged and lucky'* to go through the process. When discussing the use of PAR, Lili also discussed the issue of professional change and transformation. She declared:

> [PAR] is just fantastic and it's really opened the door to a person who wants a change, a person who wants new insight, wants new knowledge and then it's up to the person to play with it and carry this with them wherever they go.

Lili mentioned that after developing and implementing the *languaculture* modules in this subject, she felt like she wanted to 'run the personal training' process again because having reached a higher level of awareness in her own *languaculture* teaching practices meant that *'she would be able to gain much more'*. She declared that she is *'desperate, passionate about the area'* and found participating in such a collaborative teaching project to be a 'rare opportunity' for her professional and personal growth.

Conclusion

This chapter presented and analysed four exploratory case studies of curriculum innovation. These case studies in two language programmes at an Australian university set out to explore how language educators can begin to advance the development of curricula aimed to foster critical *languaculture* awareness. I organised the qualitative data obtained from the multiple data sources – classroom observations, semi-structured interviews with academics and students, and samples of classroom activities – to provide a snapshot of the main outcomes and limitations that emerged from implementing the *languaculture* modules. As such, my analysis of the data collected in each case study has provided a bottom-up perspective on what may be pedagogically achievable in the university classroom through a *languaculture* approach. Before delving into a re-examination of the framework based on this perspective, it is important to consider the data obtained through the case studies in light of the literature reviewed. In the following chapter I draw together common threads from the theoretical and empirical findings discussed in these chapters.

Notes

(1) Here 'language programme' is equivalent to 'language major' or specialisation, and thus refers to a sequence of courses from beginners to advanced levels over a projected three-year degree programme of studies. A 'course' refers to a set of learning activities (including lectures, tutorials and workshops) underpinned by a coherent syllabus. This terminology may vary depending on the institution, for instance, many universities use the term 'unit' or 'subject' rather than 'course'.

(2) Pseudonyms are used throughout Chapters 3 and 4 to refer to all participants. Other ethical issues concerning the identity of the participants, as well as the design of data collection tools, were duly addressed following institutional channels as well as guidelines in relevant literature, particularly Merriam (1998), Silverman (2000) and Creswell (2007).

(3) Even though 'good' and 'best' do not carry the same meanings, literature in the field of education tends to refer to 'good practice' and 'best practice' interchangeably. In this book, 'good practice' is understood as the lessons learned through implementing the framework. As such, 'good practices' provide evidence-based insights into aspects that worked, or did not work, in the context of this study and which may be adapted to other contexts (*cf.* Coffield & Edward, 2009).

(4) 'Subject outlines' refers to the official subject description and other useful information provided to students. Outlines generally include the subject coordinator's contact details, a summary of the learning content and activities, assessment expectations, and required and recommended weekly readings, as well as resources and websites relevant to the subject.

(5) *Dialetti d'Italia*, dialects of Italy, such as Sicilian, Vèneto, Piedmontese, are not varieties of Italian but related languages (neo-romance, other descendants of Latin). Their grammar, syntactic features and vocabulary can be very different from Italian (Lepschy & Lepschy, 1988).

4 The Good, The Bad and The Feasible

The investigation underpinning the case studies presented in Chapter 3 set out to explore avenues for bridging the gap between theory and practice in the field of language and culture pedagogy. The underlying assumption of this investigation was that without carefully informed remedial attention, this seemingly irreconcilable gap will stay in place, or perhaps widen. Only an explicit conceptual and empirical effort to understand this gap would open the way to a new space for developing pedagogy and practice in this field.

The four case studies presented in Chapter 3 therefore set out to problematise the selected subjects' cultural goals and objectives and in so doing to question their realisation in the enacted curriculum. Problematising the curriculum led to designing specific curriculum innovation projects aimed to foster critical *languaculture* awareness. These projects were underpinned by a framework developed to build a bridge between theory and practice, between the theoretical trends in the development of critical *languaculture* awareness discussed in Chapter 2 and the actual limitations of their implementation in the everyday university language classroom. In this chapter I synthesise the outcomes and exemplars of good practice that emerged through these case studies *vis-à-vis* the recurrent limitations identified in discussion of the data. Polarising these aspects for analytical purposes, I have thus divided this chapter into three main sections: the good (exemplars of good practice), the bad (recurrent limitations) and the feasible, in the current higher education context.

Extrapolating Exemplars of Good Practice

I conceptualise exemplars of good practice as evidence-based insights into the implementation of the framework presented in Chapter 2, which may be beneficially transferable to other educational contexts. Given the wide variety of higher education contexts around the world, there is scope for many different approaches to implementing this framework, which may offer valuable insights and ideas. From this perspective, I argue that the term 'best practice' evokes ideas of standards or benchmarking that are not only unnecessarily limiting, but also largely unrealistic (cf. Coffield & Edward, 2009). These exemplars of good practice therefore aim to highlight the positive aspects extrapolated from the data. It is hoped that in the spirit of action research and critical pedagogy, these exemplars can serve as catalysts for further research and self-reflection.

To facilitate discussion of these exemplars, I provide Table 4.1, which presents a comparative 'at a glance' summary of the four subjects' pedagogic interventions. This table presents the number of interventions scheduled in each subject as well as the duration and main type of activities carried out in these interventions. The table also indicates the materials used throughout the process, which in all four cases was a language-pertinent set reading from Lo Bianco and Crozet's monograph (Lo Bianco & Crozet, 2003), as well as some complementary materials such as intercultural sensitisers, film excerpts and documentaries. Assessment in all four case studies focused mainly on the students' participation in in-class discussions owing to ethical clearance constraints. As well as participation during class discussions, all four subjects included an item of asynchronous written reflection that would encourage students to elaborate on their experiences and reflections outside the classroom.

The exemplars of good practice can be discussed in terms of goals (why?), syllabus or content (what?), and teaching techniques and activities (how?).

Why?

The teacher–participants' review of curriculum goals and learning objectives was the first step in establishing curriculum alignment. The questions I asked in the initial interview were important to ensure a move from a 'tick-the-box' approach, to including (inter)cultural learning goals in the language curriculum, to a principled, rationalised formulation and integration of critical *languaculture* awareness. While most of the subjects included at least one (inter)cultural learning goal, in all four cases enactment of this goal was problematised to unveil underlying conceptualisations of culture and its relationship to language in interaction, and to explore the potential contribution of a *languaculture*-driven framework in each of the selected subjects.

Data derived from the teacher–participants' subject outlines and their initial interviews revealed an underlying tendency to define goals in linguistic terms, specifically in relation to acquisition of grammatical structures.

Table 4.1 Comparative summary of *languaculture* interventions

Elements of the curriculum/Data collection details	Case Study A – Italian Culture Context Subject	Case Study B – Italian Language Subject	Case Study C – Chinese Language Subject	Case Study D – Chinese Culture Context Subject
Teacher	Maria Full-time, non-native, Italian language teacher	Valentina Full-time, native Italian language teacher	Mei Full-time, native Chinese language teacher	Lili Full-time, native Chinese language teacher
Weekly contact hours	3 (1 hr lecture + 2 hr workshop)	4 (2 hr workshop + 2 hr tutorial)	5 (2 hr Lecture + 2 hr workshop + 1 hr writing workshop)	3 (1 hr lecture + 2 hr workshop)
Student cohort	19 enrolled	14 enrolled	48 enrolled	18 enrolled
Number of *languaculture* modules	5 × 20/30 minute modules presented at the end of the 2 hr workshop	5 × 40 minute modules presented during the 2 hr workshop	6 × 15/20 minute modules presented at the beginning of each 2 hr workshop	8 modules presented during each 2 hr workshop

Rationale for *languaculture* modules	Analysis of *languaculture* features	Analysis of *languaculture* features in interaction with native speakers	Analysis of speech acts	Analysis of miscommunication based on *languaculture* dissonance
Set reading	*Assigned Reading (Carroli et al.)*		*Assigned Reading (Li Kaining)*	
Additional teaching materials	Migrant Blogs	Film excerpts Migrant blogs as intercultural sensitisers	The course's textbook	DVD Documentary Intercultural sensitisers, biographical accounts
Assessment	Participation in in-class discussion and the course's online Electronic Discussion Forum	Participation in in-class discussions Inclusion of a reflective section on the students' *scheda*	Participation in in-class discussions and quizzes	Participation in in-class activities and discussions Discovery page (reflective worksheet)

Although the subjects' instructional objectives contemplated a 'cultural' component, this was limited to developing a 'basic understanding' of the target culture through 'the study of selected texts structured around set topics'. This finding was consistent with not only the literature examined in Part 1, but also the notion that cultural goals continue to be subordinated to linguistic goals in most language subjects. Such vague goals and instructional objectives meant that no specific assessment items were needed to demonstrate their attainment. All four teacher–participants acknowledged the resulting incidental, *ad hoc* nature of their culture teaching rationale and were willing to reconceptualise it.

Subsequently, Table 2.1, presented in Chapter 2, provided a working definition and articulation of the level of critical *languaculture* awareness and related cognitive skills. This was particularly useful in helping teachers formulate specific learning objectives in each of the *languaculture* modules and corresponding lesson plans. In addition, mapping the *languaculture* conceptual framework against these goals helped the teachers prioritise specific foci for the development of critical *languaculture* awareness, giving their overall goals a conductive thread. For instance, in Case Study C, the analysis of speech acts rationale *vis-à-vis languaculture* provided a foundation for formulating clear, concrete learning outcomes. In the context of this investigation and given its focus on beginner subjects, the formulated goals related to lower levels of awareness described in Table 2.1. However, these provided a springboard for mapping a progressive path to higher levels of *languaculture* awareness.

Notably, in the intermediate language learning subjects, the type of critical reflection generated by the reflective tasks provided evidence of progression to higher levels of critical awareness. As such, Table 4.1 was also useful for generating indicators of what was achieved in class and in some of the assessment tasks implemented. In other research contexts it may be used as a tool in creating criteria for assessment items, which would enhance accountability in making the intercultural learning goals explicit for both teachers and learners.

To sum up, while the scope of this investigation was limited to two of the several subjects within a programme, the goal alignment created within these subjects is indicative of the type of alignment that may be extended throughout the curricula of a whole programme. The formulation of specific goals and learning objectives is directly related to the design of assessment tasks. The articulation of goals and assessment is key to ensuring alignment of curriculum elements and to monitoring the development of critical *languaculture* awareness. I discuss issues concerning assessment in subsequent sections.

What?

With regard to the syllabus, the key exemplar of good practice was the mapping of *languaculture* aspects against the syllabus in all four case studies, that is, across languages and across subject types. Here, the conceptual frameworks of Crozet (Crozet, 2003; Young, 2008) served as the backbone for selecting specific content and the design of learning activities conceived as *languaculture* modules. This conceptual framework helped teachers and learners identify where culture is located in language use, specifically the linguistic content they were to cover in class. Its various axes – levels of verbosity, ritualisation, expression of emotions and feelings, and approaches to interpersonal relationships and politeness – served as touchstones for exploring both native and target *languaculture*(s). These five axes gave teachers a blueprint to guide the deliberate incorporation of *languaculture* in relation to the traditionally linguistically driven syllabus. This was possible in both beginner and intermediate subjects.

In Case Study C, the elementary Chinese language subject, Crozet's conceptual framework was used to complement the linguistic input presented in the textbook. Lili and I purposefully selected various *languaculture* aspects to be explored, based on the speech acts students were to learn. For instance, where students were to learn about offering drinks or food, and making, accepting and refusing dinner invitations, we would integrate discussion of different approaches to politeness and the hidden values they may reveal. Here, notions of insisting, and of never accepting an offer of this kind straight away, were some of the issues discussed in English rather than in the target language. We complemented these notions with relevant excerpts from films as well as learners' experiences. We used discussion of these *languaculture* aspects to promote the students' critical engagement with their conceptualisation of politeness in their native culture(s). Similarly, in Case Study B, the intermediate Italian language subject, Valentina and I used the themes she had established for the meetings with the community members and mapped them against various *languaculture* aspects. We then incorporated each of these aspects into the workshops and the learners' *schede* to promote learners' critical reflection.

Because the case studies had a particular focus on beginner subjects (three out the four case studies), additional aspects of curricular progression using this framework could not be explored. However, students enrolled in the Italian programme taking subjects with Valentina and Maria were able to start drawing links between the concepts explored in both, giving them an added sense of cohesion and coherence in the programme. Indeed, student–interviewees indicated that having taken two subjects in the Italian programme with shared information gave them a sense of consistency across subjects and helped them to explore the same theoretical concepts in different contexts and classroom environments through different activities, which in turn helped them consolidate such concepts and their meaning.

In all the case studies, the selection of material to explore relevant *languaculture* input proved challenging, however, the set reading served as a particularly suitable springboard for reflection. Use of authentic material, such as immigrant literature, intercultural autobiographies and online resources such as immigrant blog posts in both native and target languages, also provided us with the opportunity to introduce an emic perspective that could be unpacked and problematised within the safety of the classroom environment. This was particularly useful given that only one of the subjects – Case Study B – included a component comparable with ethnographic-type fieldwork through which learners could obtain and explore such an insider's perspective.

How?

As a key point of articulation between goals and content, the *how* of a curriculum development framework is surely at the crux of the process. I refer here to three specific aspects of this articulation: (1) its overall transparency; (2) its realisation in classroom materials and activities; and (3) its assessment. In this context, one of the key aspects in implementing the framework was that the exploration of *languaculture* was transparent for both teachers and learners. This meant that they could actively participate in bringing it into operation. For the teachers, who were in the foreground of this investigation, transparency enabled flexible, principled pedagogical action. For learners, who were in the background of this investigation, transparency served to promote active, conscious learning and engagement in their overall learning experience. Presenting this conceptual framework explicitly to students also legitimised its integration throughout the subject.

This conceptual framework also gave teachers and learners a 'common language' to talk about *languaculture*. As Valentina, teacher of the intermediate Italian language subject stated, this gave her a 'metalanguage' to share with the learners; a metalanguage they could use to discuss instances of *languaculture* dissonance. Indeed, the explicit presentation of the notion of *languaculture* and its conceptual framework provided both teachers and learners with specific concepts and terms to discuss the effect of *languaculture* in communication. This can be compared with teaching students about 'adjectives', 'verbs' and 'nouns', 'tenses' and 'moods'; these 'technical' grammatical terms give teachers and learners the tools to discuss linguistic problems such as 'wrong verb conjugations', 'lack of adjective–noun agreement' and so forth. By explaining 'politeness', 'verbosity', 'dissonance' and so forth as *languaculture*, teachers and learners can resort to a 'metalanguage' to talk about *'languaculture* dissonance' and its effect in creating and perpetuating stereotypes. It can also be used to discuss the importance of silence or 'levels of verbosity' in communication, in both their native and target *languacultures*. By sharing with learners the conceptual framework underlying their learning process, teachers can foster an engaged, attentive, conscious learning experience for themselves as well as for their students.

Finding adequate suitable material remains a challenge. Nonetheless, the data derived from all four case studies indicates that it is the techniques used to most effectively 'work' the material that can make all the difference. Various strategies can be useful: problematising potentially stereotypical views in the available activities in textbooks or set of readings; accessing suitable online discussion forums, blogs, etc.; and using autobiographical accounts such as the one analysed in the Chinese culture context subject (Ye, 2007) may provide ideal starting points for discussion. For Valentina, the lack of material, particularly audio-material, presented a significant challenge that motivated her to address the issue herself. At the time of our final interview she was embarking on a new project collecting audio-recorded interviews with native and non-native speakers living in Italy. The main aim in this project was to use the weekly topics planned for the intermediate Italian subject as conversation starters with native and non-native speakers, and in so doing to elicit their views on specific areas of potential *languaculture* dissonance, such as 'level of verbosity' (turn-taking and overlapping), 'approaches to interpersonal relationship' (register) and 'level of ritualisation' (specifically, greetings, taking leave and so forth).

In generating and guiding classroom discussions, the purposeful selection of trigger or prompt questions that would promote higher-order thinking was extremely useful (*cf.* Morgan, 2008). Here, implementing Mezirow's principles for transformative learning was particularly effective in designing the types of disorienting-dilemma activities and subsequent dialectic processes in class. Methodologically, these questions and principles were also useful during the data collection process, particularly during the interviews with teacher–participants in guiding their own self-reflective, transformative learning processes. In addition, data from classroom observations and discussion of classroom activities with teachers became the source of 'disorienting-dilemmas' for teacher–participants to reflect on the *languaculture* framework.

In Chapter 1 I discussed the myriad of challenges that the assessment of intercultural competence (IC) yields: from the dearth of available assessment tools to provide evidence of IC development, to the difficulty of establishing developmental sequences and assessing the various dimensions of IC. I suggested that formative assessment tasks underpinned by a *languaculture* conceptual framework could provide a suitable starting point for teachers to promote instances of 'perspective transformation' (Mezirow, 1991). Nevertheless, providing evidence of an actual *increase* in the nature of students' levels of critical *languaculture* awareness proved to be a particularly challenging task.

Two main types of formative assessment strategies were implemented in the case studies: participation in class discussions and reflective tasks. The first, common in all four case studies, aimed to encourage students to share their thoughts with each other, in small groups and with the class as a whole. Discussions were triggered by questions or statements that served as catalysts for students to share their opinions, experiences and observations in general. This type of strategy aimed to promote instances of 'perspective transformation' through a type of Socratic-style dialogic discussions (Morgan, 2008). The main caveats in implementing this strategy concern the teacher's disposition and ability to guide this type of discussion. Maria, the Italian cultural context subject teacher, indicated that she found this strategy particularly challenging. Because the discussions are largely underpinned by students' experiences and opinions, Maria was concerned by the difficulty of the teacher's need to challenge the often uncritical views of students and of students challenging each other's views, and the possibility of perpetuating stereotypes. This critique of students' discussions based on anecdotal evidence reveals a genuine and sensitive concern and I discuss this further in 'Acknowledging recurrent limitations in the framework's building blocks'.

This strategy of students participating in class discussions was complemented by use of an online forum where students could contribute to the class discussion in an asynchronous manner outside the classroom (O'Dowd, 2007). The discussion threads were initiated by the teacher, with the trigger questions posed in class. Using this online discussion forum aimed to encourage students who did not feel comfortable sharing their thoughts in class to participate in the discussion in an alternative arena. The forum also gave all class members time for further reflection on the trigger questions and the opportunity to elaborate on their comments and ideas in a more critical fashion.

The second strategy for alternative formative assessment implemented through the case studies of curriculum innovation aimed to explore the developmental nature of critical *languaculture* awareness through reflective tasks. In Case Study B, the intermediate Italian language subject, learners were expected to complete a minimum of four *schede* or worksheets after meeting their assigned Italian community member. These worksheets, in particular their fifth section, were designed to raise students' levels of critical *languaculture* awareness and thus provide evidence of their 'perspective trans-formation' processes. As such, this section included specific questions formu-lated to foster students' reflective processes. Students could write these reflections in the target language or in English, and they were not required to share their reflections with the rest of the students.

Students' comments in this section of the *schede* provided more promis-ing results than the discussion forums. Since this task was styled as keeping a private journal, students provided their answers mainly in English, as observed in earlier work by Liddicoat (2008), and in a stream of conscious-ness fashion. This type of narrative portrayed the students' flows of thought in replying to the questions the teacher had posed. Their thought flows included rhetorical questions, perceptions, wonderings and feelings held at conscious and subconscious levels. This comments task provided an oppor-tunity for students to document their critical reflectivity. However, in terms of the student cohort as a whole, some of the students' written reflections made it difficult for Valentina and myself to gauge whether there was an 'increased' level of critical reflexivity among the students as a result of the *languaculture* intervention.

Overall, these exemplars of good practice provide evidence of the poten-tial benefits of formalising a *languaculture*-driven curriculum. However, the recurrent limitations that emerged throughout this investigation need to be acknowledged and considered carefully for further advancing our initial 'intervention' model.

Acknowledging Recurrent Limitations in the Framework's Building Blocks

Limitations of our model that recurred across the four case studies can be divided into two interrelated, overarching dimensions. The first is con-cerned with issues of *integration* at the macro and micro-level. At the macro-level this includes the overall integration of the *languaculture* framework within both the particular subject, e.g. the first-year Italian cultural con-text subject, and the specific language programme, e.g. the Italian language programme. At the micro-level of curricular development I also consider issues of integration *vis-à-vis* the syllabus and teaching materials. The second overarching dimension concerns issues of *assessment*. Here I isolate assessment from other curricular elements as the fulcrum for establishing sustainable development and implementation of a *languaculture*-driven curriculum.

The pedagogic intervention modules were designed to integrate both a newly conceptualised rationale for *languaculture* exploration and the development of critical *languaculture* awareness. However, the level of integrating this rationale with the *languaculture* exploration modules into the existing subjects varied from subject to subject. At one end of the continuum we find Case Study D, a newly established Chinese cultural context subject, in which the *languaculture* interventions were designed from the grassroots giving them a strong driving force and resulting in their full integration into the curriculum. At the other end of the continuum we find Case Study C, the Chinese language subject, in which the interventions remained an add-on component. Here, Mei's underlying convictions and concerns about fulfilling a predominantly grammar-driven curriculum did not allow for the schedule of interventions to be completed as planned.

In between these extremes we find the two case studies in the Italian language programme: Case Study A, the Italian cultural context subject, and Case Study B, the Italian language subject. While the former also presented a number of challenges to fully integrating the *languaculture* modules, the teacher's concerns were with other matters. Maria's concerns ranged from the lack of readily available teaching material and the dearth of academic readings, to the influence of her own teaching style in implementing the *languaculture* discussions. In Case Study B, Valentina's efforts to extend the effect of the modules into the rest of the subject resulted in students having a strong sense of coherent and cohesive integration.

Articulating the re-framed goals and selected content with classroom practice presented several challenges. Here teachers' and learners' beliefs about the inclusion of an intercultural dimension in the classroom emerged as a distinct factor affecting the integration of curricular innovation. The most evident manifestation of these beliefs was in teachers' and learners' concern with 'time'. In all four case studies, both teacher–participants and student–interviewees reported that time spent discussing 'cultural' issues implied 'time away' from the study of linguistics aspects.

In Case Studies A and C, for instance, the *languaculture* intervention modules were perceived overall by the students as add-ons to the subject, rather than as aspects that could be interwoven with the rest of the subject. In Mei's case in particular, the modules were understood as 'time away' from the linguistic content that needed to be covered for assessment. It appears that the teacher's mindset tended to guide students to conceptualise their language subject as almost exclusively concerned with grammatical structures and vocabulary to be taught and learned as tacit goals. Divergence from this narrow scope signified time away from these goals, which learners understood as downtime when they could slacken off and which made the teacher feel guilty for dedicating time to such interesting but 'unnecessary' discussions. Overall, this response not only reflected the tendency for teachers and students to focus narrowly on what is assessed, but also it provided evidence of the challenges language teachers face as they attempt to reconceptualise the link between language and culture, and ultimately what it actually means to teach language in a changing educational paradigm.

As such, concern with 'time' is also symptomatic of assumptions that underlie the structuralist tradition in language teaching. If 'language' in languages education is conceptualised narrowly as the study of grammatical systems, isolated from the cultural dimension of interaction, it is understandable that teachers feel 'guilty' when dedicating time to the latter, and learners feel they can disregard this work as it will not be 'assessed'. This mirrors shortcomings in the theoretical underpinnings of available language teaching approaches: the lack of a conceptual 'touchstone' or reference point from which teachers can draw on their understandings of culture and, as a corollary, conceptualise how culture interacts with language.

Despite the small sample in my investigation, its findings are consistent with those of Sercu *et al.* (2005) in their larger international research project. Their project focused on the study of secondary school teachers' convictions about language and culture learning and the conditioning that may prevent them from putting into practice what they actually believe in terms of culture teaching and learning. The data in this, mostly quantitative, study revealed that across countries and target languages, whether favourably or unfavourably disposed to the integration of an intercultural dimension, all teachers complained about 'lack of time, lack of interest on the pupil's side and lack of suitable teaching materials or training' (Sercu, 2007: 77).

Another challenge to integrating curricular innovation that was highlighted in the case studies, was the difficulty in ensuring a programmatic approach to developing critical *languaculture* awareness. Even in relatively coherent and cohesive language programmes, such as the Italian one in case studies A and B where a programmatic approach to the study of *languaculture* aspects could be feasible, it proved challenging to reach agreement between teachers' beliefs, their conceptualisations of what needed to be taught and the articulation of these in practice. This becomes ever more challenging in language programmes that lack articulation among their subjects and agreement among teaching staff on the underlying language and culture teaching rationale. This was the case in the Chinese programme, whose syllabus was largely guided by the textbook. The current lack of a sequential, incremental view of the development of students' critical *languaculture* awareness adds to the difficulty of mapping out a programmatic approach to curriculum development.

An additional hurdle for integrating *languaculture* is associated with the syllabus. Use of the textbook as a *de facto* curriculum/syllabus presented a significant constraint for integrating the *languaculture* modules. For instance, in Case Study C, the Chinese elementary language subject, the *languaculture* intervention was dealt with by mapping various *languaculture* aspects *vis-à-vis* the speech acts introduced by the textbook. However, this approach is likely to be restrictive in more advanced subjects where linguistics structures and *languaculture* aspects reflected in interaction are more complex and extend beyond the speech act level of analysis.

Similarly, the lack of readily available material for studying and exploring *languaculture* aspects emerged as an equally significant constraint. This was the case in the Italian programme in particular. The common source material in all four case studies was the set readings from Lo Bianco and Crozet's (2003) monograph. While Valentina, Lili and Maria readily took on board the set reading, Mei explicitly expressed that it felt like an imposition on the students and the subject itself. She considered some of the vocabulary used in the reading – terms such as 'collectivism' and 'individualism' in relation to the various axes under examination – too technical for the first-year students. Student–interviewees indicated that they did not find the reading technical or difficult, but that they found it hard to relate this reading to the rest of the subject. Once again, this pointed to the lack of integration and the teacher's underlying belief about what is to be taught in a language subject. This issue was further substantiated by Mei's reticence to using the term *languaculture*, which could be clearly contrasted with Valentina's embracing of this term and acceptance of it as an exciting, enabling metalanguage for her and students to discuss important aspects of culture in language learning.

The teacher–participants indicated that the dearth of adequate readily available teaching material to promote *languaculture* awareness-raising activities also represented a challenge to innovation in the curriculum. It is useful to note that more teaching material was found concerning Chinese *languaculture* traits (*cf.* Brick, 2005; Wang *et al.*, 2000; Ye, 2006; Ye, 2007) than concerning Italian *languaculture*. As described in 'Extrapolating Exemplars of Good Practice', this may be overcome by utilising available material as sources of 'disorienting-dilemmas'. Two of the teacher–participants, Valentina and Lili, explained how they used the limited descriptions and interpretations presented in the assigned set readings (Carroli *et al.*, 2003; Li, 2003, respectively) as a starting point for discussing and promoting critical analysis of the text. Lili indicated she would ask students to provide additional areas of *languaculture* dissonance they may have experienced that could be added to discussion of the reading.

Let us now turn to the second overarching dimension of limitations: assessment. This was arguably the most challenging element of the curriculum to develop and implement. First, owing to ethical clearance constraints, student–participants' performance could not be assessed. Nonetheless, I was able to negotiate with each of the teacher–participants to include tasks that students had to complete in lieu of assessment. In all four cases, these tasks were included under the subject's 'participation' assessment item, and in two of the subjects, Lili's and Valentina's, as a reflective worksheet. In the context of these case studies, the challenge of evaluating students' participation during class discussions emerged. Promoting dialogue and being able to communicate in a comfortable environment should also be considered variables in this context.

In Case Study A, for instance, the online discussion forum was designed to provide an alternative to in-class discussions, giving students time to asynchronously formulate their opinions and interact with each other outside face-to-face circumstances. Nonetheless, two main caveats became evident in using this online strategy. First, because this was not an assessable task, student participation was rather poor, which reinforces the idea of the 'backwash effect' in assessment. Second, students' comments online, just as in class, require monitoring and guidance by the teacher to ensure the electronic discussion continues to generate and promote awareness-raising processes. In other words, students' comments need to be probed by teachers when necessary, so that they can be clarified, elaborated upon and therefore instructive to all forum users, but above all so that they do not offend other class members or perpetuate uncritical convictions.

Here it is important to note that using this type of information and communication technology (ICT) tool is enticing for university language teachers as they are increasingly required to incorporate ICTs into their curriculum (O'Dowd, 2007). This type of tool includes online discussion forums, blogs, wikis and podcasting, generally available through the university's online platform. The aim is to use different types of social networking technologies that are familiar to most of the student cohort, as tools for engaging them in online learning communities. ICTs, which in the context of language pedagogy fall under the umbrella of computer-assisted language learning (CALL), are therefore rationalised as tools that promote the design and implementation of learner-centred tasks for developing more autonomous, self-directed learners who can continue their learning experience outside the classroom. ICTs also represent a solution to teachers' concern about 'lack of class time' to dedicate to this type of discussion.

Nonetheless, as the example discussed here suggests, ICT-related tasks need to be purposefully and explicitly integrated into the curriculum.

The literature reveals several attempts to do so (*cf.* Belz, 2003; Belz & Mueller-Hartmann, 2003; Belz & Thorne, 2006; Elola & Oskoz, 2008; O'Dowd, 2003, 2007; Thorne, 2003; Vogt, 2001, 2006; Ware, 2005; Ware & Kramsch, 2005; *inter al.*). However, many of these attempts were marred by the 'stumbling blocks' identified in earlier chapters, namely: inconsistent definitions and applications of IC in their research designs, lack of a clear outline of the relationship between IC and the rest of the intercultural communicative competence (ICC) sub-components, and above all, lack of a clear outline for IC to help teachers monitor, assess and document the degree of its development.

Therefore, the issue of assessment presented two specific challenges: identifying *what* tasks were the most suitable to assess students' critical *languaculture* awareness, and identifying *how* to evaluate those tasks, that is, formulating specific assessment criteria that would help the teacher monitor attainment of the instructional goals. For the first, many suggestions were put forth by both the student–participants and the teacher–participants. It was agreed that a 'reflective task' was necessary. The 'Discovery Page' used in Case Study D or the *Languaculture* section of the *schede* in Case Study B proved particularly useful for some students. Other suggestions included using a 'reflective essay', and including critical incident analysis in the final written exams. However, both give rise to a further challenge about *how* to evaluate such tasks. Here suggestions included designing specific criteria for reflective activities, which would need to combine the integration of theoretical content with students' personal interpretations.

A final challenge concerning assessment of critical *languaculture* awareness remains to be addressed. The lack of a sequential, incremental conceptualisation of the development of students' critical *languaculture* awareness makes monitoring its development difficult. 'Diagnostic' assessment tools to establish students' initial levels of awareness and critical reflectivity would need to be developed to be able to gauge 'increased' levels of critical reflexivity from some of the students' reflections. As such, from a methodological point of view, the formative assessment strategies implemented in the case studies can offer only a relatively narrow, cross-sectional, snapshot of the students' levels of awareness.

Much of the literature in language and culture pedagogy reveals that this type of formative assessment tasks, equivalent to portfolio assessment, is a preferred alternative assessment tool. However, Jacobson *et al.* (1999) rightly note that portfolios reveal only a one-dimensional picture of the learning process, from the learners' point of view:

> Because portfolios rest on how students choose to represent their learning, and because they may value different types of learning or may not

know how to best represent themselves, the portfolios themselves may provide only a limited picture of what students have learned. (Jacobson *et al.*, 1999: 488)

This observation raises further concerns about the underlying assumptions of this type of assessment strategy, for instance, its implementation in just one subject rather than throughout a programme of studies. Limiting the use of portfolios to one subject within a programme exponentially reduces potential benefit. This type of assessment can be found in many language programmes, but it is rarely integrated at programme level. Usually it is implemented on the basis of two underlying assumptions: (1) that learners are adequately prepared or trained to track their awareness-raising process; and (2) that teachers are adequately prepared or trained to help students increase their levels of reflection. If integrated at programme level, some of these assumptions may be offset. Learners may be trained from beginner levels about their meta-learning, and how to talk about their level of meta-awareness. Learners also require training in processes of critical reflection to further their degree of criticality and foster instances of 'perspective trans-formation'. Once again, the need for a programmatic approach to language and culture teaching emerges as paramount. Nevertheless, pertinent research reveals that, in attempts to integrate 'culture' within language learning pro-grammes, both language and non-language subject components almost inevi-tably lose the complexity and dynamic essence of culture in communication. 'Culture' becomes a static, one-dimensional, piecemeal representation of the complex whole and tends to be assessed through equally one-dimensional, quantifiable assessment tasks.

Recent attempts to counteract this largely positivist conception of assess-ment entail the shift to a new, emerging 'assessment culture' (Dervin & Suomela-Salmi, 2010b) in language and culture pedagogy. This emerging 'assessment culture' is characterised by 'the systematic and reflexive integra-tion of assessment into teaching and learning, the active role of the student in assessment processes, [and the] assessment of both product and process instead of a numerical score' (Dervin & Suomela-Salmi, 2010a: 12).

Yet, even within this new vision for assessing intercultural competence, issues of validity, interpretation and objectivity remain unresolved. Moreover, as Sercu (2010) highlights, the assessment dimension of intercultural compe-tence and, in this case, critical *languaculture* awareness, raises more questions than answers. There are no available instruments to assess this dimension in a holistic fashion, nor are there instruments to document, monitor or determine the development of acquisition. If such a tool existed, teachers would have something to hold on to when planning practice activities and designing learning paths fit to promote individuals' or groups' learning, sharing with learners what specific goals they should achieve and what criteria will be used to assess goal achievement (Sercu, 2010: 25).

I argue that the lack of such an assessment tool traces to not only superimposing intercultural goals onto an ill-equipped field, but also the lack of feasible conceptualisation of the goals themselves, as my discussion in earlier chapters has made clear. Assessment will remain a contentious element in the language and culture curriculum, particularly if users of the new, emerging 'assessment culture' (Dervin & Suomela-Salmi, 2010a) do not contemplate an alternative way to conceptualise both evaluation and the place of assessors' subjectivity. And without reconceptualising and adequately addressing the underlying notion of IC, or critical *languaculture* awareness, no advancements can be made here.

The preceding critical discussion of empirical findings prepares us for considering the path to rebuilding connections between theory and practice, and in so doing, establishing *praxis*-driven, feasible implementation of the *languaculture* curriculum framework.

Revisiting the Framework's Foundations

Spolsky (1988) argued more than 20 years ago that theorists of second language learning continue to be 'seduced by language teachers' natural longing for simple solutions' that can be translated into 'a teaching method rather than accounting for empirical facts' (Spolsky, 1988: 377). This longing has generated a plethora of 'should be' models, with very little in common other than catchy slogans and overall ambitious claims regarding the 'all-encompassing' nature of their approach to language and culture teaching.

Rather than a specific teaching approach, and in concert with a post-method stance (Kumaravadivelu, 2001, 2003), I proposed formalising a curriculum development framework that researchers, curriculum designers and above all, teachers, could use as a guide as they endeavour to integrate language and culture in the classroom. This framework was underpinned by building blocks that acknowledge and embrace the complexities of language culture teaching discussed in earlier chapters. But above all, in conceptualising this framework I rejected the idea that there is a conventional teaching approach of what 'should be', to focus on what is possible (or at least, what teachers are realistically able to draw on given the imperfect nature and limitations of the classroom, the teachers themselves, the students and the institution). This entailed forfeiting 'seductive' claims of effectiveness, generalisability, definite answers and prescriptive guidelines typical in ready-made solution-like approaches.

What can a framework offer theorists and practitioners if not a definite solution and prescriptive guidelines? I argue that it can offer descriptive guidelines and examples of good practice with which to make informed choices regarding curriculum development. Striving to conceptualise this particular framework forced me to consider as many of the theoretical and real-world attributes as possible, attributes that would otherwise continue to be camouflaged or pass unnoticed in the complex web of interrelated elements. In addition, 'accounting for empirical facts' yielded by the case studies, provided me with the opportunity to consider the framework's overall feasibility in the Australian context and its potential transferability into other contexts.

In this third and final section of this chapter, I revisit the framework's building blocks presented in Chapter 2 and critically reflect upon them *vis-à-vis* the exemplars of good practice and the recurrent limitations discussed in earlier sections. In revisiting these building blocks, I also consider studies published in recent years (*cf.* Houghton, 2012; Houghton & Yamada, 2012; Johnston *et al.*, 2011; Lee *et al.*, 2012), which largely support and complement various aspects of the findings discussed in this chapter. This critical reflection is inspired by Levine and Phipps' call for a newly framed understanding of the theory/practice gap in which 'theory is practice is theory' (Levine & Phipps, 2012: 4).

Theoretical building blocks

I would like to start by revisiting the theoretical building blocks: (1) having an explicit conceptualisation (or, at the very least, working definition) of the language and culture nexus; (2) articulating this conceptualisation for language teaching; and, in turn, (3) mapping the progressive study of this conceptualisation against a curricular sequence of study.

I have argued that having a clear conceptualisation of these notions is pivotal to addressing the theory/practice gap in language and culture pedagogy, especially since language teachers still lack an understanding of these notions (Fantini, 1995; Sercu, 2005). I argue that, in the context of my investigation, this remains one of the key reasons preventing language teachers from planning the explicit, deliberate integration of a cultural dimension into their teaching practices. I have substantiated this contention with data from my initial interviews with teachers in the case studies. The teacher–participants' responses revealed that in the language lesson, teachers largely still introduce 'culture', however it may be conceptualised (some mix of practices, artistic traditions, geography, history and so forth), in an *ad hoc*, incidental fashion, whenever they find it suitable.

Theorists continue to overlook that most practitioners, language teachers, teacher trainers, curriculum developers and language learners, still operate under the assumption that language learning is mainly a linguistically driven activity. This assumption is a product of the historical development of the field, largely influenced by the Saussurean, structuralist tradition (Agar, 1994; Risager, 2006b). The legacy of this structuralist-tradition language teaching appears to have perpetuated the idea of studying a 'language' in the 'language classroom' and the study of 'languages' as grammatical systems, and thus on the assessment of 'language' learners' knowledge of grammatical structures (cf. Freadman, 1998).

At a theoretical level, several post-structuralist waves have challenged these views in favour of a more social, communicative view of language. Manifestations of these waves include communicative language teaching approaches in the 1970s (cf. Savignon, 1983, 2007) and intercultural language teaching approaches from the mid-1990s (cf. Risager, 2007). However, in practice these pedagogical waves have largely reduced understanding of the relationship between language and culture to the notion that they are related implicitly. This implicit relation has led both teachers and learners to assume that by teaching and learning languages, they are automatically teaching and learning about culture, an assumption that Robinson-Stuart poetically refers to as the magic-carpet-ride-to-another-culture syndrome (Robinson, 1978; Robinson-Stuart & Nocon, 1996).

As a result, the structuralist tradition remains entrenched in teachers' and learners' convictions and expectations about the language learning process. As Eisenchlas (2010) points out, 'despite the espoused adoption of a communicative rhetoric, many of the practices implemented in classrooms are still guided by grammar-driven agendas' (Eisenchlas, 2010: 19). I contend that this critique may also be extended to the 'intercultural rhetoric' in languages pedagogy. I argue that even in cases where language teachers claim to have adopted an (inter)cultural stance, their teaching practices remain largely linguistically oriented. This claim is supported by findings informing case studies B and C, respectively. There were ostensible discrepancies between the cultural objectives described in the subject outlines and the enactment of them. These discrepancies were underpinned by the lack of specific syllabi and assessment tasks to ascertain how these objectives were being addressed. Both syllabus and assessment were driven by the linguistic content to be covered.

Here it is important to establish that there is nothing inherently wrong about linguistically driven practices and the assumptions or premises that underpin them. Yet, it is the incompatibility of these underpinning assumptions or premises with the assumptions or premises necessary to address the widened educational mission teachers are currently facing that we should consider. This means that, in addition to the need for an explicit, working conceptualisation of the language and culture nexus, what is truly required is a reconceptualisation of what it means to teach and learn a language. The 'language classroom', the 'language teacher' or 'language teaching/learning' as constructs, or as they are still conceptualised, are not compatible with the new educational mission teachers are facing. As such, notions such as being a *languaculture* teacher/learner in a *languaculture* classroom may be conducive to establishing alignment between ends and means, and goals and practices in place to achieve them.

In the United States, Byrnes' (2008, 2012) research shares similar foci, but argues for the use a *genre*-based pedagogy within a theoretical framework underpinned by Halliday's systemic functional linguistics (SFL). According to Byrnes, SFL helps to establish a dialogue between language and culture in which:

> [T]exts become the unit of analysis for linking forms of language, the code, to a particular situation and, beyond that, to its larger cultural context. That includes the possibility for learners, through an evolving rich repertoire of situated texts, to develop both an understanding of culture and the ability to use situationally and culturally appropriate language. (Byrnes, 2008: 109–110)

In this context, she highlights the potential of *genre*-base pedagogy to inform a curricular progression that uses text to introduce and assess: (1) lexico-grammatical resources/content; (2) the development of multiple perspectives; and (3) a reflective stance in the study of intermediate and early advanced German language subjects (Byrnes, 2012). The preliminary results of this study resonate with both the theoretical and pedagogical building blocks in this *languaculture* framework. The overall implementation of Byrnes' framework provides complementary insights into the use of text as a unit of study beyond the elementary proficiency level, which was the focus of my study. On the other hand, the implications of Byrnes' framework remain to be explored in non-European language contexts.

Pedagogical building blocks

Key to traversing the theory/practice divide, pedagogical building blocks are concerned with three tenets: (1) formulating learning objectives coherent with overall conceptualisation of 'critical *languaculture* awareness' and corresponding awareness raising processes; (2) purposefully selecting *languaculture* aspects to be explored; and (3) embedding these goals and syllabi within a post-method paradigm. Overall, the four case studies provided evidence to support the relevance of these tenets. However, the limitations concerning *integration* and *assessment* discussed in earlier paragraphs make it plain that additional cycles of pedagogic inquiry are needed.

With regard to the first tenet, new learning objectives were formulated, particularly within the context of *languaculture* lesson plans and the design of specific critical *languaculture* awareness-raising activities. However, additional research may shed more light on how these learning objectives may extend into longer sequences of study beyond the subject level. This will entail additional research into two specific aspects of criticality: (1) its incremental and developmental nature; and (2) its transformative capacity.

In this context, and building on the third tenet of the theoretical building block, we find studies that can complement and inform the developmental notion of critical *languaculture* awareness, specifically, Johnston *et al.* (2011), Houghton (2012), as well as Houghton and Yamada (2012). They all draw from Barnett's work on critical thinking in higher education (Barnett, 1997), specifically the three domains – knowledge, self and world – and provide insights into the sequential progression of these skills with particular attention to language learning (*cf.* Brumfit *et al.*, 2005). Johnston *et al.* (2011) provide a *Framework for Criticality Development*, which outlines three broad and overlapping levels: (1) early criticality; (2) guided criticality; and (3) late criticality. They map specific descriptors and skills against each of these levels and examine their realisation, or lack thereof, within a Modern Languages programme in a United Kingdom university. This examination included 'content' subjects (history, literature, etc., taught in English), language subjects (intermediate and advanced levels) and the Year Abroad experience.[1] The major finding yielded by this investigation is that all three types of learning contexts can develop criticality in various ways.

This finding supports the findings yielded by the case studies in this investigation, which provided data from both content and language subjects, one of which included an 'ethnographic' component, comparable with the experiential learning expected to take place in the Year Abroad programme. Mapping by Johnston *et al.* (2011) of content subjects' learning activities (oral presentations and written tasks) in the first, second and third year can complement future iterations of Maria's and Lili's cycles of inquiry in their respective content subjects. Here, one of the caveats to consider is that offerings of these types of content subjects are in decline, which means that a focus on the development of criticality, and in this case, critical *languaculture* awareness, from elementary, *ab initio* levels, is imperative.

Houghton (2012) and Houghton and Yamada (2012) provide specific insights into the transformative capacity of criticality from both top-down (teacher-guided) and bottom-up (student-guided) approaches to the exploration of self and other in these levels. In both approaches they characterise the criticality learning process as cyclical, spiral and open-ended. This characterisation mirrors the description of critical *languaculture* awareness provided in Chapter 2 and the examples of students' work presented in the various case studies.

Houghton's study, in particular, makes specific reference to Bloom's taxonomy (*cf.* Anderson & Krathwohl, 2001; Bloom, 1956) of cognitive skills, from basic (knowledge, comprehension and application) to higher-order thinking skills (analysis, synthesis and evaluation) as a way of mapping learning objectives and activities in the language classroom. The insights and strategies in these studies support and complement the pedagogical tenets upheld in this building block. First, through synergistic use of top-down and bottom-up approaches to *languaculture* exploration, and second, through the use of the taxonomy of skills *vis-à-vis* critical *languaculture* awareness that teacher–participants use to map against and articulate into their programme, subject curricula, but also everyday classroom activities.

Houghton's Intercultural Dialogue (ID) Model (2012) – studied and implemented in English-as-a-foreign-language classes in a Japanese university – provides a particularly useful strategy to look into the relationship between the cognitive development of criticality and the affective implications in evaluating difference. Both are largely articulated by the suspension of judgement as a cornerstone for the development of criticality and, in the context of this study, 'perspective transformation'. The ID Model can thus complement and further inform future cycles of inquiry into the development of critical *languaculture* awareness with a focus on value judgement.

Mapping learning objectives onto the curriculum has additional implications for the coherent alignment, explicit articulation and design of assessment tasks that may provide evidence (both descriptive indicators and measurable outcomes) to monitor student learning. While assessment was not the primary concern in this investigation, the case studies provided examples of how this curriculum dimension may be approached. As outlined earlier in this chapter, additional research in this area will provide tools that may aid accountability and therefore, enhance internal and external quality assurance mechanisms.

Overall, while these studies do not make specific reference or draw implication *vis-à-vis* traditional language teaching approaches such as 'communicative language teaching' (except for Houghton & Yamada, 2012: 155–156), they all implicitly support the notion made explicit by the third tenet in this pedagogical building block. Namely, (1) frameworks such as the ID Model and the *languaculture* exploration framework can offset teachers' concerns with specific teaching methodologies as they are borne by a post-method stance to language teaching practices; and that (2) a focus on criticality from early stages in the language-learning process necessarily requires teachers to break free from the limitations of specific teaching approaches. In this sense, a post-method stance allows teachers to be able to make pedagogical decisions based on principles that are informed by specific working definitions or working frameworks of the complex relationship between language and culture and the development of criticality, or as argued in this book, critical *languaculture* awareness. As such, rather than supporting claims of effectiveness, this stance enhances the feasibility, and promotes the potential transferability, of these frameworks to other learning contexts, thereby narrowing further the perceived theory/practice gap in the field. Yet, given the centrality of teachers in this pedagogical stance, implications also emerge for their roles and teaching styles. In this investigation, these aspects were particularly evident in the concerns expressed by Maria and Mei in Case Studies A and C. I explore these implications in Chapter 5.

Finally, additional research remains to be conducted to explore how *languacultural* aspects may be progressively integrated and studied within a language programme. This will require institutional support, a point that is elaborated under 'Institutional building blocks'.

Institutional building blocks

These building blocks are underpinned by three tenets: (1) alignment of institutional graduate profile with *languaculture* goal; (2) increasing flexibility in degree structure; and (3) ensuring a programmatic approach when developing and implementing innovative curricula. The findings presented in the case studies are particularly concerned with the third tenet.

The potential positive effect of any subject innovation – in this case, through inclusion of a critical *languaculture* dimension – may ultimately be undermined by failure to formulate an integrative articulation of innovation within programmes as a whole. As pointed out by Valentina, the Italian language teacher, students in her second-year class would have benefited from introduction of this framework in the first year. It would also have 'saved time' spent in the modules on presentations to students and familiarising them with the terminology used in the framework. Similarly, in Case Study D, the Chinese cultural context subject, successful integration of the *languaculture* exploration modules was limited to the non-language component of the programme.

The four case studies that informed this investigation involved two language programmes: Chinese and Italian. The Chinese language programme lacked both articulation among subjects and agreement among teaching staff about the underlying language and culture teaching rationale. The Italian programme, however, displayed a relatively coherent and cohesive rationale among subjects and teachers involved. Both Maria and Valentina, the teacher–participants in this programme, embraced the programmatic approach to curriculum innovation, albeit with different levels of integration in the subjects where the participatory action research (PAR) projects were implemented. This view was supported by Valentina, who specifically mentioned the need to familiarise students with the terminology early in their *languaculture* learning journey. Maria also acknowledged the need for such a programmatic approach, despite students' reported views on the lack of integration of the *languaculture* modules in the cultural context subject.

Nonetheless, efforts to commit to a programmatic approach to develop *languaculture* may pose some other challenges that need to be addressed from the onset of the curriculum innovation process. A programmatic approach entails not only the re-definition of goals at programme level and at subject level so that specific instructional objectives may be identified at each stage, it also entails involvement of the whole teaching team and their willingness to embrace this type of curriculum innovation. As established in earlier paragraphs, agreement among teachers on their beliefs and conceptualisations of what needs to be taught, as well as how and why, is essential.

These findings are supported by a recent volume published by the Association for the study of Higher Education (ASHE) in the United States higher education context. This volume, titled *Engaging Diversity in Undergraduate Classrooms: A Pedagogy for Developing Intercultural Competence* (Lee *et al.*, 2012), highlights the need for institutions to develop a comprehensive, integrated approach to engaging with diversity and the development of intercultural competences. Here, they place particular emphasis on avoiding the tendency to produce 'islands of innovation' approaches whose cumulative effect is a 'piecemeal approach' that targets diversity but does not embed it into the fabric of the institution as a comprehensive pedagogy across curricular contexts. They claim that 'each classroom has the potential to foster the skill of problem solving in new contexts, the attitude of being open to multiple perspectives, or the practice of trying multiple approaches to tackle a complex question' (Lee *et al.*, 2012: 9).

Here, the first and second tenets underpinning institutional building blocks come into play. The overall lack of organisation support is reflected in the absence of coherent alignment between the 'globally prepared' vision for graduates and the role of foreign language and culture learning. This is mirrored in the largely restrictive structure of degrees. The lack of support, coupled with the conflicting imperatives of an increase in their teaching workload and research output targets, alongside an increase in uncertainty about employment, means that, in many cases, revisiting the curriculum's '(inter)cultural dimension' becomes a relatively low-ranking priority for most language educators. I will explore this and other implications for higher education institutions in the following chapter.

Conclusion

In this chapter I have synthesised the outcomes and exemplars of good practice that emerged through these case studies *vis-à-vis* the recurrent limitations identified in discussion of the data. On the basis of this synthesis, I turned to the building blocks of the *languaculture* framework presented in Chapter 2 and considered them under a new light provided by these findings as well as by current research in the field.

While the nature of this framework and its building blocks is largely descriptive, the empirical dimension grounds this description in *praxis*. The tenets binding together each of the building blocks are not *ad hoc* stipulations, but principles I have extrapolated from, and strengthened through, my discussion of the theoretical and empirical findings presented in this investigation. The latter, in particular, stem from curriculum innovation projects that involved a PAR component. As such, these findings integrate bottom-up perspectives of the participants involved and thus provide a unique convergence of theory and practice.

This investigation moves away from attempting to claim the 'effectiveness' of the *languaculture* exploration modules proposed to foster the development of 'critical *languaculture* awareness'. A focus on 'effectiveness' would have entailed a prescriptive approach and its generalisability across contexts – cultural, linguistic, educational, geographic and so forth – which, as discussed in the literature, may prove largely unfeasible when considering the range of variables involved in a given educational research design. Alternatively, my inquiry into the development and implementation of *languaculture* exploration modules was exploratory, and as such sought to provide models of curriculum designs that may help teachers to bridge the gap between the broadened educational aim of languages education and the practical challenges involved.

Owing to its exploratory nature, this investigation focused on a relatively small sample of subjects. Sacrificing breadth for depth enabled me to have extended engagement with the teacher–participants involved and provided valuable insight into four different curriculum innovation experiences.

Because of the time constraints inherent in subject delivery over the academic calendar, I could be involved with only two subjects at a time, per semester. I sought to study at least one language subject component and one non-language subject component within two different language programmes. Nevertheless, the scope of this investigation may encourage further research to confirm, extend or even disconfirm the results I have obtained.

Note

(1) A programme of studies that requires third-year language majors to spend a year or a year and a half in a country where their language of study is spoken.

Part 3

Bridging the Gap Without Falling into the Precipice

5 Articulating the Feasible with Sustainable Innovation

The impetus for this investigation arose from a desire to help university language teachers like myself, revisit their teaching philosophies and practices in light of a widened educational mission exhorting us to embrace our role as curriculum innovators for the development of intercultural learners. Throughout the book I have thus tried to take the teacher's perspective, considering external and internal forces impinging on our practices. In Part 1 of the book I examined the theoretical, conceptual and structural 'stumbling blocks' standing in the way of innovation and proposed a way to transform these into the 'building blocks' of a framework that may enable and support curriculum innovation. In Part 2, I presented and discussed empirical data yielded by case studies illustrating implementation of this framework in practice. The research design underpinning the case studies also took the teacher's perspective. This was achieved through incorporation of a Participatory Action Research (PAR) component that allowed teacher–participants to engage directly in innovation within the context of their own subjects. The main rationale for the use of this PAR component was the central role attributed to teacher–participants as potential drivers and enablers of sustainable innovation. The argument here is that focusing on teachers' professional learning is potentially more conducive to long-term impact on the field.

The challenge now becomes how to articulate feasible, innovative practices into 'sustained improvement' that may lead to 'systemic change across programme, department and institutional boundaries' (LanQua, 2010). In other words, how to overcome the 'islands of innovation' scenario described in Chapter 2 in order to ensure innovative practices are transferred beyond the context that generated them with a view to feeding back into the field, making the 'theory is practice is theory' loop come full circle. In this chapter

I address this challenge by identifying three interlinked, sustainability enabling mechanisms: (1) re-imagining the role of teachers as curriculum innovators; (2) scaffolding innovation through continuing professional development; and (3) designing active embedding strategies. In the spirit of ensuring theory/practice alignment, I explore how theories and rhetoric supporting these mechanisms may operate at a practical level, against the sometimes limiting realities in which they are rooted. Finally, I also consider the proposed *languaculture* framework in the broader higher education context, paying particular attention to the conceptualisation of intercultural graduate outcomes *vis-à-vis* current demands in the internationalised higher education scene.

Revisiting the Teacher's Role as Curriculum Innovator

In the context of this investigation, curriculum innovation had a key role in redressing and aligning 'ends' and 'means' in language and culture pedagogy. As such, curriculum innovation served as a catalyst for teacher–participants to consider more closely the curriculum itself as a construct, the reflective nature underpinning of innovation and, above all, their own role in enabling innovation. In so far as it relates to innovation and overall reform, the curriculum is a construct that has remarkably escaped the critical lens of professional discussions in higher education, at least, until recently (Fraser & Bosanquet, 2006; Vidovich *et al.*, 2011).

In this context, it is important to remember that, as Byrnes points out, 'there is curriculum as wishful intention, at times as imposed prescription of "what should happen"; and there is curriculum as reality, "what does happen"' (Byrnes, 2008: 111). The task of helping teachers to bridge the seemingly unbridgeable chasm between 'what should happen' and 'what does happen' is at the core of sustainable curricular innovation. Here Byrnes suggests we turn to the well-known curriculum specialist Lawrence Stenhouse, who argues that teachers should think of a curriculum as 'an attempt to communicate the essential principles and features of an educational proposal in such a form that it is open to critical scrutiny and capable of effective translation into practice' (Stenhouse, 1975: 4, in Byrnes, 2008: 111). In the context of this investigation, the role of the teacher in translating this 'educational proposal' into practice entailed developing a critical stance toward their own teaching philosophies and teaching practices to become what Giroux (1988) calls 'transformative intellectuals'. This term conceives of teachers as professionals with the task of engaging critically with social realities. Giroux argues that teachers should develop a capacity for self-reflection and for conscious action directed at dealing with the perceived social inequalities. The term reflects Giroux's adoption of Freire's view of 'transformation' as a process that results from the interplay between *action* and *critical analysis*.

Here the adoption of a critical stance by the teacher presupposes the understanding of reality 'as a *process*, undergoing constant transformation' (Freire, 1970: 56; emphasis in original). Freire argued that such an understanding of reality should aim towards conscious participation in the process of transforming this reality (Freire, 1970, 1973). Freire conceptualised this process of conscious participation through the Gramscian concept of *praxis*, the process of 'reflection and action upon the world in order to transform it' (Freire, 1970: 33). This notion of *praxis* is thus consistent with the reflective processes both teacher and student–participants were asked to engage in.

In addition, the notion of teachers as 'transformative intellectuals' is consistent with the theory of 'transformative learning' I discussed in earlier chapters. Indeed, Mezirow's theory of adult learning is also underpinned by Freirian views of education. As such, the process of curricular innovation places teachers, as adult learners, in a position of transformation, which Kumaravadivelu (2003) argues should be the main role of teachers as educators. Before delving further into the 'critical' dimension of this role and its impact on curriculum innovation, it is important to consider how it compares with alternative teachers' roles.

Kumaravadivelu has explored the historical development of language teachers' roles and identified the main features in Table 5.1. He argues that these roles should not be treated as absolute opposites, but rather as relative tendencies, with teachers leaning toward one or the other at different moments.

In Table 5.1, Kumaravadivelu compares three types of teacher roles. The first type of role refers to teachers as *passive technicians* whose primary task is to act as conduits of professional knowledge and the empirical research conducted by experts. In this role, teachers tend to maximise their knowledge through prescribed activities anchored in a discipline informed by the experts in the field. The second type of role conceives teachers as *reflective practitioners* whose primary task is to act as facilitators of professional knowledge as well as their knowledge informed by action research activities. In this role, teachers tend to focus on maximising learning through problem-solving activities anchored in the interface between their own experience in the classroom, their learners' experience and the experts in the field. Finally, the third type of role concerns teachers as *transformative intellectuals* whose primary task is to act as *agents of change*. This type of change is reflected in personal transformation anchored in professional knowledge, their personal knowledge and experiences in the classroom, but more importantly, in an exploratory pro-

Table 5.1 The roles of the teacher

	Teachers as passive technicians	Teachers as reflective practitioners	Teachers as transformative intellectuals
Primary role of teacher	Conduit	Facilitator	Change agent
Primary source of knowledge	Professional knowledge + empirical research by experts	Professional knowledge + teacher's personal knowledge + guided action research[a]	Professional knowledge + teacher's personal knowledge + self-exploratory research by teachers
Primary goal of teaching	Maximising content knowledge through prescribed activities	All above + maximising learning potential through problem-solving activities	All above + maximising socio-political awareness through problem-posing activities
Primary orientation	Discrete approach, anchored in the discipline	Integrated approach, anchored in the classroom	Holistic approach, anchored in society
Primary players in the teaching process (in rank order)	Experts + teachers	Teachers + experts + learners	Teachers + learners + experts + community activists

Note: [a]I refer to Action Research, and in particular, PAR and its role in this investigation in Chapter 3.
Source: This table is reproduced with permission from Kumaravadivelu (2003) *Beyond Methods: Macrostrategies for Language Teaching* (p. 16). London: Yale University Press.

cess of self-reflection. In this role, teachers tend to focus on maximising the socio-political awareness through problem-solving activities in a holistic approach that includes learners, experts and the community as a whole.

Kumaravadivelu (2003) also argues that the essential feature of teachers as transformative intellectuals is 'their ability and willingness to go beyond the professional theories transmitted to them through formal teacher education programmes and try to conceive and construct their own personal theory of teaching' (Kumaravadivelu, 2003: 17). In other words, the process of transformative teaching demands that 'teachers take a critical look at the dichotomy between theory and practice, between theorists and practitioners'

(Kumaravadivelu, 2003: 17). Kumaravadivelu's arguments are supported by Kincheloe's seminal book *Teachers as Researchers: Qualitative Inquiry as a Path to Empowerment* (Kincheloe, 2003). Kincheloe extends the notion of teachers as 'transformative intellectuals' to support the type of critical, constructivist and participatory inquiry underpinning this investigation and the kind of classroom-based research teacher–participants were asked to engage in.

The above discussion points to a recurring aspect of this investigation: *criticality*. This is not fortuitous. For language and culture pedagogy, it is evidence of an emerging shift. Dasli (2011a) refers to this shift or 'moment' as a transition towards *critical intercultural language pedagogy*. In practice, a critical stance emerges, not only as self-reflection, but also as an 'investigative orientation' to our practices. The latter refers to the intentional, systematic processes involved in 'noticing, analysing, interpreting and making sense of the actions of teachers and learners, motivated by an ongoing interest in using information about classroom interactions to develop teaching and learning' (Crichton, 2007: 3). For the languages and cultures 'transformative intellectuals', this 'investigative orientation' or stance is conceived as an *integral* part of teaching practices, that is:

> Not as a 'noun', an 'add on' to teaching and learning, but 'adverbially': a way of doing teaching, of being alert to interactions, in which teachers continuously notice, compare, reflect on and apply information about teaching and learning back into how they do and how they understand teaching and learning. (Crichton, 2007)

This stance is strongly advocated in the Australian compulsory education system as a key aspect of languages teachers' professional standards (AITSL, 2011; Scarino *et al.*, 2012). In the higher education context, both in Australia and the world, it is largely embedded in the notion of 'scholarship of teaching and learning' (SOTL) (Hutchings *et al.*, 2011). Criteria underpinning SOTL points to the need for: high levels of discipline-related expertise, an understanding of who the learners are, how they learn and what practices are most effective in the context of the discipline (pedagogical content knowledge). Additional features of SOTL include promoting innovation and having the potential to be replicated and elaborated; which in turn, requires it to be documented and subjected to peer review (Gossman *et al.*, 2009; Kreber, 2010).

As such, the role of language teachers as 'transformative intellectuals', and therefore, as agents of change and innovation, is strongly supported at a rhetorical level in the higher education context. However, the current reality university teachers are facing reveal contradictory forces are at play. Language teachers find themselves in 'survival mode', trying to cope with simultaneous employment uncertainty, increasing teaching workloads and conflicting demands made by universities in relation to research outputs and teaching standards (Nettelbeck *et al.*, 2007; White & Baldauf, 2006).

The findings yielded by this investigation revealed that university language teachers are indeed in a precarious situation. The case studies revealed that teacher–participants were largely unfamiliar with current trends in language and culture pedagogy within the field and with relevant language-in-education policies in the sector. Given the critical situation of university language departments across Australia (Go8, 2007), this is not surprising. Overall, reduction of funding in the higher education sector has resulted in shrinking departments, increased workloads and, for the humanities, in particular for foreign language programmes, the systemic (if not systematic) de-professionalisation, through erosion of senior leadership, and widespread juniorisation and casualisation of staff (Nettelbeck *et al.*, 2012; Newfield, 2009).

This raises critical questions about the role of university language teachers in the process of curriculum innovation. The first is: how can in-service university language teachers provide an adequate model of language and culture learning for future language teachers if they are unfamiliar with the current developments in the field? Moreover, how can teachers who are unfamiliar with these developments be aware of their own development of intercultural competence/critical *languaculture* awareness? And, how can native teachers of Eastern languages have developed these if their education system does not contemplate this type of notions? This last question in particular, has recently generated much discussion regarding intertwined educational values and traditional cultural values that may influence teaching philosophies, beliefs and overall pedagogical practices, even while teaching in a foreign context (see for instance: Hsieh, 2011; Jiang *et al.*, 2010).

A number of additional questions from Sercu and St John (2004) concern raising teachers' critical awareness of their changing roles and educational mission:

> How can teachers foster learner responsibility in the classroom, unless they themselves are bearing the intellectual responsibility for their own professional development? How can they encourage reflectivity among their students, without developing a capacity for critical reflection themselves? How can they help learners acquire intercultural competence, if they are not intercultural learners themselves? How can they promote change in the skills and attitude of their students, if they are unable to see a need for change in themselves and are not taking systematic action

to develop their approaches to foreign language teaching? (Sercu & St John, 2004: 59)

Thus, if language departments are even to survive, let alone fulfil the expectation upon them to produce a flow of inter-culturally competent communicators to meet national requirements, language educators need to be adequately informed and equipped to fight for their survival. They need to be familiar with current trends in theory, with national language policies and university internationalisation policies, and with their newly formulated intercultural goals. This will best prepare them to embrace their role as agents of educational change (Stenhouse, 1975) and ultimately, to be better prepared collectively to position language studies at the forefront of such policies. A core aspect in ensuring the sustainability of innovative practices therefore, consists in engaging teachers in suitable professional learning processes.

Scaffolding Innovation Through Professional Development

Having taken the teacher's perspective in bridging the theory/practice gap in language and culture pedagogy is thus not fortuitous. Despite the many 'stumbling blocks' to bridging this gap identified along the way, it has become clear that language teachers hold the key to promoting the type of centrifugal force necessary to turn these 'stumbling blocks' into the 'building blocks' of sustainable innovation. Furthermore, as Sercu and St John (2004) point out, 'it has [also] become clear that to become an *agent of change*, a teacher needs to become an achiever of personal and professional change' (Sercu & St John, 2004: 59, emphasis added). This uncovers the centrality of teacher's professional development, not only in the context of individual classroom contexts, but the entire field of foreign language education and the prospects of our profession. Given the precarious situation of university language departments, it is important to consider what type of approaches to professional development may best promote effective and sustained innovation to meet the critical needs of these teachers.

Historically, faculty professional development, also referred to as educational development, has not been considered a priority, at least, in relation to teaching practices (Amundsen & Wilson, 2012). However, recently, a pressing need to rationalise and substantiate the quality of learning and teaching has led many Australian universities (Dearn *et al.*, 2002), and universities around the world, (Calkins *et al.*, 2009; Gosling, 2009; Saroyan &

Frenay, 2010) to introduce formal programmes for professional induction of new academic staff and development and support of continuing staff. However, these programmes are largely underpinned by top-down prescriptive perspectives on teachers' practices and tend to focus on generic teaching skills, rarely targeting specific areas such as language teaching. Indeed, as Pauwels points out 'although universities in some countries make it increasingly mandatory for new staff to undertake some training in university-level teaching, it remains largely voluntary for existing staff. Furthermore, the type of training they provide is generic rather than subject-specific' (Pauwels, 2011: 252).

Languages education is one of perhaps many university departments, or sections within them, that have much to gain from subject-specific professional development. Here it is also important to consider characteristics of university language teachers' professional backgrounds in various geographical locations. In Australia, for instance, the majority of university language teachers do not have a background in language pedagogy. White and Baldauf's 2006 report on Australia's Tertiary Language Programmes indicated that while most universities aspire to employ staff with pedagogical training, this is not a requirement. Moreover, 'where there is shortage of skilled language teachers in a particular language, universities would settle for native speakers with some teaching experience' (White & Baldauf, 2006: 29). And as in most areas of the university system, there is increasing employment of casual staff and postgraduate research students whose educational background and professional experience vary widely (Nettelbeck et al., 2012). Their teaching practices rely heavily on their own experiences as language learners. As such, while it may be unreasonable to expect universities to set up independent professional development programmes within language departments (Klapper, 2001a), there is still considerable room for conducting and promoting bottom-up, collaborative professional development initiatives like the one I have carried out in this investigation.

Over the last few decades, the traditional top-down approaches to professional development of language teachers have come under increasing scrutiny. Even though research has indicated that top-down approaches are largely ineffective in promoting and supporting ongoing advancement of teachers' knowledge and skills (Klapper, 2001b; Knight et al., 2006; Richards & Lockhart, 1994; Wallace, 1991), universities continue to rely on this mode. Bottom-up approaches like the one implemented through this investigation become central to the sustainability of innovative practices because they are driven by the needs of the agents involved and they are underpinned by the iterative nature of reflective practice (Richards & Farrell, 2005; Richards & Lockhart, 1994; Schön, 1987; Zeichner & Liston, 1996).

Reflective practices underpinning bottom-up approaches are concerned with the critical examination of teaching practices through which teachers are able to develop awareness of their own practices and their underlying convictions. Roberts (1998) argues that increased levels of awareness are often made possible through collaboration between professionals. As such, in my investigation I used a PAR component to generate and scaffold teachers' reflective processes on language and culture pedagogy. Zuber-Skerritt (1992a) explains that using PAR as a professional development strategy 'is not only a possible alternative to advancing knowledge in higher education, it is also a more effective and immediate way of improving learning and teaching practice' (Zuber-Skerritt, 1992: 10).

In this investigation, the starting point for teacher–participant reflection was problematising the subjects' cultural goals and their enactment, or lack thereof, in practice. Then came development and implementation of the *languaculture* exploration modules and the data collection tools to examine the outcomes of the interventions. Data sources of teacher–participant reflection included my semi-structured interviews and regular meetings with the teacher–participants to discuss developing and implementing the *languaculture* modules, which were complemented by the teachers' participation in delivering the modules, first as observers, and later in charge of delivery. Through the interviews and discussions, I aimed to offer teacher–participants a cognitive space to reflect on their practices. Through their participation in delivering the modules, I aimed to provide them with actual instances of teaching practices that may challenge their reflections and thus increase awareness of their convictions to potentially trigger changes in their own practices. Research suggests that teachers' convictions may change as a result of experiences that challenge their frames of reference (Schön, 1983). And as Fullan has claimed, 'the relationship between beliefs and behaviour is reciprocal – trying new practices sometimes leads to questioning one's underlying beliefs; examining one's beliefs can lead to attempting new behaviour' (Fullan, 1982: 247).

Therefore, the PAR component of this investigation mirrored both the type of learning processes used to develop critical *languaculture* awareness raising activities and Mezirow's theory of transformative learning underpinning the notion of 'perspective transformation' (Mezirow, 1981, 1991). It enabled teachers to challenge their own frames of reference through discussing critical incidents, in this case, implementation of the *languaculture* modules. That process gives this framework a clear connecting thread: *criticality*. Criticality becomes central to breaking the vicious cycle underlying the pervasive lack of coherence, which seems to perpetuate the theory/practice divide.

Critical, collaborative, systematic engagement in cyclic examination of our own teaching practices can thus lead to sustainable embedding of innovation. In this context, teacher–participants had the opportunity to continue with the research cycle and incorporate findings into their next offering of the investigated subject or other subjects. Valentina, the Italian language teacher, and Lili, the Chinese cultural context subject teacher, took on this challenge, albeit with different degrees of planning, and indicated they were able to apply the knowledge gained through this experience to other subjects. Mei and Maria both advised that at the end of the first cycle they had largely benefited from participating in the project. However, they still found it challenging to apply some of the principles explored into their teaching practices. The need for ongoing reflection and experimentation to incorporate new practices leads me to my next point.

The iterative nature of reflective practice requires the implementation of specific management strategies. This entails systematically planning each cycle of inquiry to ensure that the results obtained from one cycle can be taken up in the next to move the innovation process forward. The process requires teachers to design data collection tools to provide evidence of the interventions conducted and the outcomes resulting from them. This evidence can be incorporated into the next cycle of inquiry and so forth (McAlpine & Harris, 2002). This research approach is particularly relevant in the higher education sector as teachers are increasingly required to document their teaching practices for quality assurance purposes (Dearn et al., 2002). In the context of this investigation, data collection tools included classroom samples and the learners' reflective tasks.

In addition, teachers need to monitor the outcomes of the interventions. Monitoring strategies may include regular peer observation and subsequent discussions with teachers involved; individual interviews and focus groups with students before, during, and at the end of the subject; and subject evaluations, which are now compulsory at most Australian universities (Dearn et al., 2002). In this investigation, the collaborative nature of the interventions provided an opportunity to discuss both the progress of the interventions with the teacher–participants during the subject and the final outcomes with both the teacher and student–participants. However, the structural and logistical limitations inherent to subject offerings at university level prevented our use of additional monitoring strategies that may have strengthened the research design. For instance, one possibility could have been to have control groups, that is, two different subject cohorts, possibly in two different campuses (cf. Kember, 2003).

Overall, the PAR component proved to be a useful avenue to promote the bottom-up professional development of the teacher–participants. Indeed, despite her overall concerns regarding various aspects of the project, Mei's comments summarise the overall perceptions of the teacher–participants in this regard:

> With this project, I have learned through doing, which is quite different from traditional professional development workshops. I have gathered some first-hand information, which may work and which may not. I don't believe this can be achieved through traditional workshop talks and discussion.

Yet, the case studies also revealed a stark truth: putting teachers at the forefront of innovation is not enough. Of the four teachers who participated in this investigation, only two seemed to fully embrace the opportunity to generate bottom-up innovation in their subjects. The other two expressed genuine concerns and an overall perceived level of resistance to their changing roles and teaching practices. Indeed, in Mei's case in particular, this resistance seemed to stem from her own level of *languaculture* awareness. This relates to the question posed earlier on native teachers of Asian languages and their own attitudes and beliefs with regards to language teaching coming from an education system that does not integrally contemplate this type of notion.

Significantly, as Hartley noted, often these types of continuing professional development programmes in higher education are 'likely to be resisted by the very agents for whom they are designed' (Hartley, 2003: 63). This is understandable given that, as mentioned earlier in this chapter, language teachers are being constrained by conflicting imperatives. On the one hand are the beliefs underlying their teaching practice – and their own attitudes and beliefs with regards to language teaching and *languaculture* awareness – and on the other hand are increases in their teaching workload and research output targets juxtaposed with an increase in employment uncertainty.

Higher education institutions around the world need to recognise these strained circumstances and ensure that, as part of their commitment to quality assurance, language teachers are offered continuing professional development opportunities suitable to their needs. For language teaching professionals, remaining abreast of the latest developments in the field and the constantly changing higher education environment is an imperative that also relates to the future of the field as a whole as it impacts upon the education of the next generation of language scholar–teachers (*cf.* Allen & Maxim, 2013; Norris, 2010).

Ensuring Sustainability Through Active Embedding of Innovation

The discussion above leads me to the third and final mechanism stakeholders should consider in promoting and enabling the sustained improvement of teaching practices. This mechanism is concerned with effectively moving beyond the 'islands of innovation' phenomena. Indeed, pedagogic innovation does not accrue passively or automatically. Nor does it guarantee systemic transformation. This may only be achieved through the active engagement of all stakeholders in the integral embedding of innovation at both discipline and institutional levels.

Embedding is conceived as the last stage in an innovation process and it is understood as the integration of the new practices, or set of practices, as a core aspect of the given curriculum, programme of studies, discipline or institutional structure in which it was generated (Southwell *et al.*, 2005: 81). Given the current state of the foreign language teaching field and its critical standing in the internationalised higher education sector, embedding innovation is a challenging task. However, research conducted in this area presents several useful strategies (Hinton *et al.*, 2011; Smith, 2012) that may be tactically adapted and implemented in the field of language and culture pedagogy.

The challenges of embedding the sustainable development of interculturally sensitive practices in higher education are documented widely in the literature (for recent discussion in this regard see Lee *et al.*, 2012). This is particularly true in the context of university business programmes, which is not surprising given the pressing need to deal with the development of intercultural competences in internationalised business environments (Witte, 2010). In the Australian context for instance, Treleaven *et al.* (2011) propose an active embedding methodology enacted within three organisational domains of action: (1) the capacity of 'communities of practice' and distributed leaders to generate organisational commitment and seed activities; (2) formal and informal organisational policies and procedures for initiating and systematically sustaining curricular change; and (3) accessible resources, tools and databases that support implementation of innovation. According to their study, of these three, it is the first one that holds the most potential to catalyse sustainable systemic change. Here communities of practice refers to 'groups of people who share a commitment to, and an understanding of, the work practices they undertake as a group, a network or distributed/dispersed group' (Treleaven *et al.*, 2011: 9). In this context, they argue that PAR methodologies are particularly useful in generating the type of active engagement and iterative action-oriented collaboration necessary to promote and embed innovation in the curricula. In so doing, they also acknowledge PAR's potential for academic development and its correspondence with 'not only the complexity and self-reflective nature of developing intercultural competence itself, but also with developing a conceptual framework for embedding' (Treleaven et al., 2011: 6). These findings are corroborated in numerous studies on embedding of innovation (for a thorough review of literature in this area see Smith, 2012).

In line with these embedding strategies, in the context of this investigation, the systematic iterative nature of the PAR component used largely enhanced potential for embedding and up-scaling of good practice. PAR facilitated the active engagement of language teachers in curriculum innovation projects within the context of their own subjects and also provided a platform to explore the feasibility of the critical *languaculture* framework. The findings provided evidence to suggest that various levels of embedding at subject and programme level were taking place. Yet, owing to the exploratory, small-scale nature of this investigation, additional embedding strategies, such as policy changes and creation of publicly available resources, remain to be explored.

Nevertheless, this discussion suggests that, in addition to its potential to foster professional development, the creation of communities of practice (Lave & Wenger, 1991), even at small-scale, also has the potential to support effective dissemination of innovation, and in turn, the systematic, sustainable embedding of it within subjects, programmes, disciplines and institutions (Hinton et al., 2011). Their inherently participative and voluntary nature provides a strong platform for stakeholders to collectively encourage, enact and enable sustained improvement of teaching practices. In addition, within these communities there are usually activities carried out at various levels of influence within organisations that have been referred to as *distributed* or *shared leadership*. This type of approach to leadership in learning and teaching supports an informal but systematic, bottom-up process of collaboration whereby individuals, groups and teams who trust and respect each other's contribution, 'willingly take responsibility and generate ideas and initiatives' (Bolden et al., 2009: 271).

Extensions of these groups and activities at a larger-scale have emerged around the world in response to a 'call to action' in our field. Indeed, despite its critical state as a field in transition and its precarious state within higher education, there are reasons to remain optimistic about its prospects. As Nettelbeck, Hajek and Woods argue 'there remain strong currents of resilience, dynamism and innovation' (Nettelbeck et al., 2012). These currents have been largely driven by the heartening formation of grassroots movements aimed to counter and repair further erosion and fragmentation in the field (Hajek *et al.*, 2012; Modern Language Association, 2007; Woods *et al.*, 2011). These movements are stimulating critical self-reflection and re-envisioning of the overall sense of community in the language teaching profession, particularly in relation to the teaching of languages and cultures. It is within this renewed sense of community that collaboration and sharing can thrive at a local and, almost imperatively, at an international level. The momentum gained from the grassroots level is indeed a testament to the passionate commitment of the profession.

Articulating Innovation and Sustainability with Current Demands in Higher Education

As the preceding discussion makes plain, in order to ensure coherent articulation of innovation at subject and programme levels, it is important to avoid an 'add-on', cumulative approach to its dissemination and embedding. This is ever more imperative at discipline level. Indeed, if we are to traverse effectively the theory/practice divide, we need to break the patterns perpetuated by the 'seemingly endless array of proposals, recommendations, and new 'theories' competing for attention in professional discussion and praxis' (Byrnes, 2013: 18). The question is thus how to articulate sustainable innovation with the current demands of the field and the higher education sector as a whole. In other words, how to ensure that bottom-up movements articulate and complement top-down ones for the coherent alignment of efforts. The answer, I argue, lies in harnessing the potential of internationalisation and quality assurance strategies being developed and implemented worldwide.

As discussed throughout the book, reconfiguration of higher education underway across continents is being driven by analogous trends. This is especially true in relation to foreign language teaching in the United States, England and Australia. Analogous top-down frameworks are thus being employed to channel these trends (Cañado, 2010: 392). As such, despite its many complexities, the parallelisms drawn by this increasingly internationalised education context provide fertile ground in which to frame sustainable innovation endeavours.

Here two specific paths for action can be identified: (1) revisiting intercultural graduate outcomes in an international context; and (2) providing frameworks for systemic, whole curriculum reform. A shift in emphasis to graduate outcomes as the basis for judgements of educational quality in many parts of the world has intensified efforts to generate convincing evidence that students are achieving or are making progress towards the graduate outcomes specified for a given programme of study. In this context, the discussion presented throughout this book, together with emerging research, suggests that it is ever more imperative to revisit the ways in which graduate outcomes are conceptualised in relation to the 'intercultural'. I argued that in re-examining these conceptualisations, efforts should be made to acknowledge the central role of language learning as a meaning-making process for knowledge production and reproduction, and above all, as a tool to facilitate and promote transformative, critical self-reflection and the ongoing destabilising and restabilising of our *languaculture* schemas. Indeed, taking an imaginary 'excursion into the future', Byrnes reminds us of the central role language will play 'in the world for which our educational efforts are intended' (Byrnes, 2013: 21). Her considerations highlight the increasing need to develop highly literate abilities in several languages as increasingly deterritorialised contexts of communication continue to emerge.

While constructive alignment of intercultural graduate outcomes is underway – albeit under many guises – in many institutions around the world, soon, alignment strategies will also have to address matters of quality assurance (QA). In preceding chapters I explored how QA initiatives are working towards generating internationalised descriptions of graduate outcomes. More recently these strategies are converging at international levels to promote and facilitate dialogue between higher education institutions (HEIs) around the world. In September 2012, the United States-based Council for Higher Education and Accreditation (CHEA) – a non-profit advocacy group that represents accredited American colleges and universities – launched an international division – the CHEA International Quality Group, or CIQG – which aims to streamline efforts around the globe to continue striving for the transparency and rationalisation of academic achievements and overall graduate outcomes (Moodie, 2012). This will be achieved by sharing information on quality standards, identifying trends in quality assurance and promoting international cooperation in improving academic quality in higher education. Here, initiatives such as the LanQua project in Europe (LanQua, 2010) have the potential to support greater sharing of practice in QA across languages and institutional contexts.

Macro-level QA initiatives like these ones will also have to meet micro-level, teacher-driven strategies like the one presented in this book. Indeed, a critical dimension of QA has to do with teachers' accountability in relation to the continuous improvement of their practices. In this context, institutional support for teachers' classroom-based learning is indispensable to the sustained provision of high quality education. In addition, as discussed above, institutional support should also be provided in terms of professional development opportunities that may scaffold the type of bottom-up, teacher-driven curriculum reform required for sustainable innovation.

This takes me to the second path for action. This path is guided by efforts to support institution-wide embedding of innovation through whole curriculum reform. A growing number of universities around the world are currently engaged 'in radical curriculum policy transformations as a key strategy to strengthen their competitive position in a global knowledge era' (Vidovich *et al.*, 2011: 283). Yet, as Vidovich *et al.* point out, more empirical research is needed, across nations, institutions and disciplines in order to inform the decision-making of stakeholders: scholars, policy makers and practitioners working in higher education. They argue that institutions should aim for a 'whole curriculum' approach to innovation and policy transformation in which the trilogy of curriculum content, pedagogy and assessment are treated as parts of a complex whole rather than separate domains.

This argument resonates with the development of the critical *languaculture* awareness framework presented in this book. Even if at a small-scale, this *praxis*-driven framework provided teacher–participants with the tools to generate constructive alignment of *languaculture* curriculum content, pedagogy and assessment within the context of their own subjects and programmes. As discussed in previous chapters, this framework was never conceived as a ready-made solution for the theory/practice divide in language and culture pedagogy. Rather, I envisaged this framework as a blueprint to provide a systematic account of the elements that can support the meeting of the two.

The largely exploratory, descriptive nature of this framework is thus not fortuitous. I argue that future empirical research in this area should avoid falling in to the trap of prescribing, striving instead to retain balance between the competing and often conflicting forces of structure and freedom. That is, at one end, providing practitioners with explicit and coherent structural guidelines to maximise the chance of achieving the goals sought in language and culture pedagogy. At the other end, providing the freedom and flexibility for them to make the difficult pedagogical choices in adapting such guidelines to their own educational environment. This tension notwithstanding, the efforts to provide such a curriculum development framework are vital if we are to help each other make informed and deliberate choices that best enable us to address the demands of our broadened educational mission.

Conclusion

This chapter focused on how to ensure that innovations brought about by the need to bridge the theory/practice gap are sustained over time through active dissemination and systematic and systemic embedding. The mechanisms identified through the literature and partially exemplified through the current investigation aimed to provide guidance to all stakeholders involved in promoting innovation. While emphasis was placed on the paramount role of language and culture teachers as curriculum innovators an overall 'transformative intellectuals', the discussion also highlighted the need for HEIs to provide 'environments that both stimulate innovatory practices and facilitate change' (Smith, 2012: 178).

Here the literature highlighted the benefits of bottom-up processes of professional development rooted in concerted, active collaboration. In this context, the creation of communities of practice emerged as a suitable strategy for effective embedding of innovation and the type of contributions the field and the sector so urgently need. As the discussion makes plain, there is indeed a sense of urgency for the field to ensure effective embedding of innovation, both at discipline and institutional levels, locally and internationally. Indeed, at international level, similar forces are at work in shaping foreign language teaching, particularly in the United States, Australia and England. Theorists and practitioners should thus capitalise on these similarities by promoting creation of analogous policy frameworks that may support alignment of intercultural graduate outcomes through institution-wide curriculum reform.

In order to achieve sustainable innovation in practice as well as theory, theorists (i.e. linguists and applied linguists) and practitioners (i.e. teachers, teacher trainers and curriculum designers) as well as other stakeholders involved (i.e. policy makers and university leaders) need to accept and embrace the inherent complexities of the current educational landscape. As knowledge producers and life-long learners themselves, theorists and practitioners need to consider both top-down and bottom-up perspectives on the structural and logistical features of an increasingly internationalised higher education sectors. These perspectives may provide not only limitations but also opportunities for creatively implementing and embedding innovation in the field of language and culture pedagogy.

Conclusion: Prospects for a Field in Transition

It is undeniable. Profound changes over the last few decades are still reshaping, redefining and reconfiguring the way we communicate across languages and cultures across and within national borders. The unprecedented rise in population mobility and the ubiquitous availability of instant international communication fuel the ever-increasing frequency of intercultural encounters in everyday life. The pace of these global changes is paralleled by the energy that many people devote to keeping up with them.

This energy seems to be driven by opposing yet complementary forces: the need to respond to an increasingly globalised context against locally and nationally contextualised priorities; the demand for immediate solutions against the more deliberate pace of conceptual developments; and the need to generate comparable results against a concern about homogenisation. The dynamic interplay of these conflicting forces has served to complicate rather than reconcile the tension between what is advocated in theory and what is manifested in practice.

As we have explored throughout this book, these observations resonate strongly within the field of foreign language teaching in the context of higher education. Two specific changes have been singled out here: first, the unrelenting processes of internationalisation of higher education (HE), and second, the intercultural turn in the field of language education. These changes or shifts in the way we think about HE and language education in general have emerged concomitantly and, to a certain extent, synergistically. They point largely to the same overarching goal: the need to develop students' ability to function in an increasingly globalised world that requires them to convey, negotiate and critically interpret meanings across languages and cultures for effective communication.

This final chapter revisits the aims and scope of this investigation and outlines its main findings presented over the preceding chapters. It discusses the implications of this investigation for language and culture pedagogy, and for the overarching HE sector where this pedagogy can beneficially be put into practice. These implications in turn shine a light on the paths for emerging research agendas that will further develop understanding of *languaculture* conceptually and in practice. By improving the ability of foreign-language teachers and learners to teach and learn about the language–culture nexus, *languaculture* will serve to enhance effective communication across languages and cultures while our shared need for this has never been greater.

Aims Revisited

Two specific aims motivated my investigation. The first was to *understand* the reasons behind the pervasive discrepancy between 'ends' and 'means', theory and practice in language and culture pedagogy, particularly, within the HE context. The second was to *identify* ways to address this discrepancy, particularly through avenues that may help university language teachers bridge the theory/practice gap, and in so doing, point towards paths of viable, sustainable curricular innovation that may lead to the development of interculturally competent graduates. As a result, the scope of this study had two trajectories. First, the study focused on critically re-examining discrepancies between the expected goals of languages education in relation to culture learning and the teaching approaches and practices in place to achieve them. Second, it focused on empirically examining curriculum development and implementation strategies of university language teachers to address these discrepancies.

These aims were respectively addressed in Part 1 and Part 2 of the book. In Part 1, this investigation began by problematising the seemingly unbridgeable gap between theory and practice in language and culture pedagogy within the internationalised HE context. I identified the complex web of elements responsible for this gap and systematically untangled them to explore their connections and impact on one another. In doing so, I was able to turn theoretical and practical limitations or 'stumbling blocks' into the 'building blocks' that may support the enactment of more coherent teaching practices aimed to develop interculturally competent graduates. This led to articulating and formalising a curriculum development framework aimed to foster what I have termed 'critical *languaculture* awareness'. This framework was subsequently implemented through four consistent curriculum innovation projects conducted in four language subjects within two language programmes (Chinese and Italian) at an Australian university. These projects and corresponding findings were explored in detail in Part 2 of this book.

In Part 3, I presented a synthesis of the findings from this empirical work and on this basis re-envisioned the framework as a *praxis*-driven tool to support sustainable innovation. In so doing, I also considered a number of implications for the main audience of this investigation: university language teachers like myself. I discussed the re-envisioning of our role and practices in light of what may be considered a 'critical' turn in the field. Finally, I formulated a call to action for universities around the world to re-examine current conceptualisations of intercultural graduate attributes. I argued that in re-examining these conceptualisations, efforts should be made to acknowledge the central role of language learning as a meaning-making process for knowledge production and reproduction, and above all, as a tool to facilitate and promote transformative, critical self-reflection and the ongoing destabilising and restabilising of our *languaculture* schemas.

Overall, since the focal context of this investigation was language programmes at university level, this investigation brought to the fore adult learning in terms of both the teacher–participants and the student–participants in my empirical investigation. In terms of the teacher–participants, this investigation shed light on the under-researched area of continuing professional development for university language teachers and their own development of critical *languaculture* awareness. As concerns the student–participants, this investigation contributed to the exploration of adult learners' intercultural language learning processes.

Implications for Language and Culture Pedagogy

From the time this investigation was conceptualised and as it was being implemented, some concurrent studies were being carried out that coincide with several underlying views presented in this book. These studies, published in recent years, (*cf.* Houghton, 2012; Houghton & Yamada, 2012; Johnston *et al.*, 2011; Lee *et al.*, 2012; Levine & Phipps, 2012; Tsai & Houghton, 2010), largely support and complement various aspects of this book, which I hope contributes and actively engages with the dialogue they collectively inspire.

While several implications for the field of language education have been explored widely in preceding chapters, here I would like to synthesise these into two main areas and relate them to emerging research in the field. First is the need to revisit the ultimate goal for languages education. As I discussed in Chapter 1, focus on 'intercultural competence' (IC) has largely eclipsed its overarching intercultural communicative competence (ICC) model. Yet, despite widespread agreement on its central role in language education, IC remains a largely problematic construct. Indeed, the limitations outlined in this book clearly point to the need to reconsider the role of IC in the field of language education, which is itself undergoing deep transformation.

Undoubtedly, the presence of IC will remain a cornerstone in the field of language pedagogy. Its contribution to the way language and culture pedagogy has evolved in the last few decades cannot be ignored. Its rhetorical appeal also will continue to be relevant as we advance into a 21st century of evermore complex communication. However, its reified, almost tokenistic use, together with inconsistent ontological and epistemological applications in research designs cast doubt upon its reliability. In light of the current progressive shift towards a 'critical' stance in relation to language and culture pedagogy, the development of learners' 'criticality' emerges as a feasible alternative, particularly in the context of adult education.

In this investigation, students' development of 'criticality' focused on the exploration of *languacultures*. This exploration, however, was largely limited to specific aspects of this conceptual framework – its semantic and pragmatic dimensions in particular – owing to the contextual constraints of each case study. However, future research may focus more specifically on the identity dimension of *languaculture* to dig deeper into *languacultural* ideologies and power struggles relevant to minority *languacultures* as well as *categorisation* and discrimination based on *languacultures*.

As such, a focus on 'criticality' helps us move away from the definitional and operational uncertainties inherent to 'competence' in order to consider a type of learning goal that can be transversally applied across disciplines. Let me forestall here possible objections to this argument by acknowledging some points. Criticality is also a contentious concept. Comprehensive examination by Johnston *et al.* (2011) of 'criticality' in the literature across many disciplines attests to this. However, in the context of HE, and particularly given the internationalisation of graduate outcomes, it presents attractively. While the development of language learners' 'criticality' requires further research, continuing to think critically about this concept, as well as about IC, takes us to the very level of iterative metacriticality at the core of the language and culture learning process.

At an overarching level, 'criticality' serves as a conductive thread weaving together the previously mentioned works and the current investigation. This focus on criticality is also significant. It is evidence of an emerging shift in language and culture pedagogy, a shift or, as Dasli (2011a) labels it, a 'moment' that she defines as *critical intercultural language pedagogy*. According to Dasli (2011a, 2011b), this shift hinges on reassessment of 'what it means to live interculturally on the threshold of the twenty-first century' (Dasli, 2011a: 33). She explains that this shift brings to the fore 'questions of cultural identity by sensitising learners to the various limitations that dominant ideologies bring to intercultural *praxis* within the context of education for cosmopolitan citizenship' (Dasli, 2011a: 22). Here, the emphasis on *critical pedagogy* brings into play educational theories and philosophies (Dewey, 1933, 1938; Freire, 1970, 1973; Giroux, 1988; Guilherme, 2002) that have been gradually driving this paradigmatic shift in the field of language education. In turn, these theories and philosophies also weave into the type of classroom inquiry advocated by action research. This type of inquiry is underpinned by what Guilherme (2002) describes as:

> [A] reflective, exploratory, dialogic and active stance towards cultural knowledge and life that allows for dissonance, contradiction and conflict as well as consensus, concurrence, and transformation. It is a cognitive and emotional endeavour that aims at individual and collective emancipation, social justice, and political commitment. (Guilherme, 2002: 219)

As a direct corollary, we have a second set of implications concerned with language teachers' call to action in the current educational landscape. This call to action is eloquently encapsulated by Levine and Phipps as a 'continued commitment to deep reflection and analysis, a continued critique of the *status quo* and a willingness to work carefully and with compassion' (Levine & Phipps, 2012: 232), and I would add, collaboratively, to re-envisage the theory/practice gap as *praxis*-driven understandings of our work. This process is what Houghton describes as 'throwing a loop from theoretically driven practice back to theory itself with a view to illuminating both in new ways that prove useful to theorists and practitioners alike' (Houghton, 2012: 74). Only through this continued commitment will we be able to overcome the serious obstacles preventing us from creating the type of internal consistency the field so urgently needs.

Indeed, as Byrnes incisively observes, the 'inconsistencies, discontinuities and even contradictions' embedded in the field have ultimately resulted in 'a reduced sense of purpose, accomplishment and sense of community, along with reduced external persuasive power regarding the value of humanities education in contemporary higher education' (Byrnes, 2013: 17–18). Byrnes argues that foreign language teaching as a discipline needs to reassess its foundational educational philosophies to generate coherence and, in so doing, remove the 'obstacles to the accumulation of research-based effective educational practice' (Byrnes, 2013: 18).

Thus, in order for this continued commitment to be enacted and coherently articulated within the language and culture teaching profession as a whole, it is necessary to provide strong scaffolding strategies. As Levine and Phipps observe 'new reflective embodiments of theories in practice (or *praxis*, as Freire defined it) are fragile things unless nourished structurally' (Levine & Phipps, 2012: 229). The type of trial and error they encourage for the individual classroom resonates with the collaborative nature of case studies underpinning this investigation.

This investigation brought teacher–researcher collaboration to the foreground of the research design, thus highlighting our paramount role as curriculum developers and potential agents of educational innovation. As such, from a methodological perspective, we can see a recurrent focus on the teacher–researcher and the use of action research as an increasingly prevalent mode of inquiry. This is not coincidental. Action research, individual and collaborative or participatory, is at the heart of critically re-examining our practices and of promoting sustainable ongoing professional development. Future research agendas may thus continue to focus on teachers but engage in longitudinal study of their practices. A teacher-focused longitudinal study underpinned by a participatory action research design may shed valuable light on the various processes of professional development that emerge from the iterative cycles of inquiry.

Notably, in the Australian compulsory education sector (primary and secondary school contexts) this type of 'investigative stance' towards understanding classroom practice has become a cornerstone in the way the profession is conceptualised (Crichton, 2008). Nevertheless, the lack of articulation between compulsory and non-compulsory education sectors has meant that this stance is largely undermined. As discussed in Chapter 5, higher education institutions (HEIs) around the world are placing increased emphasis on the Scholarship of Teaching for both professional development and the development of curriculum innovation. Australian HEIs are not the exception. However, when it comes to foreign language education, less emphasis is being placed on narrowing the gaps between compulsory and non-compulsory language education. Indeed, from an organisational perspective, there are a number of issues that need to be addressed. Among these, the most salient being the lack of connection between the training of pre-service teachers at university level. This training entails a two-pronged process. On the one hand the inclusion teacher education content that addresses intercultural language teaching practices in a post-method era and the development of an 'investigative stance' throughout their pre-service education. On the other hand, and perhaps an even more difficult challenge to address, is assisting in-service teachers (at university and primary and secondary schools) to articulate and integrate intercultural teaching practices to transcend the 'rather mechanistic, instrumental approach to its coverage in second languages [...] [as] a bolt-on element in the curriculum, sitting somewhat outside of the main activities of language teaching' (Woodgate-Jones & Grenfell, 2012: 342). I argue that this lack of articulation between what is expected once languages teachers begin their practice and what is provided to them during their education and training is one of the major obstacles that remains to be addressed in order to bridge the gap between policy and practice. Building bridges between educational contexts puts us in a better position to respond to the needs of a changing professional paradigm (Allen & Maxim, 2013).

Additional emerging research agendas concern specific aspects of the research design. At least two paths are evident for future research designs. One is selection of a larger sample of subjects within a language faculty across a larger number of language programmes; the other is selection of a larger number of subjects within a given language programme. Future research designs may also consider long-term engagement with participants. Here the options may vary in terms of focus and scope.

Future research may focus on the development of data collection tools to explore the transformative theory of adult learning used in this investigation and involved in 'perspective transformation' processes. In addition to teaching practices, the findings suggested that teachers' own level of critical *languaculture* awareness may be a relevant variable worth investigating. If so, inclusion of additional data collection tools, such as teachers' reflective journals, may provide further insights into their reflective processes. Alternatively, bringing the learner variable to the foreground may also present a significant contribution to the field. Future researchers may thus shift their focus to the development of learners' 'critical *languaculture* awareness' and, in so doing, engage in long-term examination of perspective transformation processes. A learner-focused longitudinal study on the development of different levels of 'critical *languaculture* awareness', for instance, may enable delineation of a path for learners' life-long journey to becoming increasingly aware of the *languaculture* dimension in communication.

Finally, future research agendas may also be concerned with innovating specific elements of the curriculum. This investigation looked at the curriculum as a whole, however, focusing on specific elements, such as the materials and tasks that may have useful input to promoting 'cognitive dissonance' and by leading to 'perspective transformation', can make a significant contribution to the present under-endowment of material.

Implications for the HE Sector

As Cañado contends, 'the time is ripe for a necessary reorientation in tertiary language education worldwide' (Cañado, 2010: 408). Progress toward a view of internationalisation and interculturally competent graduates that acknowledges languages' central role in knowledge production and reproduction largely hinges on a shift in the organisational philosophy of the HE sector (Eisenchlas *et al.*, 2003; Lee *et al.*, 2012). This shift should play a key role in creating structural alignment between universities' mission statements, curriculum goals and everyday teaching practices. Such a shift would entail reconceptualising the meanings and values underlying what it actually means to be an interculturally competent speaker in today's globalised world and, ultimately, to 'communicate effectively across human difference' (Lee *et al.*, 2012: 103). From the discussion developed throughout the book, together with the empirical findings yielded by this investigation and emerging research in the area, there are three clear sets of implications that seem to be channelling this shift.

The first set of implications concerns avoiding the piecemeal development of interculturally competent graduates, particularly within internationalisation rhetoric. To create structural alignment of intercultural graduate goals and their enactment in practice, HEIs around the world need to move from isolated, compartmentalised strategies to more comprehensive, integrative, institution-wide strategies that can support the 'systemic transformation' (Lee *et al.*, 2012) of the institution *vis-à-vis* its commitment to 'improving student preparedness for an internationalised world' (Egron-Polak & Hudson, 2010). Indeed, while excellent initiatives continue to emerge in various disciplines and programmes of study (e.g. medicine, engineering and business), concerted efforts are needed at the cross-disciplinary, institution-wide level to enable curriculum reform (*cf.* Leask, 2013; Vidovich *et al.*, 2011).

This can be achieved only through the systematic embedding of strategies across the curriculum and across disciplines to support interculturally inclusive practices and overall engagement with diversity (Lee *et al.*, 2012). These strategies mirror the institutional building blocks discussed in this book. They are: (1) mapping the sequential, incremental, and at the same time, iterative progression of learning goals that may lead to the achievement of interculturally competent graduates throughout a programme of studies; (2) intentionally prioritising their integration in the curriculum both vertically and horizontally, across programmes and disciplines; and (3) purposefully ensuring their enactment in a variety of learning contexts inside and outside the classroom. Above all is the strategy of promoting and scaffolding teachers' adoption of a critical reflective stance towards rationalising and enacting these goals.

Here, foreign language education offers a unique milieu for bringing these strategies to fruition. Indeed, as Dlaska (2012) highlights, 'language programmes attract a mix of home and international students from all disciplines and engage them in learning dialogues relevant to mobile learners and future global citizens' (Dlaska, 2012: 2). This is true for HEIs around the world. As I have discussed in preceding chapters providing the rationalisation of theoretical and pedagogical building blocks proposed in this book, language programmes offer a unique opportunity to support and advance the coherent development of interculturally competent graduates and thus, of institution-wide re-envisioned internationalisation processes.

This crystallises the second set of implications for HEIs: making concerted efforts to embed strategies that may support language studies across disciplines, degrees and curricula. While this lies beyond the scope of my investigation, it is supported by a growing body of research urging HEIs to consider the vital role of languages in promoting internationalisation processes (cf. Byram, 2012b; Cañado, 2010; Dlaska, 2012; Trevaskes et al., 2003). Here, in light of the critical turn described earlier, the role of foreign language education should be considered beyond the instrumentalist notion of language as a commodity. Instead, its role should be re-envisioned as a medium for engaging critically in meaning-making processes that can illuminate and enhance communication 'across human difference'.

Committing to reconceptualising intercultural goals in this light necessarily requires the development of supporting policy frameworks. In the currently internationalised HE scenario, such frameworks will most likely be driven by quality assurance (QA) mechanisms. This is the subject of the third and final set of implications for the HE sector. Here the main task for HEIs is extending QA efforts beyond the current focus on providing English language learning. This is particularly true for the Australian context (cf. Burdett & Crossman, 2012; Lane, 2011; Lane, 2012). Considering QA initiatives such as the Language Network for Quality Assurance (LanQua) project for languages other than English is likely to boost critical engagement in teaching practices and enhance the enactment of coherent practices.

While QA processes remain contested practices that lie beyond the scope of this investigation, they invoke issues of accountability that are at the core of curriculum alignment advocated in this book. From this perspective, QA can indeed be considered at many levels within the HE context: internal, external, top-down, bottom-up and so forth. Returning to the focus on the teacher, the type of professional development advocated throughout the book supports and integrally complements the notion of internal QA. Accountability also concerns the alignment of practices with HEI's espoused graduate outcomes. The increasingly regulated, internationalised HE sector is required to explicitly rationalise its academic practices, share information on quality standards and identify trends in QA. It is expected that HE institutions will promote international cooperation to enhance comparability and compatibility of programmes of study, transparency and transferability of grades, and learning outcomes that will facilitate implementation of other internationalisation activities, such as student mobility and offshore delivery. Foreign language teaching is no exception.

Today we have easy accessibility of national, other government and intergovernmental reports, communiqués and formal reviews from around the world, as well as numerous academic publications concerning the analogous limitations and possibilities for languages in HEIs around the world. The time appears ripe to start unifying efforts and collaborating to establish a shared global system of quality assurance that may help promote international cooperation and enhance the academic quality of language teaching in HE. Initiatives promoting QA dialogue between and among HEIs around the globe are already underway in many disciplinary areas. Foreign language education should follow suit.

Concluding Remarks

This investigation was motivated by my desire to 'make sense' of a complex educational landscape rife with discrepancies and to find innovative ways to address them. I contend that innovations brought about by the need to further develop the critical *languaculture* dimension of the curriculum will drive future pedagogical debates and teaching practices in the field of languages education. Furthermore, as the imperative to produce interculturally competent citizens strengthens further, frameworks such as the one I have articulated in this study will become ever more relevant and valuable for the future of nations and their citizenry as a whole. In this context, the need to reconceptualise the role of language from its usual ancillary position to its central role in knowledge production and reproduction will become ever more crucial.

The opposing yet complementary forces explored throughout the book become catalysts of change, innovation and growth. As *languaculture* teachers, *praxis*-driven curriculum innovators and overall *transformative intellectuals*, we need to push forward with our commitment to this change, innovation and growth. We can use it to shape the future of, not only the field and our learners, but also of the societies in which we live, where we seek to communicate effectively with others for our common benefit. The responsibility for action is ours, for as renowned Uruguayan journalist, writer and novelist Eduardo Galeano presciently observed, *'At the end of the day, we are what we do to change who we are'*.

Appendix 1: Case Study A: *Languaculture* Workshop Presentation in Italian Culture Context Subject

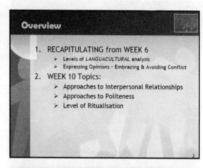

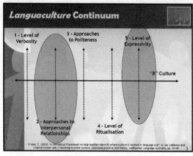

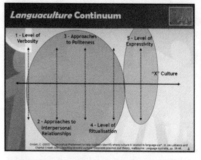

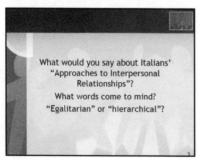

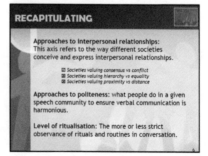

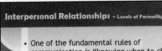

Interpersonal Relationships – Levels of Formality

- One of the fundamental rules of communication is "knowing when to change attire" (*sapersi cambiare d'abito*).
- Therefore, it is important to know which "attire" to wear in which context - *ad ogni contesto, l'abito giusto*.
- Transgression of these rules can lead to miscommunication or complete communication breakdown.

(p. 82)

7

Terms of Address

- Whenever speakers of Italian wish to address one another, they are immediately confronted with a decision: whether to use formal or informal terms of address. (Musumeci, 1991, p. 434)
  - What factors affect their choice?
  - How do they make the transition from formality to informality?

8

Research-based trends (Musumeci, 1991)

- Reciprocal and non-reciprocal use is highly context-based.
- Subjects' comments:
  - Subject (North, rural): "Snobs always use *Lei*. *Lei* is impersonal: you use it more in the city; *in paese* you use *tu*."
  - Subject (South, rural): "*Lei* keeps a distance between you and the other person. When I want to stay by myself I keep using *Lei*, never switch [to *tu*], and people finally leave me alone."
  - Subject (South, urban): "If I don't know which to use, I use *voi*."
- "*Tu* vs *Lei*" becoming egalitarian or extending the meaning of the pronouns?

9

Terms of Address, titles and other formulas

- Do you know any titles in Italian?
- Have you ever used them?
- Do you use titles in English?

10

The Italian Perspective on "mate"

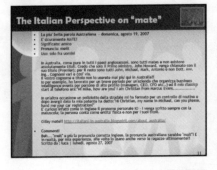

11

DISCUSSION

- What do you think about Sobrero's definition of "hypocritical informality" (Sobrero cited in Carroli, et. al.,p. 183)?

- Have you ever experienced misunderstandings based on different "Approaches to interpersonal relationships"? How did you react? Why?

- How do these levels of analysis help you conceptualise differences and similarities between the *languacultures* of Italian speakers and your own?

12

Appendix 2: Case Study B: Italian Language Subject Sample Lesson Plan

Italian Language Course - WEEK 2
INTERVENTION 1 (30 minuti)

Aims:
1. To discuss Italian Levels of Politeness and Approaches to Interpersonal Relationships in relation to "formal & informal" register in contemporary standard Italian.
2. Development of "basic awareness" skills (identification/comparison).
3. Development of "meta-awareness" skills (challenging/questioning stereotypes).

Materials:
- PPT – Language & Culture
- DVD – Italia Contemporanea
- OHT with Comprehension questions
- Handout with the transcription of the DVD dialogue.
- Handout – DISCOVERY SHEET
- Handout – Assigned reading

1-   The relationship between Language & Culture (5-10 minutes)
- Tutor will present a brief and general introduction to the course's conceptualisation of the intertwined relationship between language and culture and how it may be reflected in interaction.

2-   Exploring register (20 minutes)
- **TC – MOTIVAZIONE (Warm-up)** – Use of formal & informal with the CM.
- What have we learnt in previous years of study about the use of formal and informal?
- Why do you think it is important to explore this aspect of communication?
- **TC – GLOBALITÀ (Presentation)** - Teacher introduces this aspect by presenting the DVD – Italia Contemporanea – Chapter 20 – Segment 6 – Time 1:20:34.
- Context: two actors discuss the current situation regarding the use of formal and informal pronouns and corresponding expressions in contemporary Italian.
- Students watch the DVD for general comprehension and discuss the content with a partner.
- In a centralised way the teacher asks students regarding the speakers' opinions on the rules for the formal & informal.

COMPREHENSION QUESTIONS:
- According to the two actors:
- What are the aspects that affect the choice of tu/lei?
- What about the use of the formal form to maintain distance? (Strategic use)
- What does the lady say is an indication that someone is getting old?
- The teacher distributes a handout with a transcription of the dialogue. (Square brackets indicate places where the two speakers are talking at the same time).
- Teacher checks the meaning of new vocabulary.
- Teacher asks students about any other aspects observed in the video (gestures, interjections, etc.)

- **TC - ANALISI – (Practice) ACTIVITY SHEET – 'Formale & Informale'**
- Students are asked to order the utterances according to levels of formality.
- The teacher discusses Italy's contemporary situation, from a more structured class society (which is also mentioned in the DVD) where social divide was significant and clearly reflected in the language, to a more flexible "egalitarian" society where egalitarianism has become politically correct and distance between people tend to diminish.
- If time runs out students will be asked to complete this exercise for homework.
- The teacher reminds students that this activity will be followed-up in the tutorial with specific activities on the linguistic component of "formal & informal" registers.
  (The SINTESI /Production Stage section will be completed in the TUTORIAL)
- **RIFLESSIONE:** Students to complete a DISCOVERY SHEET (10 minutes)
- If time runs out in class, this document will be available on *blackboard* to be handed it at the following class.

NEXT ACTIVITY'S TOPIC: WEEK 5 in preparation for the Second Meeting with the CM.
- The next activity will be based on the assigned reading, which will be discussed in class.
- ASSIGNED READINGS for WEEK 5 – (Remind students to read the assigned reading material as soon as possible, as it is useful for all the meetings).
- Carroli, Piera; Pavone, Adriana & Tudini, Vincenza (2003) "Face Value: teaching Italian verbal and social-cultural interaction". In Joe LoBianco and Chantal Crozet (eds.) *Teaching invisible culture: classroom practice and theory*, Melbourne: Language Australia.

CODE: TC = Teacher Centred task.

Appendix 3: Case Study B: *Languaculture* Workshop Presentation in Italian Language Subject

---

La comunicazione non-verbale & il silenzio

WEEK 7

Il Codice Cinesico

- In ogni interazione "faccia a faccia" il messaggio orale viene in qualche modo completato dai movimenti del corpo (non-verbali) che possono *rafforzare* o *conferire* significati aggiuntivi alle parole a cui si accompagnano.
- Si parla in questo caso di "codice cinetico" (dal greco kynesis = movimento) e ci si riferisce in particolare:
  - all'espressione del volto,
  - agli sguardi,
  - alla postura del corpo,
  - al contatto fisico fra gli interlocutori (haptics),
  - <u>alla gestualità.</u>

Covered in "Approaches to Interpersonal Relationships" - Kinesic Behaviour - Gestures (and posture) particular facial expressions, eye contact and gaze - pp 180-182- Handout WEEK 2

Avete notato se i vostri CM utilizzano/fanno dei gesti durante i vostri incontri?

Quali sono i gesti italiani più comuni?

Quando si usano i gesti?

- Quando si vuole esprimere qualcosa difficile da tradurre a parole (pensate agli insulti o al gesto che in Italia indica che qualcuno è "cornuto");
- Quando si vuole trasmettere un concetto più rapidamente senza ricorrere a una lunga spiegazione (pensate agli insulti o agli apprezzamenti per strada);
- Quando ci sono impedimenti fisici che possono limitare l'uso della voce (distanza fra gli interlocutori, comunicazione attraverso un vetro).

Levels of Verbosity - Il Silenzio

- "Findings tend to confirm that Italians generally avoid silence in conversation, as they *value* a flowing, lively conversation."
- "Turn-taking rules in Italian conversation do not allow for silent pauses which are *perceived* as a lack of interest in the subject or an inability to carry a conversation."
- "It is not [*considered*] rude, for example, not to wait for one's turn when speaking (...) so that voices overlap and get louder and louder."

Covered in "Importance placed on speaking" - Level of Verbosity - Silence - pp 179-180- Handout WEEK 2

Durante I vostri incontri...

Ci sono delle "pause vuote"?
Ci sono delle "pause piene"?
(Uso di "fillers")
Ci sono degli "accavallamenti"?

Appendix 4: Case Study C: Chinese Language Subject

WEEK IV LANGUACULTURE DISCUSSION

Overview

- Recap from WEEK 3
  - Approaches to "Chinese Politeness"
    - Lǐmào 礼貌 & kèqi 客气
- WEEK 4 – Topics
  1. Making an offer/invitation (pp. 86-88)
  2. Paying after dinner (p. 88)

Making an offer/invitation (pp. 86-88)

shìbùguòsān
事不过 三

Only if an invitation is rejected three times can one be sure that the invitation/rejection is genuine.

What do you think?
Have you had this experience?

Would you like a coke?

甲：喝点儿可乐！
A: Drink a bit of coke

乙：我不渴，你不用客气！
B: I'm not thirsty. You don't need to be polite.

甲：喝点儿吧！
A: Have it please!

乙：我真 不渴。
B: I'm really not thirsty。

甲：看你，怎么那么客气！
A: How come you are so polite?

乙：那好吧，谢谢了。
B: Ok, thank you.

Dinner Invitations

- Inviting people to eat is an important element in Chinese culture
  请客吃饭，是 中 国 文 化 先 朋 的一 道风景线
- Relevance in the business world
- Host responsibility — 吃好喝好 Eat well, drink well.
- Guest responsibility – Leave some food/drink unfinished
- Sharing a meal 大家坐在一起吃个饭就都是自己人了
  "Now that you are one of us, we can talk about anything"

Paying for Dinner (p. 88)

- "A favourite Chinese sport is fighting over the bill."
- Whoever initiates the invitation pays the bill.
- However, "it's considered polite to offer to pay once, or even twice, even if you are clearly the guest. Protests may be made loudly to show sincerity, even when it's a bluff." You can say jokingly:

"You invited, but I pay"

nǐqǐngkè wǒfùqián
你 请 客，我 付 钱

Reciprocity

- Repay the favour by returning the invitation.

回 请

- The rule here is: "it's not polite to receive without giving something back."

yǒu lái wú wǎng fēi lǐ yě
有来无 往 非礼也

- Principle of reciprocity: 报bào

DISCUSSION

- Were you ever made aware (by friends, language exchange partner, your teacher, etc.) of these rules of politeness regarding invitations and offers?

- Have you ever been in these situations?

- How would you deal with situations in which miscommunication may be caused by such differences?

- Do you see yourself ever adopting these Chinese rules of politeness? Why? Why not?

Appendix 5: Case Study D: Discovery Page

Discovery Page

Student's Name:

Date:

What did you learn today about the way *languaculture* is reflected in intercultural encounters?

_____

_____

_____

_____

_____

What did you learn today about <u>interpreting</u> miscommunication in intercultural encounters?

_____

_____

_____

_____

_____

What did you learn about <u>negotiating</u> meaning in intercultural encounters?

_____

_____

_____

_____

_____

How are you going to apply what you learnt in today's lesson outside the classroom?

1. _____

2. _____

3. _____

4. _____

5. _____

What would you like to explore in future *languaculture* sessions?

_____

_____

_____

References

AACU and National Leadership Council (2007) *College Learning for the New Global Century: A Report from the National Leadership Council for Liberal Education & America's Promise.* Washington, DC: Association of American Colleges and Universities.

ACTFL (2006) *Standards for Foreign Language Learning in the 21st Century* (3rd edn). Yonkers, NY: National Standards in Foreign Language Education Project.

ADFL (2012) *Association of Departments of Foreign Languages (ADFL) – Guidelines and Policy Documents,* accessed 28 May 2012. http://www.adfl.org/resources/index.htm

Agar, M. (1994) *Language Shock: Understanding the Culture of Conversation.* New York: Perennial.

AITSL (2011) National Professional Standards for Teachers.

Allen, H.W. and Maxim, H.H. (eds) (2013) *Educating the Future Foreign Language Professoriate for the 21st Century.* Boston, MA: Heinle Cengage Learning.

Allen, J.P.B. (1984) General-purpose language teaching: A variable focus approach. In C. Brumfit (ed.) *General English Syllabus Design: Curriculum and Syllabus Design for the General English Classroom* (pp. 61–74). Oxford: Pergamon Press, in association with the British Council.

Amundsen, C. and Wilson, M. (2012) Are we asking the right questions? *Review of Educational Research* 82 (1), 90–126.

Anderson, L.W. and Krathwohl, D.R. (2001) *A Taxonomy for Learning, Teaching, and Assessing: A Revision of Bloom's Taxonomy of Educational Objectives.* New York: Longman.

Arabski, J. and Wojtaszek, A. (eds) (2011) *Aspects of Culture in Second Language Acquisition and Foreign Language Learning.* Berlin Heidelberg: Springer.

AUQA. (2009) *Good Practice Principles for English Language Proficiency for International Students in Australian Universities.* Canberra, ACT: Department of Education, Employment and Workplace Relations.

Bachman, L. (1990) *Fundamental Considerations in Language Testing.* Oxford: Oxford University Press.

Bandura, A. (1986) *Social Foundations of Thought and Action: A Social Cognitive Theory.* Englewood Cliffs, NJ: Prentice Hall.

Barnett, R. (1997) *Higher Education: A Critical Business.* Buckingham, UK: Bristol, PA Society for Research into Higher Education & Open University Press.

Bawden, A. (2007) Chattering classes. *The Guardian,* accessed 23 March 2010. http://www.guardian.co.uk/education/2007/mar/13/highereducation.cutsandclosures

Béal, C. (1992) Did you have a good week-end? Or why there is no such thing as a simple question in cross-cultural encounters. *Australian Review of Applied Linguistics* 15 (1), 23–52.

Belz, J. (2003) Linguistic perspectives on the development of intercultural compentence in telecollaboration. *Language Learning & Technology* 7 (2), 68–117.

Belz, J. and Mueller-Hartmann, A. (2003) Teachers as intercultural learners: Negotiating German–American telecollaboration along the institutional faultline. *Modern Language Journal* 87 (1), 71–89.

Belz, J. and Thorne, S.L. (eds) (2006) *Internet-Mediated Intercultural Foreign Language Education*. Boston: Heinle and Heinle.

Bennett, M.J. (1986) Towards ethnorelativism: A developmental model of intercultural sensitivity. In R.M. Paige (ed.) *Cross-cultural Orientation: New Conceptualizations and Applications* (pp. 27–70). NewYork: University Press of America.

Bennett, M.J. (1993) Towards ethnorelativism: A developmental model of intercultural sensitivity. In R.M. Paige (ed.) *Education for the Intercultural Experience* (pp. 21–71). Yarmouth, ME: Intercultural Press.

Bennett, M.J. (1998) *Basic Concepts of Intercultural Communication: Selected Readings*. Yarmouth, ME: Intercultural Press.

Bergan, S. and van't Land, H. (2010) *Speaking Across Borders: The Role of Higher Education in Furthering Intercultural Dialogue*. Strasbourg: Council of Europe Pub.

Bernhard, A. (2012a) *Quality Assurance in an International Higher Education Area a Case Study Approach and Comparative Analysis*. Wiesbaden: VS Research.

Bernhard, A. (2012b) Quality assurance in an international higher education area: A summary of a case-study approach and comparative analysis. *Tertiary Education and Management* 18 (2), 153–169.

Bialystok, E. (1993) Symbolic representation and attentional control in pragmatic competence. In G. Kasper and S. Blum-Kulka (eds) *Interlanguage Pragmatics* (pp. 42–57). New York: Oxford University Press.

Bloom, B.S. (ed.) (1956) *Taxonomy of Educational Objectives: The Classification of Educational Goals*. New York, Toronto: Longmans, Green.

Blum-Kulka, S. (1982) Learning to say what you mean in a second language: A study of speech act performance of learners of Hebrew as a second language. *Applied Linguistics* 3 (1), 29–59.

Bolden, R., Petrov, G. and Gosling, J. (2009) Distributed leadership in higher education. *Educational Management Administration & Leadership* 37 (2), 257–277.

Bourn, D. (2010) Studens as global citizens. In E. Jones (ed.) *Internationalisation and the Student Voice: Higher Education Perspectives* (pp. 18–29). New York: Routledge.

Brick, J. (2005) *China: A Handbook in Intercultural Communication* (2nd edn). Sydney: National Centre for English Language and Teaching Research.

Brooks, N. (1968) Teaching culture in the foreign language classroom. *Foreign Language Annals* 1 (3), 204–217.

Broughton, J. (1977) "Beyond formal operations": Theoretical thought in adolescence. *Teachers College Record* 79 (1), 87–97.

Brown, H.D. (1980) Learning a second culture. In J.M. Valdes (ed.) *Culture Bound: Bridging the Cultural Gap in Language Teaching* (pp. 33–48). Cambridge: Cambridge University Press.

Brumfit, C., Myles, F., Mitchell, R., Johnston, B. and Ford, P. (2005) Language study in higher education and the development of criticality. *International Journal of Applied Linguistics* 15 (2), 145–168.

Bruner, J. (1960) *The Process of Education*. Cambridge, MA: Harvard University Press.

Bruner, J. (1996) *The Culture of Education*. Cambridge, MA: Harvard University Press.

Burdett, J. and Crossman, J. (2012) Engaging international students: An analysis of the Australian Universities Quality Agency (AUQA) reports. *Quality Assurance in Education* 20 (3), 207–222.

Buttjes, D. and Byram, M. (1991) *Mediating Languages and Cultures: Towards an Intercultural Theory of Foreign Language Education*. Clevedon: Multilingual Matters.

Byram, M. (1989) *Cultural Studies in Foreign Language Education*. Clevedon: Multilingual Matters.

Byram, M. (1997) *Teaching and Assessing Intercultural Communicative Competence*. Clevedon: Multilingual Matters.

Byram, M. (2001) *Developing Intercultural Competence in Practice*. Clevedon: Multilingual Matters.

Byram, M. (2008) *From Foreign Language Education to Education for Intercultural Citizenship: Essays and Reflections*. Clevedon: Multilingual Matters.

Byram, M. (2009a) Afterword – Education training and becoming critical. In A. Feng, M. Byram and M. Fleming (eds) *Becoming Interculturally Competent through Education and Training* (pp. 211–213). Bristol: Multilingual Matters.

Byram, M. (2009b) Intercultural competence in foreign languages: The intercultural speaker and the pedagogy of foreign language education. In D. Deardorff (ed.) *The SAGE Handbook of Intercultural Competence* (pp. 321–332). Thousand Oaks, CA: SAGE Publications.

Byram, M. (2012a) Language awareness and (critical) cultural awareness – relationships, comparisons and contrasts. *Language Awareness* 21 (1–2), 5–13.

Byram, M. (2012b) A note on internationalisation, internationalism and language teaching and learning. *The Language Learning Journal* 40 (3), 375–381.

Byram, M., Esarte-Sarries, V. and Taylor, S. (1990) *Cultural Studies and Language Learning: A Research Report*. Clevedon: Multilingual Matters.

Byram, M., Gribkova, B. and Starkey, H. (2002) *Developing the Intercultural Dimension in Language Teaching: A Practical Introduction for Teachers*. Strasbourg: Council of Europe.

Byram, M. and Morgan, C. (1994) *Teaching-and-Learning Language-and-Culture*. Clevedon: Multilingual Matters.

Byram, M. and Zarate, G. (1994) *Definitions, Objectives and Assessment of Socio-Cultural Competence*. Strasbourg, France: Report for the Council of Europe.

Byrnes, H. (2008) Articulating a foreign language sequence through content: A look a the culture standards. *Language Teaching* 41 (1), 103–118.

Byrnes, H. (2010) Revisiting the role of culture in the foreign language curriculum. *The Modern Language Journal* 94 (2), 315–317.

Byrnes, H. (2012) Reconsidering Crosscultural Abilities: The Link to Language Learning and Assessment. Paper presented at the Third International Conference on the Development and Assessment of Intercultural Competence (ICC 2012) – Intercultural Competence and Foreign/Second Language Immersive Environments, Tucson, AZ, accessed 12 August 2012. http://cercll.arizona.edu/doku.php/development/conferences/2012_icc/speakers

Byrnes, H. (2013) Reconsidering graduate students' education as scholar-teachers: Mind your language! In H.W. Allen and H.H. Maxim (eds) *Educating the Future Foreign Language Professoriate for the 21st Century* (pp. 17–42). Boston, MA: Heinle Cengage Learning.

Calkins, S., Cox, R. and Light, G. (2009) *Learning and Teaching in Higher Education: The Reflective Professional*. Thousand Oaks, CA: Sage.

Cañado, M.L.P. (2010) Globalisation in foreign language teaching: establishing transatlantic links in higher education. *Higher Education Quarterly* 64 (4), 392–412.

Canale, M. (1983) From communicative competence to communicative language pedagogy. In J. Richards and R. Schmidt (eds) *Language and Communication* (pp. 2–27). London: Longman.

Canale, M. and Swain, M. (1980) Theoretical bases of communicative approaches to second language teaching and testing. *Applied Linguistics* 1 (1), 1–47.

Carroli, P., Pavone, A. and Tudini, V. (2003) Face value: Teaching Italian verbal and sociocultural interaction. In J. Lo Bianco and C. Crozet (eds) *Teaching Invisible Culture – Classroom Practice and Theory* (pp. 177–210). Melbourne: Language Australia.

Chambers, A. (2003) *A Language Policy in Higher Education in Europe: A Pilot Survey*, accessed 26 November 2010. http://www.atriumlinguarum.org/contenido/LangPolicy.pdf

Chow, P. and Bhandari, R. (2011) *Open Doors 2011: Report on International Educational Exchange*. New York: Institute of International Education.

CIGE (2012) *Mapping Internationalization on U.S. Campuses*. 2012 edition. Washington, DC: ACE [American Council on Education] and CIGE [Center for Internationalization and Global Engagement].

Clyne, M. (2005) *Australia's Language Potential*. Sydney: UNSW Press.

Clyne, M., Pauwels, A. and Sussex, R. (2007) The state of languages education in Australia: A national tragedy and an international embarrassment. *ACSSO Australian Council of State School Organisations or the Australian Parents Council – Opinion Paper*, accessed 18 August 2009. http://www.curriculum.edu.au/leader/the_state_of_languages_education_in_australia,19754.html

Coffield, F. and Edward, S. (2009) Rolling out 'good', 'best' and 'excellent' practice. What next? Perfect practice? *British Educational Research Journal* 35 (3), 371–390.

Coleman, J.A. (2011) Modern Languages in the United Kingdom. *Arts and Humanities in Higher Education* 10 (2), 127–129.

Coperías Aguilar, M.J. (2002) Intercultural communicative competence: A step beyond communicative competence. *ELIA (Estudios de Lingüística Aplicada)* (3), 85–102

Coperías Aguilar, M.J. (2007) Dealing with intercultural communicative competence in the foreign language classroom. In E. Alcón Soler and M.P. Safont Jordá (eds) *Intercultural Language Use and Language Learning*. Dordrecht, The Netherlands: Springer.

Crawford-Lange, L. and Lange, D.L. (1984) Doing the unthinkable in the second language classroom. In T.V. Higgs (ed.) *Teaching for Proficiency, the Organising Principle* (pp. 139–177). Lincolnwood, IL: National Textbook.

Creswell, J. (2007) *Qualitative Inquiry & Research Design – Choosing Among Five Approaches* (2nd ed.). Thousand Oaks, CA: SAGE Publications.

Crichton, J. (2007) *Why an Investigative Stance Matters in Intercultural Language Teaching and Learning: An Orientation to Classroom-Based Investigation*. Canberra: DEST.

Crichton, J. (2008) Why an investigative stance matters in intercultural language teaching and learning: An orientation to classroom-based investigation. *Babel* 43 (1), 31–35, 39.

Crichton, J. and Scarino, A. (2007) How are we to understand the 'intercultural dimension'? An examination of the intercultural dimension of internationalisation in the context of higher education in Australia. *Australian Review of Applied Linguistics* 30 (1), 4.1–4.21.

Crichton, J., Paige, M., Papademetre, L. and Scarino, A. (2004) *Integrated Resources for Intercultural Teaching and Learning in the Context of Internationalisation in Higher Education*. University of South Australia – School of International Studies – Research Centre for Languages and Cultures Education.

Crozet, C. (2003) A conceptual framework to help teachers identify where culture is located in language use. In J. Lo Bianco and C. Crozet (eds) *Teaching Invisible Culture – Classroom Practice and Theory* (pp. 39–49). Melbourne: Language Australia.

Damen, L. (1987) *Culture Learning: The Fifth Dimension in the Language Classroom*. Reading, MA: Addison-Wesley.

Dasli, M. (2011a) Reviving the 'moments': From cultural awareness and cross-cultural mediation to critical intercultural language pedagogy. *Pedagogy, Culture & Society* 19 (1), 21–39.

Dasli, M. (2011b) Theorizations of intercultural communication. In G.S. Levine and A. Phipps (eds) *Critical and Intercultural Theory and Language Pedagogy* (pp. 95–111). Boston, MA: Heinle, Cengage Learning.

Davies, M. and Devlin, M. (2007) *Interdisciplinary higher education and the Melbourne model*. Paper presented at the Creativity, enterprise, policy: New directions in education, Philosophy of Education Society of Australasia Conference, Wellington, NZ, accessed 22 June 2011. http://hdl.handle.net/10536/DRO/DU:30006786

Deardorff, D.K. (2006) Identification and assessment of intercultural competence as a student outcome of internationalisation. *Journal of Studies in International Education* 10 (3), 241–266.

Deardorff, D.K. (2011) Assessing intercultural competence. *New Directions for Institutional Research* 2011 (149), 65–79.

Dearn, J., Fraser, K. and Ryan, Y. (2002) *Professional Development for University Teaching in Australia: A Discussion Paper*. Canberra, ACT: Department of Education, Science and Training.

Della Chiesa, B., Scott, J. and Hinton, C. (eds) (2012) *Languages in a Global World: Learning for Better Cultural Understanding*. Paris, France: OECD Organisation for Economic Co-operation Development and Centre for Educational Research Innovation.

Denzin, N.K. and Lincoln, Y.S. (2005) *Handbook of Qualitative Research* (3rd edn). Thousand Oaks, CA: Sage.

Department of Education, Employment and Workplace Relations (DEEWR) (2008) *Review of Australian Higher Education: Final Report*. Canberra, ACT: Department of Education, Employment and Workplace Relations.

Dervin, F. and Suomela-Salmi, E. (2010a) Introduction: Three keys to understanding the new *culture* of language and (inter-)cultural assessment in higher education. In F. Dervin and E. Suomela-Salmi (eds) *New Approaches to Assessing Language and (Inter-)Cultural Competences in Higher Education* (pp. 9–22). Frankfurt am Main: Peter Lang.

Dervin, F. and Suomela-Salmi, E. (eds) (2010b) *New Approaches to Assessing Language and (Inter-)Cultural Competences in Higher Education*. Frankfurt am Main: Peter Lang.

Dewey, J. (1933) *How We Think: A Restatement of the Relation of Reflective Thinking to the Educative Process*. Boston: D.C. Heath.

Dewey, J. (1938) *Experience and Education*. New York: Collier Books.

Díaz, A. (2012) Intercultural competence through language education in Australian higher education: Mission (im)possible? In J. Hajek, C. Nettelbeck and A. Woods (eds) *The Next Step: Introducing the Languages and Cultures Network for Australian Universities*. Selected Proceedings of LCNAU's Inaugural Colloquium, Melbourne, 26–28 September 2011 (pp. 285–298). Australia: LCNAU.

Dlaska, A. (2000) Integrating culture and language learning in institution-wide language programmes. *Language, Culture and Curriculum* 13 (3), 247–263.

Dlaska, A. (2003) Language learning in the university: Creating content and community in non-specialist programmes. *Teaching in Higher Education* 8 (1), 103–116.

Dlaska, A. (2012) The role of foreign language programmes in internationalising learning and teaching in higher education. *Teaching in Higher Education* 18 (3), 260–271.

Donato, R. (2000) Sociocultural contributions to understanding the foreign and second language classroom. In J. Lantolf (ed.) *Sociocultural Theory and Second Language Learning* (pp. 27–50). Oxford: Oxford University Press.

Donmall-Hicks, B.G. (1997) The history of language awareness in the UK. In L. van Lier and D. Corson (eds) *Encyclopedia of Language and Education* (Vol. 6: Knowledge about Language pp. 21–30). Netherlands: Kluwer Academic Publishers.

Egron-Polak, E. and Hudson, R. (eds) (2010) *Internationalization of Higher Education: Global Trends, Regional Perspectives – IAU 3rd Global Survey Report*. Paris: International Association of Universities (IAU).

Eisenchlas, S. (2010) Conceptualising 'communication' in foreign language instruction. *Babel* 44 (2), 12–21.

Eisenchlas, S. and Hortiguera, H. (1999) Beyond the classroom: The Hispanic community as a resource for teaching and learning. *Babel* 34 (3), 16–20.

Eisenchlas, S. and Trevaskes, S. (2003) Creating cultural spaces in the Australian university setting: A pilot study of structured cultural exchanges. *Australian Review of Applied Linguistics* 26 (2), 84–99.

Eisenchlas, S. and Trevaskes, S. (2007) Developing intercultural communication skills through intergroup interaction. *Intercultural Education* 18 (5), 413–425.

Eisenchlas, S., Trevaskes, S. and Liddicoat, A.J. (2003) Internationalisation: The slow move from rhetoric to practice in Australian universities. In A.J. Liddicoat, S. Eisenchlas and S. Trevaskes (eds) *Australian Perspectives on Internationalising Education* (pp. 141–149). Melbourne: Language Australia.

Elola, I. and Oskoz, A. (2008) Blogging: Fostering intercultural competence development in foreign language and study abroad contexts. *Foreign Language Annals* 41 (3), 454–477.

Fairclough, N. (1992) *Critical Language Awareness*. London; New York: Longman.

Fantini, A.E. (1991) Bilingualism: Exploring language and culture. In L.M. Malavé-López and G. Duquette (eds) *Language, Culture, and Cognition: A Collection of Studies in First and Second Language Acquisition* (pp. 110–119). Clevedon: Multilingual Matters.

Fantini, A.E. (1995) Introduction – Language, culture and world view: Exploring the nexus. *International Journal of Intercultural Relations* 19 (2), 143–153.

Feng, A., Byram, M. and Fleming, M. (eds) (2009) *Becoming Interculturally Competent through Education and Training*. Bristol: Multilingual Matters.

Festinger, L. (1957) *A Theory of Cognitive Dissonance*. Evanston, IL: Row & Peterson.

Flamini, E. and Jiménez Raya, M. (2007) Action Research: Professional Development through Enquiry. In M. Jiménez Raya and L. Sercu (eds) *Challenges in Teacher Development: Learner Autonomy and Intercultural Competence* (Vol. 10, pp. 105–124). Frankfurt: Peter Lang.

Fraser, S.P. and Bosanquet, A.M. (2006) The curriculum? That's just a unit outline, isn't it? *Studies in Higher Education* 31 (3), 269–284.

Freadman, A. (1998) Models of genre for language teaching. *South Central Review* 15 (1), 19–39.

Freire, P. (1970) *Pedagogy of the Oppressed*. New York: Seabury Press.

Freire, P. (1973) *Education for Critical Consciousness*. New York: Continuum.

Freire, P. (1998) *Teachers as Cultural Workers: Letters to Those Who Dare Teach*. Boulder, CO: Westview Press.

Friedrich, P. (1989) Language, ideology, and political economy. *American Anthropologist* 91 (2), 295–312.

Fullan, M.G. (1982) *The Meaning of Educational Change*. Toronto: OISE Press.

Furman, N., Goldberg, D. and Lusin, N. (2010) *Enrollments in Languages Other Than English in United States Institutions of Higher Education,* Fall 2009, accessed 27 July 2011. http://www.mla.org/pdf/2009_enrollment_survey.pdf.

Gabrys, D. (2002) A universal or unique and amorphous feeling of ANGER: On conceptualizing emotions and language awareness. In J. Arabski (ed.) *Time for Words: Studies in Foreign Language Vocabulary Acquisition* (pp. 22–34). Frankfurt: Peter Lang.

Gallagher-Brett, A. and Broady, E. (2012) Teaching languages in higher education. *The Language Learning Journal* 40 (3), 263–271.

Gieve, S. and Cunico, S. (2012) Language and content in the modern foreign languages degree: a students' perspective. *The Language Learning Journal* 40 (3), 273–291.

Giroux, H.A. (1988) *Teachers as Intellectuals: Toward a Critical Pedagogy of Learning*. New York, NY: Bergin & Garvey.

Go8. (2007) *Languages in Crisis – National Languages Summit*. Canberra, ACT: National Press Club, accessed 1 June 2008. http://www.go8.edu.au/_documents/university-staff/agreements/go8-languages-in-crisis-discussion-paper.pdf

Godsland, S. (2010) Monolingual England: The crisis in foreign language enrollments from elementary schools through college. *Hispania* 93 (1), 113–118.

Goffman, E. (1967) *Interaction Ritual: Essays on Face-to-face Behavior*. New York: Anchor Books, Doubleday.

Gosling, D. (2009) Educational development in the UK: A complex and contradictory reality. *International Journal for Academic Development* 14 (1), 5–18.

Gossman, P., Haigh, N.H. and Jiao, X. (2009) *The Status of the Scholarship of Teaching and Learning (SoTL) in New Zealand Universities: Three Institutional Case Studies*. Auckland, NZ: Final Report to the Ministry of Education and Ako Aotearoa: The National Centre of Tertiary Teaching Excellence.

Guba, E.G. and Lincoln, Y.S. (1994) Competing paradigms in qualitative research. In N.K. Denzin and Y.S. Lincoln (eds) *Handbook of Qualitative Research* (pp. 105–117). London: Sage.

Gudykunst, W.B. (1991) *Bridging Differences: Effective Intergroup Communication*. Newbury Park, CA: Sage.

Gudykunst, W.B., Ting-Toomey, S. and Chua, E. (1988) *Culture and Interpersonal Communication*. Thousand Oaks, CA: Sage.

Guilherme, M. (2002) *Critical Citizens for an Intercultural World: Foreign Language Education as Cultural Politics*. Clevedon: Multilingual Matters.

Guilherme, M., Glaser, E. and Mendez Garcia, M.d.C. (2009) The pragmatics of intercultural competence in education and training: A cross-national experiment on 'diversity management'. In A. Feng, M. Byram and M. Fleming (eds) *Becoming Interculturally Competent through Education and Training* (pp. 193–210). Bristol: Multilingual Matters.

Gumperz, J.J. and Hymes, D.H. (1986) *Directions in Sociolinguistics: The Ethnography of Communication* (Rev. ed.). Oxford: Blackwell.

Habermas, J. (1971) *Knowledge and Human Interests*. Boston: Beacon Press.

Hall, J.K. and Ramírez, A. (1993) How a group of high school learners of Spanish perceives the cultural identities of Spanish speakers, English speakers and themselves. *Hispania* 76 (3), 613–620.

Hajek, J., Nettelbeck, C. and Woods, A. (eds) (2012) *The Next Step: Introducing the Languages and Cultures Network for Australian Universities*. Selected Proceedings of LCNAU's Inaugural Colloquium, Melbourne, 26–28 September 2011. Australia: LCNAU.

Harden, T. (2011) The perception of competence: A history of a peculiar development of concepts. In A. Witte and T. Harden (eds) *Intercultural Competence: Concepts, Challenges, Evaluations* (pp. 75–87). Bern, Switzerland Peter Lang.

Hartley, B. (2003) Just return for dedicated investment: Internationalisation, Japanese language teacher education, and student expectations. In A.J. Liddicoat, S. Eisenchlas and S. Trevaskes (eds) *Australian Perspectives on Internationalising Education* (pp. 53–64). Melbourne: Language Australia.

Henerson, M.E., Morris, L.L. and Fitz-Gibbon, C.T. (1987) *How to Measure Attitudes*. Newbury Park: Sage.

Heron, J. and Reason, P. (1997) A participatory inquiry paradigm. *Qualitative Inquiry* 3 (3), 274–294.

Hewstone, M. and Giles, H. (1986) Social groups and social stereotypes in intergroup communication: A review and model of intergroup communication breakdown. In W.B. Gudykunst (ed.) *Intergroup Communication* (pp. 10–26). London: Edward Arnold.

Hinton, T., Gannaway, D., Berry, B. and Moore, K. (2011) *The D-Cubed Guide: Planning for Effective Dissemination*. Sydney: Australian Teaching and Learning Council.

Houghton, S. (2010) Savoir se transformer: Knowing how to become. In Y. Tsai and S. Houghton (eds) *Becoming Intercultural: Inside and Outside the Classroom* (pp. 194–228). Newcastle upon Tyne: Cambridge Scholars.

Houghton, S. (2012) *Intercultural Dialogue in Practice: Managing Value Judgment through Foreign Language Education*. Bristol: Multilingual Matters.

Houghton, S. and Yamada, E. (2012) *Developing Criticality in Practice through Foreign Language Education*. Oxford: Peter Lang.

House, J. (2007) What is an 'intercultural speaker'? In E. Alcón Soler and M.P. Safont Jordá (eds) *Intercultural Language Use and Language Learning* (pp. 7–21). Dordrecht, The Netherlands: Springer.

Hsieh, H.-h. (2011) Challenges facing Chinese academic staff in a UK university in terms of language, relationships and culture. *Teaching in Higher Education* 17 (4), 371–383.

Hutchings, P., Huber, M.T. and Ciccone, A. (2011) *The Scholarship of Teaching and Learning Reconsidered: Institutional Integration and Impact*. Princeton, N.J: Carnegie Foundation for the Advancement of Teaching.

Hymes, D.H. (1972) On communicative competence. In J.B. Pride and J. Holmes (eds) *Sociolinguistics: Selected Readings* (pp. 269–293). Harmondsworth: Penguin.

Hymes, D.H. (1974) *Foundations in Sociolinguistics: An Ethnographic Approach*. Philadelphia: University of Pennsylvania Press.

Ingram, D., Kono, M., Sasaki, M., Tateyama, E. and O'Neill, S. (2004) Cross-cultural attitudes among language students in Australia and Japan. *Babel* 39 (1), 11–19.

ITL (2012) *The National Graduate Attributes Project – GAP*, accessed 13 June 2011. http://www.itl.usyd.edu.au/projects/nationalgap/introduction.htm

Jackson, J. (2011) Cultivating cosmopolitan, intercultural citizenship through critical reflection and international, experiential learning. *Language and Intercultural Communication* 11 (2), 80–96.

Jacobson, W., Sleicher, D. and Burke, M. (1999) Portfolio assessment of intercultural competence. *International Journal of Intercultural Relations* 23 (3), 467–492.

Jiang, X, Di Napoli, R., Borg, M., Maunder, R., Fry, H. and Walsh, E. (2010) Becoming and being an academic: the perspectives of Chinese staff in two research-intensive UK universities. *Studies in Higher Education* 35 (2), 155–170.

Johnson, V.C. and Mullholland, J. (2006) Open doors, secure borders: Advantages of education abroad for public policy. *International Educator* 15 (3), 4–7.

Johnston, B., Mitchell, R., Myles, F. and Ford, P. (2011) *Developing Student Criticality in Higher Education*. London; New York: Continuum.

Kember, D. (2003) To control or not to control: The question of whether experimental designs are appropriate for evaluating teaching innovations in higher education. *Assessment & Evaluation in Higher Education* 28 (1), 89–101.

Kemmis, S. and McTaggart, R. (1988) *The Action Research Planner*. Waurn Ponds, Victoria: Deakin University Press.

Kemmis, S. and Wilkinson, M. (1998) Research and the study of practice. In B. Atweh, S. Kemmis and P. Weeks (eds) *Action Research in Practice: Partnerships for Social Justice in Education* (pp. 21–36). London: Routledge.

Kerbrat-Orecchioni, C. (1994) *Les Interactions Verbales*. Paris: Armand Collin.

Kerbrat-Orecchioni, C. (2000) Quelle place pour les émotions dans la linguistique du XXᵉ siècle? Remarques et aperçus. In C. Plantin, M. Doury and V. Traverso (eds) *Les Émotions dans les Interactions*. Lyon: ARCI Presses Universitaires de Lyon.

Kincheloe, J.L. (2003) *Teachers as Researchers: Qualitative Inquiry as a Path to Empowerment* (2nd ed.). London: Routledge.

Kincheloe, J.L. (2005) *Critical Constructivism Primer*. New York: Peter Lang.

King, R., Findlay, A. and Ahrens, J. (2010) *International Student Mobility Literature Review*. Bristol: Higher Education Funding Council for England (HEFCE).

Kinginger, C. (2009) *Language Learning and Study Abroad: A Critical Reading of Research*. Basingstoke; New York: Palgrave Macmillan.

Kitchenham, A. (2008) The evolution of John Mezirow's transformative learning theory. *Journal of Transformative Education* 6 (2), 104–123.

Klapper, J. (2001a) Introduction: Professional development in modern languages. In J. Klapper (ed.) *Teaching Languages in Higher Education: Issues in Training and Continuing Professional Development* (pp. 1–15). London: CILT (The National Centre for Languages).

Klapper, J. (ed). (2001b) *Teaching Languages in Higher Education: Issues in Training and Continuing Professional Development*. London: CILT (The National Centre for Languages).

Klapper, J. (2006) *Understanding and Developing Good Practice – Language Teaching in Higher Education*. London: CILT (The National Centre for Languages).

Klee, C. A. (2009) Internationalization and foreign languages: The resurgence of interest in languages across the curriculum. *The Modern Language Journal* 93 (4), 618–621.

Knight, J. (2006) *Internationalisation of Higher Education: New Directions, New Challenges – IAU 2005 Global Survey*. Paris: UNESCO, International Association of Universities.

Knight, P., Tait, J. and Yorke, M. (2006) The professional learning of teachers in higher education. *Studies in Higher Education* 31 (3), 319–339.

Korhonen, K. (2010) Interculturally savvy or not? Developing and assessing intercultural competence in the context of learning for business. In A. Paran and L. Sercu (eds) *Testing the Untestable in Language Education* (pp. 35–51). Bristol: Multilingual Matters.

Kramsch, C. (1987) Foreign language textbooks' construction of foreign reality. *Canadian Modern Language Review* 44 (1), 95–119.

Kramsch, C. (1993) *Context and Culture in Language Education*. Oxford: Oxford University Press.

Kramsch, C. (1998a) *Language and Culture*. Oxford: Oxford University Press.

Kramsch, C. (1998b) Teaching along the cultural faultine. In R. M. Paige, D. L. Lange and Y. A. Yershova (eds) *Culture as the Core: Interdisciplinary Perspectives on Culture Teaching and Learning in the Second Language Curriculum* (pp. 15–32). Minneapolis: CARLA, University of Minnesota.

Kramsch, C. (2009) *The Multilingual Subject: What Foreign Language Learners Say About Their Experience and Why it Matters.* Oxford: Oxford University Press.

Kreber, C. (2010) Empowering the Scholarship of Teaching and Learning: Towards an Authentic Practice. Paper presented at the SOTL Commons Conference, Statesboro, Georgia, Georgia Southern University.

Kumaravadivelu, B. (2001) Toward a postmethod pedagogy. *Tesol Quarterly* 35 (4), 537–560.

Kumaravadivelu, B. (2003) *Beyond Methods: Macrostrategies for Language Teaching.* London: Yale University Press.

Lane, B. (2011) *TEQSA Role to Safeguard Language Standards.* The Australian, Higher Education, accessed 28 September 2011. http://www.theaustralian.com.au/higher-education/teqsa-role-to-safeguard-language-standards/story-e6frgcjx-1226148430401.

Lane, B. (2012) *National Regulator Sharpens Focus on English Language Standards.* The Australian, Higher Education, accessed 22 August 2012. http://www.theaustralian.com.au/higher-education/national-regulator-sharpens-focus-on-english-language-standards/story-e6frgcjx-1226455260799

LanQua. (2010) *A Quality Toolkit for Languages – Frame of Reference for Quality in Languages in Higher Education.* Highfield, Southampton: University of Southampton, accessed 13 June 2012. http://www.lanqua.eu/sites/default/files/LanQua_frame_of_reference.pdf

Lantolf, J. and Thorne, S. (2006) *Sociocultural Theory and the Genesis of Second Language Development.* New York: Oxford University Press.

Lave, J. and Wenger, E. (1991) *Situated Learning: Legitimate Peripheral Participation.* Cambridge: Cambridge University Press.

Le Page, R. and Tabouret-Keller, A. (1985) *Acts of Identity: Creole-based Approaches to Language and Ethnicity.* Cambridge: Cambridge University Press.

Leask, B. (2013) Internationalizing the curriculum in the disciplines—imagining new possibilities. *Journal of Studies in International Education* 17 (2), 103–118.

Lee, A., Poch, R., Shaw, M. and Williams, R. (2012) *Engaging Diversity in Undergraduate Classrooms: a Pedagogy for Developing Intercultural Competence.* Ashe Higher Education Report, Vol. 38 (2). Hoboken, NJ: Jossey-Bass Inc Pub.

Leithwood, K., Begley, P.T. and Cousins, J.B. (1994) *Developing Expert Leadership for Future Schools.* London: Falmer Press.

Lepschy, A.L. and Lepschy, G. (1988) *The Italian Language Today.* London; New York: Routledge.

Levine, G.S. (2011) Stability, crisis, and other reasons for optimism. *Arts and Humanities in Higher Education* 10 (2), 131–140.

Levine, G.S. and Phipps, A. (eds) (2012) *Critical and Intercultural Theory and Language Pedagogy.* Boston, MA: Heinle, Cengage Learning.

Li, K. (2003) Chinese. In J. Lo Bianco and C. Crozet (eds) *Teaching Invisible Culture – Classroom Practice and Theory* (pp. 53–100). Melbourne: Language Australia.

Li, L., Singh, M. and Robertson, S. (2012) Australian languages education in the Asian century: Deepening of linguistic and intellectual engagements with Asia. *Journal of Local-Global – Special Issue: Globalization, Languages, Knowledge: Australian languages education in the 'Asian Century'* 9, 6–17.

Liddicoat, A.J. (2002) Static and dynamic views of culture and intercultural language acquisition. *Babel* 36 (3), 4–11, 37.

Liddicoat, A.J. (2003) Teaching languages for intercultural communication. *Berkeley Language Centre Newsletter* 19 (1), 1–4, 7.

Liddicoat, A.J. (2008) Language choices in the intercultural language classroom. *Babel* 43 (1), 18–35, 38.

Liddicoat, A.J. and Crozet, C. (2000) *Teaching Languages, Teaching Cultures*. Melbourne: Applied Linguistics Association of Australia and Language Australia.

Liddicoat, A.J. and Crozet, C. (2001) Acquiring French interactional norms through instruction. In K.R. Rose and G. Kasper (eds) *Pragmatics in Language Learning* (pp. 125–144). New York: Cambridge University Press.

Liddicoat, A.J., Eisenchlas, S. and Trevaskes, S. (2003) *Australian Perspectives on Internationalising Education*. Melbourne: Language Australia.

Liddicoat, A.J., Papademetre, L., Scarino, A. and Kohler, M. (2003) *Report on Intercultural Language Learning*. Canberra, ACT: Department of Education, Science and Training.

Liddicoat, A.J. and Scarino, A. (2013) *Intercultural Language Teaching and Learning*. New York: Wiley and Sons.

Lillie, E. (2003) *Higher Education, Languages and Quality in the United Kingdom. Thematic Network Project in the Area of Languages 2, Subgroup 3 – Quality Enhancement in Language Studies*. Germany: National reports, Universität zu Köln.

Lo Bianco, J. (2003) Culture: visible, invisible and multiple. In J. Lo Bianco and C. Crozet (eds) *Teaching Invisible Culture: Classroom Practice and Theory* (pp. 11–38). Canberra, ACT: Language Australia.

Lo Bianco, J. (2009) *Second Languages and Australian Schooling*. Camberwell, VIC: Australian Council for Educational Research (ACER) Press.

Lo Bianco, J. and Crozet, C. (2003) *Teaching Invisible Culture: Classroom Practice and Theory*. Canberra, ACT: Language Australia.

Long, M. (1996) The role of the linguistic environment in second language acquisition. In W. C. Ritchie and T. K. Bhatia (eds) *Handbook of Second Language Acquisition* (pp. 413–468). New York: Academic Press.

Lucas, C. (2000) *Italia Contemporanea – Conversations with Native Speakers*. New Haven: Yale University Press.

Luk, J.C.M. (2004) [Review of the book Teaching Invisible Culture: Classroom Theory and Practice by J. Lo Bianco (ed.)]. *TESOL in Context Volume* 14 (1&2), 28–30.

Maringe, F., Foskett, N. and Woodfield, S. (2013) Emerging internationalisation models in an uneven global terrain: findings from a global survey. *Compare: A Journal of Comparative and International Education* 43 (1), 9–36.

Martín, D. (2005) Permanent crisis, tenuous persistence: Foreign languages in Australian universities. *Arts and Humanities in Higher Education* 4 (1), 53–75.

McAlpine, L. and Harris, R. (2002) Evaluating teaching effectiveness and teaching improvement: A language for institutional policies and academic development practices. *The International Journal of Academic Development* 7 (1), 7–17.

MCEETYA (2005) *National Statement for Languages Education in Australian Schools: National Plan for Languages Education in Australian Schools 2005–2008*. Hindmarsh, SA: DECS – Ministerial Council on Education, Employment, Training and Youth Affairs.

McMeniman, M. and Evans, R. (1997) The contribution of language learning to the development of cultural understandings. *Australian Review of Applied Linguistics* 20 (2), 1–18.

Merriam, S.B. (1998) *Qualitative Research and Case Study Applications in Education* (2nd edn). San Francisco: Jossey-Bass.

Mezirow, J. (1981) A critical theory of adult learning and education. *Adult Education Quarterly* 32 (1), 3–24.

Mezirow, J. (1991) *Transformative Dimensions of Adult learning*. San Francisco: Jossey-Bass.

Mezirow, J. (2000) *Learning as Transformation: Critical Perspectives on a Theory in Progress* (1st edn). San Francisco: Jossey-Bass.

Modern Language Association (2007) *Foreign Languages and Higher Education: New Structures for a Changed World*, accessed 18 May 2011. http://www.mla.org/pdf/forlang_news_pdf.pdf

Montier, J. (2002) *Darwin's Mind: The Evolutionary Foundations of Heuristics and Biases*, accessed 7 March 2008. http://papers.ssrn.com/sol3/papers.cfm?abstract_id=373321

Moodie, A. (2012) Quality and Accreditation Body Goes Global. *University World News* (240), accessed 29 September 2012. http://www.universityworldnews.com/article.php?story=20120919165946970

Morgan, A-M. (2008) The importance of questioning and questions for consideration in programming for intercultural language learning. *Babel* 43 (1), 13–17, 38.

Mrowa-Hopkins, C.M. and Strambi, A. (2005) How angry can you be in French and Italian? Integrating research and teaching for the development of pragmatic competencies in L2 classrooms. *FULGOR – Flinders University Languages Group Online Review* 2 (2), accessed 23 August 2008. http://dspace.flinders.edu.au/xmlui/handle/2328/177

Murphy, E. (1988) The cultural dimension in foreign language teaching: Four models. *Language, Culture and Curriculum* 1 (2), 147–162.

Murphy, P. (2008) Defining pedagogy. In K. Hall, P. Murphy and J. Soler (eds) *Pedagogy and Practice: Culture and Identities* (pp. 28–39). Los Angeles: SAGE Publications.

Nemser, W. (1971) Approximative systems of foreign language learners. *International Review of Applied Linguistics* 9 (2), 115–123.

Nettelbeck, C., Byron, J., Clyne, M., Hajek, J., Lo Bianco, J. and McLaren, A. (2007) *Beginners' LOTE (Languages Other than English) in Australian Universities: An Audit Survey and Analysis*. Canberra: Australian Academy of the Humanities.

Nettelbeck, C., Hajek, J. and Woods, A. (2012) Re-professionalizing the Profession: Countering Juniorization and Casualization in the Tertiary Languages Sector. *Journal of Local-Global – Special Issue: Globalization, Languages, Knowledge: Australian Languages Education in the 'Asian Century'* 9, 60–75.

Newfield, C. (2009) Ending the budget wars: Funding the humanities during a crisis in higher education. *Profession* 2009 (1), 270–284.

Norris, L. (2010) The current state and nature of languages teacher education. In A.J. Liddicoat and A. Scarino (eds) *Languages in Australian Education: Problems, Prospects and Future Directions* (pp. 71–85). Newcastle: Cambridge Scholars.

O'Dowd, R. (2003) Understanding the "other side": Intercultural learning in a Spanish–English e-mail exchange. *Language Learning & Technology* 7 (2), 118–144.

O'Dowd, R. (ed.) (2007) *Online Intercultural Exchange: An Introduction for Foreign Language Teachers*. Clevedon: Multilingual Matters.

OECD (2012) Testing Student and University Performance Globally: OECD's AHELO, accessed 30 June 2012. http://www.oecd.org/education/highereducation-andadultlearning/testingstudentanduniversityperformancegloballyoecdsahelo.htm

Paige, R.M. and Goode, M.L. (2009) Intercultural competence in international education administration. In D. Deardorff (ed.) *The SAGE Handbook of Intercultural Competence*. Thousand Oaks, CA: SAGE Publications.

Papademetre, L. and Scarino, A. (2000) *Consider Language and Culture Teaching: Teachers' Practice, Perspectives, Reflections*. Underdale, SA: University of South Australia; Language Australia.

Parmenter, L. (2010) Becoming intercultural: A comparative analysis of national education policies. In S. Houghton and Y. Tsai (eds) *Becoming Intercultural: Inside and Outside the Classroom* (pp. 66–88). Newcastle upon Tyne: Cambridge Scholars.

Pauk, B. (2007) Student participation in developing outcomes: A survey of students majoring in European Languages. *Teaching and Learning Forum*, accessed 29 September 2009. http://otl.curtin.edu.au/professional_development/conferences/tlf/tlf2007/refereed/pauk.html

Pauwels, A. (2002) Languages in the university sector at the beginning of the third millennium. *Babel* 37 (2), 16–20, 37–38.

Pauwels, A. (2007) Maintaining a language other than English through higher education in Australia. In A. Pauwels, J. Lo Bianco and J. Winter (eds) *Maintaining Minority Languages in Transnational Contexts* (pp. 107–123). London: Palgrave.

Pauwels, A. (2011) Future directions for the learning of languages in universities: challenges and opportunities. *The Language Learning Journal* 39 (2), 247–257.

Peeters, B. (2004) "Thou shall not be a tall poppy": Describing an Australian communicative (and behavioural) norm. *Intercultural Pragmatics* 1 (1), 71–92.

Piaget, J. (1970) Piaget's theory. In P. Mussen (ed.) *Handbook of Child Psychology* (4th ed., Vol. 1, 1983, pp. 103–128). New York: Wiley.

Piasecka, L. (2011) Sensitizing foreign language learners to cultural diversity through developing intercultural communicative competence. In J. Arabski and A. Wojtaszek (eds) *Aspects of Culture in Second Language Acquisition and Foreign Language Learning* (pp. 21–33). Berlin Heidelberg: Springer.

Pitman, T. and Broomhall, S. (2009) Australian universities, generic skills and lifelong learning. *International Journal of Lifelong Education* 28 (4), 439–458.

Pratt, D.D. (1991) Conceptions of self within China and the United States: Contrasting foundations for adult education. *International Journal of Intercultural Relations* 15 (3), 285–310.

QAA (2007) *Languages and Related Studies*. Adamsway, Mansfield: The Quality Assurance Agency for Higher Education.

Rathje, S. (2007) Intercultural competence: The status and future of a controversial concept. *Language and Intercultural Communication* 7 (4), 254–266.

RCLCE – University of South Australia (2008) *An Investigation of the State and Nature of Languages in Australian Schools*. Canberra, ACT: DEEWR.

Richards, J. and Sukwiwat, M. (1983) Language transfer and conversational competence. *Applied Linguistics* 4 (2), 113–125.

Richards, J.C. and Farrell, T.S.C. (2005) *Professional Development for Language Teachers: Strategies for Teacher Learning*. New York: Cambridge University Press.

Richards, J.C. and Lockhart, C. (1994) *Reflective Teaching in Second Language Classrooms*. New York: Cambridge University Press.

Risager, K. (2005) Languaculture as a key concept in language and culture teaching. In B. Preisler, A. Fabricius, H. Haberland, S. Kjærbeck and K. Risager (eds) *The Consequences of Mobility* (pp. 185–196). Roskilde: Roskilde University, Department of Language and Culture.

Risager, K. (2006a) Culture in language: A transnational view. In H.L. Andersen, K. Lund and K. Risager (eds) *Culture in Language Learning* (pp. 27–44). Aarhus; Oakville, CT: Aarhus University Press.

Risager, K. (2006b) *Language and Culture: Global Flows and Local Complexities*. Clevedon: Multilingual Matters.

Risager, K. (2007) *Language and Culture Pedagogy: From a National to a Transnational Paradigm*. Clevedon: Multilingual Matters.

Risager, K. (2011) Linguaculture and transnationality: The cultural dimensions of language. In J. Jackson (ed.) *Routledge Handbook of Language and Intercultural Communication* (pp. 101–115). London and New York: Routledge.

Risager, K. (2013) Linguaculture. In C.A. Chapelle (ed.) *The Encyclopedia of Applied Linguistics* (pp. 3418–3421). Chichester: Blackwell Publishing Ltd.

Roberts, J. (1998) *Language Teacher Education*. London: Arnold.

Robinson, G. (1978) The magic-carpet-ride-to-another-culture syndrome: An international perspective. *Foreign Language Annals* 11 (2), 135–146.

Robinson-Stuart, G. and Nocon, H. (1996) Second culture acquisition: Ethnography in the foreign language classroom. *The Modern Language Journal* 80 (4), 431–449.

Ros i Solé, C. (2003) Culture for beginners: A subjective and realistic approach for adult language learners. *Language and Intercultural Communication* 3 (2), 141–150.

Rose, K.R. and Kasper, G. (2001) *Pragmatics in Language Teaching*. New York: Cambridge University Press.

Saran, R. and Neisser, B. (eds) (2004) *Enquiring Minds: Socratic Dialogue in Education*. Stoke on Trent, UK; Sterling, USA: Trentham Books.

Saroyan, A. and Frenay, M. (eds) (2010) *Building Teaching Capacities In Higher Education: A Comprehensive International Model*. Sterling, VA: Stylus Pub.

Sauvé, V. (1996) Working with the cultures of Canada in the ESL classroom: A response to Robert Courchene. *TESL Canada Journal* 13 (2), 17–23.

Savignon, S. (1983) *Communicative Competence: Theory and Classroom Practice*. Reading, MA: Addison-Wesley.

Savignon, S. (2007) Beyond communicative language teaching: What's ahead? *Journal of Pragmatics* 39 (1), 207–220.

Scarino, A. (2009) Assessing intercultural capability in learning languages: Some issues and considerations. *Language Teaching* 42 (1), 67–80.

Scarino, A., Crichton, J., Heugh, K. and Liddicoat, A.J. (2012) *Mentoring and Reflecting: Languages Educators and Professional Standards*. Adelaide: Australian Federation of Modern Language Teachers Associations [AFMLTA] & University of South Australia, School of International Studies, Research Centre for Languages and Cultures Education.

Schmidt, R. (1993) Consciousness, learning and interlanguage pragmatics. In G. Kasper and S. Blum-Kulka (eds) *Interlanguage Pragmatics* (pp. 21–42). New York: Oxford University Press.

Schmidt, R. (1995) Consciousness and foreign language learning: A tutorial on the role of attention and awareness in learning. In R. Schmidt (ed.) *Attention and Awareness in Foreign Language Learning* (pp. 1–63). Honolulu, Hawai'i: University of Hawai'i. Second Language Teaching & Curriculum Centre.

Schmidt, R. (2001) Attention. In P. Robinson (ed.) *Cognition and Second Language Instruction* (pp. 3–32). Cambridge: Cambridge University Press.

Schneider, G. and North, B. (2000) *Fremdsprachen können – was heisst das? Skalen zur Beschreibung, Beurteilung und Selbsteinschätzung der fremdsprachlichen Kommunikationsfähigkeit*. Zürich: Rüegger.

Schön, D.A. (1983) *The Reflective Practitioner: How Professionals Think in Action*. London: Temple Smith.

Schön, D.A. (1987) *Educating the Reflective Practitioner: Toward a New Design for Teaching and Learning in the Professions*. San Francisco: Jossey-Bass.

Scollon, R. and Scollon, S.B.K. (1995) *Intercultural Communication: A Discourse Approach*. Oxford, UK; Cambridge, MA: Blackwell.

Seelye, H.N. (1984) *Teaching Culture: Strategies for Intercultural Communication*. Lincolnwood, IL: National Textbook Company.

Selinker, L. (1972) Interlanguage. *International Review of Applied Linguistics in Language Teaching* 10 (1–4), 209–232.

Sercu, L. (2004) Intercultural communicative competence in foreign language education. Integrating theory and practice. In K. van Esch and O. St. John (eds) *New Insights into Foreign Language Learning and Teaching* (pp. 115–130). Frankfurt: Peter Lang.

Sercu, L. (2005) Teaching foreign languages in an intercultural world. In L. Sercu and E. Bandura (eds) *Foreign Language Teachers and Intercultural Competence: An International Investigation* (pp. 1–18). Clevedon: Multilingual Matters.

Sercu, L. (2007) Foreign language teachers and intercultural competence. What keeps teachers from doing what they believe in? In M. Jiménez Raya and L. Sercu (eds) *Challenges in Teacher Development: Learner Autonomy and Intercultural Competence* (pp. 65–80). Frankfurt: Peter Lang.

Sercu, L. (2010) Assessing intercultural competence: More questions than answers. In A. Paran and L. Sercu (eds) *Testing the Untestable in Language Education* (pp. 17–34). Bristol: Multilingual Matters.

Sercu, L. and Bandura, E. (2005) *Foreign Language Teachers and Intercultural Competence: An International Investigation*. Clevedon; Buffalo, NY: Multilingual Matters.

Sercu, L., Bandura, E., Castro, P., Davcheva, L., Laskaridou, U.L., Méndez García, M.d.C. and Ryan, P. (2005) *Foreign Language Teachers and Intercultural Competence: An International Investigation*. Clevedon; Buffalo, NY: Multilingual Matters.

Sercu, L. and St John, O. (2004) Teacher beliefs and their impact on teaching practice: A literature review. In L. Sercu and O. St John (eds) *New Insights into Foreign Language Teaching*. Frankfurt: Peter Lang.

Shaules, J. (2007) *Deep Culture: The Hidden Challenges of Global Living*. Clevedon: Multilingual Matters.

Silverman, D. (2000) *Doing Qualitative Research: A Practical Handbook*. London; Thousand Oaks, CA: SAGE Publications.

Smith, K. (2012) Lessons learnt from literature on the diffusion of innovative learning and teaching practices in higher education. *Innovations in Education and Teaching International* 49 (2), 173–182.

Southwell, D., Gannaway, D., Orrell, J., Chalmers, D. and Abraham, C. (2005) *Strategies for Effective Dissemination of Project Outcome*. Carrick Institute for Learning and Teaching in Higher Education. Commonwealth of Australia: The University of Queensland and Flinders University.

Spitzberg, B.H. and Changnon, G. (2009) Conceptualising intercultural competence. In D. Deardorff (ed.) *The SAGE Handbook of Intercultural Competence* (pp. 2–52). Thousand Oaks, CA: SAGE Publications.

Spolsky, B. (1988) Bridging the gap: A general theory of second language learning. *TESOL Quarterly* 22 (3), 377–396.

Stenhouse, L. (1975) *An Introduction to Curriculum Research and Development*. London: Heinemann.

Swain, M. (1995) Three functions of output in second language learning. In G. Cook and B. Seidlhofer (eds) *Principles and Practice in the Study of Language: Studies in Honour of H. G. Widdowson* (pp. 125–144). Oxford: Oxford University Press.

Taylor, D. (1988) The meaning and use of the term 'competence' in linguistics and applied linguistics. *Applied Linguistics* 9 (2), 148–168.

Taylor, E.W. (1994) Intercultural competency: A transformative learning process. *Adult Education Quarterly* 44 (3), 154–174.

Taylor, E.W. (1997) Building Upon the Theoretical Debate: A Critical Review of the Empirical Studies of Mezirow's Transformative Learning Theory. *Adult Education Quarterly* 48 (1), 34–59.

Taylor, E.W. (2007) An update of transformative learning theory: a critical review of the empirical research (1999–2005). *International Journal of Lifelong Education* 26 (2), 173–191.

Taylor, H.D. and Sorensen, J. (1961) Culture capsules. *Modern Language Journal* 45 (8), 350–354.

Thomas, J. (1983) Cross-cultural pragmatic failure. *Applied Linguistics* 4 (2), 91–112.

Thorne, S. (2003) Artifacts and cultures-of-use in intercultural communication. *Language Learning & Technology* 7 (2), 38–67.

Tomalin, B. and Nicks, M. (2007) *The World's Business Cultures and How to Unlock Them*. London: Thorogood.

Tomalin, B. and Stempleski, S. (1993) *Cultural Awareness*. Oxford; Melbourne: Oxford University Press.

Tomlinson, B. and Masuhara, H. (2004) Developing cultural awareness: Integrating culture into a language course. *Modern English Teacher* 13 (1), 5–11.

Treleaven, L., Sykes, C. and Ormiston, J. (2011) A dissemination methodology for learning and teaching developments through engaging and embedding. *Studies in Higher Education* 37 (6), 747–767.

Trevaskes, S., Eisenchlas, S. and Liddicoat, A.J. (2003) Language, culture and literacy in the internationalisation process of higher education. In A.J. Liddicoat, S. Eisenchlas and S. Trevaskes (eds) *Australian Perspectives on Internationalising Education* (pp. 1–12). Melbourne: Language Australia.

Tsai, Y. and Houghton, S. (eds) (2010) *Becoming Intercultural: Inside and Outside the Classroom*. Newcastle upon Tyne: Cambridge Scholars.

Tudor, I. (2005) *Higher Education Language Policy in Europe: A Snapshot of Action and Trends*. European Network for the Promotion of Language Learning among all Undergraduates (ENLU). http://web.fu-berlin.de/enlu/

UNESCO (2009) *UNESCO World Report: Investing in Cultural Diversity and Intercultural Dialogue*. Paris: United Nations Educational, Scientific and Cultural Organization.

Vidovich, L., O'Donoghue, T. and Tight, M. (2011) Transforming university curriculum policies in a global knowledge era: mapping a "global case study" research agenda. *Educational Studies* 38 (3), 283–295.

Vijver, F.J.R.v.d. and Leung, K. (2009) Methodological issues in researching intercultural competence. In D. Deardorff (ed.) *The SAGE Handbook of Intercultural Competence* (pp. 404–418). Thousand Oaks, CA: SAGE Publications.

Visocnik-Murray, S. and Laura, F. (2001) *Ti posso offrire un caffè? Implementing an Out-of-Class Experience in a Tertiary Italian Programme*. Paper presented at the Innovations in Italian Teaching Workshop, Brisbane, Australia.

Vogt, K. (2001) E-Mail-Projekte am Berufskolleg – Not worth a light? *Fremdsprachenunterricht* 45, 416–422.

Vogt, K. (2006) Can you measure attitudinal factors in intercultural communication? Tracing the development of attitudes in e-mail projects. *ReCALL* 18 (2), 153–173.

Vygotsky, L.S. (1978) *Mind in Society: The Development of Higher Psychological Processes*. Cambridge, MA: Harvard University Press.

Wallace, M.J. (1991) *Training Foreign Language Teachers: A Reflective Approach*. Cambridge: Cambridge University Press.

Wang, M., Williams, D., Brislin, R., Chao, J. and Wang, W-Z. W. (2000) *Turning Bricks into Jade*. Boston: Intercultural Press.

Ware, P. (2005) "Missed communication" in on-line communication: Tensions in fostering successful on-line interactions. *Language Learning & Technology* 9 (2), 64–89.

Ware, P. and Kramsch, C. (2005) Toward an intercultural stance: Teaching German and English through telecollaboration. *Modern Language Journal* 89 (2), 190–205.

Warner, C. (2011) Rethinking the role of language study in internationalizing higher education. *L2 Journal* 3 (1), 1–21.

White, P. and Baldauf, R. (2006) *Re-Examining Australia's Tertiary Language Programmes – A Five Year Retrospective on Teaching and Collaboration*. Brisbane: University of Queensland, Faculty of Arts/Faculty of Social and Behavioural Sciences.

Wiemann, J. and Backlund, P. (1980) Current theory in communicative competence. *Review of Educational Research* 50 (1), 185–199.

Witte, A. and Harden, T. (eds) (2011) *Intercultural Competence: Concepts, Challenges, Evaluations*. Bern, Switzerland: Peter Lang.

Witte, A.E. (2010) The global awareness curriculum in international business programs: A critical perspective. *Journal of Teaching in International Business* 21 (2), 101–131.

Woodgate-Jones, A. and Grenfell, M. (2012) Intercultural understanding and primary-level second language learning and teaching. *Language Awareness* 21 (4), 331–345.

Woods, A., Hajek, J. and Nettelbeck, C. (2011) A Vital Network: The First Year for the Language and Cultures Network for Australian Universities. *Babel* 46 (2–3), 56–57.

Worton, M. (2009) *Review of Modern Foreign Languages Provision in Higher Education in England*. Bristol: Higher Education Funding Council for England (HEFCE).

Yamada, E. (2010) Developing criticality through higher education language studies. In Y. Tsai and S. Houghton (eds) *Becoming Intercultural: Inside and Outside the Classroom* (pp. 146–166). Newcastle upon Tyne: Cambridge Scholars.

Ye, S. (2006) *China Candid: The People on the People's Republic of China*. Berkeley: University of California Press.

Ye, Z.V. (2004) Chinese categorisation of interpersonal relationships and the cultural logic of Chinese social interaction: An indigenous perspective. *Intercultural Pragmatics* 1 (2), 211–230.

Ye, Z.V. (2007) Returning to my mother tongue: Veronica's journey. In M. Besemeres and A. Wierzbicka (eds) *Translating Lives – Living with Two Languages and Cultures* (pp. 56–69). Brisbane: University of Queensland Press.

Yoshikawa, M. (1987) The double-swing model of intercultural communication between the East and the West. In D.L. Kincaid (ed.) *Communication Theory: Eastern and Western Perspectives*. San Diego: Academic Press.

Young, S.F. (2008) Theoretical frameworks and models of learning: Tools for developing conceptions of teaching and learning. *International Journal for Academic Development* 13 (1), 41–49.

Zamborlin, C. (2007) Going beyond pragmatic failures: Dissonances in intercultural communication. *Intercultural Pragmatics* 4 (1), 21–50.

Zeichner, K.M. and Liston, D.P. (1996) *Reflective Teaching: An Introduction*. Mahwah, NJ: Lawrence Erlbaum Associates.

Zuber-Skerritt, O. (1992a) *Action Research in Higher Education: Examples and Reflections*. London: Kogan Page.

Zuber-Skerritt, O. (1992b) *Professional Development in Higher Education: A Theoretical Framework for Action Research*. London: Kogan Page.

Index